Volume 34

ADVANCES IN LIBRARIANSHIP: LIBRARIANSHIP IN TIMES OF CRISIS

Advances in
Librarianship

Volume 34

ADVANCES IN LIBRARIANSHIP: LIBRARIANSHIP IN TIMES OF CRISIS

Advances in
Librarianship

Edited by
Anne Woodsworth

New York, USA

United Kingdom • North America • Japan
India • Malaysia • China

Emerald Group Publishing Limited
Howard House, Wagon Lane, Bingley BD16 1WA, UK

First edition 2011

British Library Cataloguing in Publication Data
A catalogue record for this book is available from the British Library

ISBN: 978-1-78052-390-3
ISSN: 0065-2830 (Series)

Emerald Group Publishing
Limited, Howard House,
Environmental Management
System has been certified by
ISOQAR to ISO 14001:2004
standards

Awarded in recognition of
Emerald's production
department's adherence to
quality systems and processes
when preparing scholarly
journals for print

INVESTOR IN PEOPLE

Contents

"Free Puppies": Integrating Web Resources into Online Catalogs   159

Robert L. Bothmann and Kellian Clink

Bringing Order Out of Chaos: Benchmarking Tools Used in Merging University Libraries in Finland   183

Ari Muhonen, Ulla Nygrén and Jarmo Saarti

Innovation for Survival: From Cooperation to Collaboration   207

Jennifer Rowley

Contents

Contributors

Numbers in parentheses indicate the pages on which the author's contributions begin.

Jennifer Weil Arns (37), School of Library and Information Science, University of South Carolina, Columbia, SC, USA

John Carlo Bertot (19), Information Policy & Access Center, College of Information Studies, University of Maryland, College Park, MD, USA

Robert L. Bothmann (159), Library Services, Minnesota State University, Mankato, MN, USA

Cynthia Churchwell (113), Knowledge and Library Services, Harvard Business School, Boston, MA, USA

Kellian Clink (159), Library Services, Minnesota State University, Mankato, MN, USA

Evelyn H. Daniel (37), School of Information and Library Science, University of North Carolina at Chapel Hill, Chapel Hill, NC, USA

Elizabeth J. DeCoster (19), Information Policy & Access Center, College of Information Studies, University of Maryland, College Park, MD, USA

Keith Michael Fiels (3), American Library Association, Chicago, IL, USA

Lisa K. Hussey (59), Graduate School of Library and Information Science, Simmons College, Boston, MA, USA

Paul T. Jaeger (19), Information Policy & Access Center, College of Information Studies, University of Maryland, College Park, MD, USA

Lesley A. Langa (19), Information Policy & Access Center, College of Information Studies, University of Maryland, College Park, MD, USA

Abigail J. McDermott (19), Information Policy & Access Center, College of Information Studies, University of Maryland, College Park, MD, USA

Ari Muhonen (183), Library, Aalto University, Espoo, Finland

Lilia Murray (139), Libraries, Murray State University, Murray, KY, USA

Ulla Nygrén (183), Library, University of Turku, Turku, Finland

W. David Penniman (97), Consultant, Columbus, OH, USA

Jennifer Rowley (207), Department of Information and Communications, Manchester Metropolitan University, Manchester, UK

Jarmo Saarti (183), Library, University of Eastern Finland, Kuopio, Finland

Kathryn Sigler (19), Information Policy & Access Center, College of Information Studies, University of Maryland, College Park, MD, USA

Mallory Stark (113), Knowledge and Library Services, Harvard Business School, Boston, MA, USA

Diane L. Velasquez (59), Independent Scholar, Westmont, IL, USA

Debra Wallace (113), Knowledge and Library Services, Harvard Business School, Boston, MA, USA

Preface

The field of librarianship has undergone traumatic shifts (mostly downward) due to the global financial meltdown that began in the fall of 2008. While libraries were not mentioned in the motion picture, *Inside Job* (Marrs & Ferguson, 2010), they were, and still are, deeply affected by the worst recession since the Great Depression. Worse yet is that current dialogues and negotiations about declining library budgets show promise of continuing well into 2012. Permanent reductions to budget support for libraries by all levels of government in the United States have resulted in library closures, loss of staff, reduced material purchases, deferred maintenance, and fewer or altered services in all types of libraries. Library associations experienced similar strains with the Canadian Library Association facing a budget crunch and the American Library Association giving staff a week's unpaid furlough in 2010. Five library systems in Illinois sought government approval to consolidate into one system and some consortia/networks merged or, like Nylink (NY), simply closed their doors.

In the United Kingdom, the budget of the Department of Culture, Media, and Sports was cut by 50% for fiscal years 2011–2012 through 2014–2015. Since this department funded public libraries, they experienced what many called "cultural vandalism" with up to 25% of the nation's library workers laid off (Global Reach, 2011). As of June 10, 2011, a blog by Anstice estimated that 455 U.K. libraries (383 buildings and 72 mobiles) out of circa 4517 were under threat, had been closed and/or were leaving council control in the first five months of the year. "Leaving council control" meant the libraries turned into "community libraries" operated by volunteers. The map on Anstice's Web site shows a frightening and graphic view of the results.

Headlines in professional journals, newspapers, and on Web sites say it all. Arns and Daniel cite a number of these about public libraries from *Library Journal*. Academic libraries, their parent institutions, and related organizations also face increasingly stringent financial futures. To wit:

- Cuts, freezes widespread in academic libraries (Kniffel, 2009)
- OCLC report: Research libraries face risks (Oder et al., 2010)

- Louisiana budget woes affect database funding, LSU [Louisiana State University], and LIS school (Blumenstein, 2010)
- U.S. higher education confronts historic financial challenges (Diverse Staff, 2011)
- University of Washington iSchool, University Libraries face budget pressures (Kelley, 2011b) and
- Challenges for academic libraries in difficult economic times (Research Information Network, 2010).

The reality behind such devastating headlines was illustrated by Florida's state's roller coaster of financial decisions. On March 10, 2011 the appropriations committees of Florida's House and Senate adopted positions eliminating all funding for the State Aid to Public Libraries program in FY 2011–2012. That was wrenching news to public libraries across the state. On March 11 the Florida Library Association issued a news release that stated:

> This devastating action will result in some Florida library branches closing and will seriously cripple libraries' ability to serve Floridians. Libraries have already taken their share of local and state budget cuts. This will be especially damaging to libraries in Florida's rural communities, as these libraries rely heavily on provisions in the program that help communities with lower tax bases (2011).

To put this in perspective, Clark (2011) provided budget data for Florida's public library state aid budgets in prior years:

```
2006–2007 31.9 million
2007–2008 30.7 million
2008–2009 23.3 million
2009–2010 21.2 million
2010–2011 21.2 million
```

A firestorm of advocacy, outcries, and lobbying by librarians and the public ensued. When the dust settled after almost two months, it was announced on May 3, 2011 that the House and Senate budget chairs had agreed to fund state aid to libraries at $21.3 million for 2011–2012, an increase of $100,000 over the previous year. Not great, but at least it was not totally devastating. In this volume, Velasquez and Hussey discuss advocacy from the perspective of two case studies and Fiels in his chapter points to a number of tools for building community advocacy provided by associations like the American Library Association.

In a survey conducted by *Library Journal*, 72% of survey respondents from all types of libraries reported that their budgets had been cut and 43% had taken staff cuts (Kelley, 2011a). This happened against a backdrop of incessant increases in serial prices and the need to adapt to changing technologies, largely driven by mobile access to serials and other library resources. Bosch, Henderson, and Klusendorf (2011) predicted that for serials, the 2010 inflation rates of 4.3% and 5.3% in 2011 would likely be in the 6–8% range in 2012. Publishers and libraries are both looking at newer models of access and delivery of content, particularly through smartphone applications as discussed in this volume by Lillia Murray.

While *Advances in Librarianship* endeavors to identify trends and innovations, the trend addressed in this volume is admittedly not a happy one. The current climate does, however, present opportunities for analysis, and far-reaching searches for solutions and innovations that can alleviate the challenges created by the clash of fiscal retrenchment with steadily increasing use of libraries. Therefore, this volume addresses the ripple effects of the economic recession from the point of view of librarianship, the need for advocacy, and the necessity to tout the value that libraries bring to their communities. Chapters focus on identifying means to change library and library related organizations so that they focus on distinctive assets and strengths, use free or low cost resources and technologies, and position themselves to take advantage of collaborative initiatives.

Keith Fiels, executive director of the American Library Association (ALA), presents a framework for the entire volume from the macro level by looking at mega issues in librarianship, at the same time as he debunks myths and points out realities. He asserts that advocacy and touting the value of libraries are critical tools for librarianship. ALA's advocacy kits and research-based reports, such as *Add It Up: Libraries Make the Difference in Youth Education* and *Value of Academic Libraries*, (American Library Association, 2011) are tools to use in times of crisis. The economic dollar value of libraries can be established if his example of the Free Library of Philadelphia is emulated. ALA's advocacy Web site provides a Library Value Calculator created by the Massachusetts Library Association, which a number of libraries are using to make the case for funding. Similarly, the National Network of Libraries of Medicine, Midcontinental Region (2011) has been building a national database to demonstrate the combined value of all health sciences libraries against which individual libraries can be measured. Another tool useful is *The Value of Libraries for Research and Researchers* from RLUK, Research Libraries UK (2011).

Following Fiels' broad context, is an analysis of the ways in which American public libraries are using the Internet to meet patron, community, and government needs by a group of researchers at the Information Policy & Access Center, College of Information Studies, University of Maryland, MD: Kathryn Sigler, Paul T. Jaeger, John Carlo Bertot, Abigail J. McDermott, Elizabeth J. DeCoster, and Lesley A. Langa. They point out that in currently harsh economic times American public libraries are using the Internet to meet patron, community, and government needs. They draw data from a 2010–2011 national survey, *Public Library Funding and Technology Access*, to analyze and examine key issues at the intersection of public libraries, the Internet, economic uncertainty, and library/e-government partnerships.

The next chapter is by Jennifer Weil Arns, associate professor, School of Library and Information Science, University of South Carolina, Columbia, SC, and Evelyn Daniel, adjunct professor at the School of Information and Library Science, University of North Carolina at Chapel Hill, NC. They focus on how cutback decisions to services and operations are made in U.S. public libraries as a result of shrinking financial support. They contend that private sector economic practices and theories have crept into the public sector but that it is a poor fit for agencies like public libraries. They suggest that open and transparent models are needed in decisions making about cutbacks to library services.

Also flowing from Fiels' broad context is a chapter by Diane K. Hussey, assistant professor, Graduate School of Library and Information Science at Simmons College, Boston, MA, and Diane L. Velasquez, independent scholar, Westmont, IL. They present two case studies that illustrate the impact of advocacy, or lack thereof, based on studies of Boston Public Library in Massachusetts and the Los Angeles Public Library in California. The two cities have different cultures and orientations and handled their fiscal crises in vastly different ways. One used public advocacy and lobbying and the other sought legislative changes to increase library funding appropriations Lessons from the two cases will serve other libraries well in terms of finding models and tactics that can reverse or offset losses in revenue.

Turning to solutions or innovations that help libraries sustain and even improve the quality of their services to their customers, the remaining chapters in the volume provide various strategies to deal with downsizing, changing mandates, and initiatives that help all types of libraries as they struggle to remain vital in rapidly changing times and climates. W. David Penniman, consultant in Columbus, OH, outlines three cases in which he personally led a private sector library, a library and information science program, and a library consortium through strategic changes. As do the authors of the last chapter, his strategies for change included heavy focus on changing the culture of organizations. His "autopsies" of each case provide pointers for others facing similar futures. In their chapter about Harvard's Baker Library, Cynthia Churchwell, Information Research Specialist, Mallory Stark, Curriculum Services Specialist, and Debra Wallace, managing director outline the processes and strategies that were used to realign library services not only to meet budget reductions, but also to change the orientation and direction of services. The results included improved relevance to the school's teaching, learning, and research environments and getting library services embedded into curriculum design and delivery and in teaching processes.

Lilia Murray, Research and Instruction Librarian at Murray State University (no relation) in Kentucky, outlines three initiatives that can be introduced in libraries to meet the demand for library access via smartphones. The applications that she describes in detail were carefully researched in terms of relatively low costs and ease of adoption into library operations. Through an intensive review of the literature she contends that libraries with tight budgets should approach mobilization projects in terms of stages, developing content, and services sequentially from passive formats, which require little input, to more dynamic interfaces which entail greater interaction. Robert Bothman and Kellian Clink, both from the University of Minnesota in Mankato, MN, approach cost savings from the perspective of incorporating free web resources in libraries' online catalogs. Using the field of social work as an illustration, they analyze the work involved in collection development and cataloging of what they call "free puppies" drawn from Web sites. They conclude that shrinking staff and materials budgets might drive a paradigm shift in which web resources are treated as part of the richer universe of recorded knowledge and hence is worthy of being included in library online catalogs.

Another question that often arises in times of financial retrenchment is how to merge operations and institutions. This question is addressed directly by three library directors from recently merged universities in Finland. Ari Muhonen, Ulla Nygrén, and Jarmo Saarti are from Aalto University, University of Turku, and the University of Eastern Finland, respectively. Three independent and autonomous institutions were formed out of what had previously been seventeen government run universities. Although they are still in the process of making decisions about shared/merged processes such as collection development and cataloging, the lessons they learned about building new organizational cultures are presented as benchmarks in effecting change and finding cost savings. On the basis of their experiences, communication and marketing internally and externally were critical for new culture shifts to succeed. Shifting from hierarchical structures to self directed teams enabled the libraries to become more responsive to the changed missions of their universities.

The final capstone to librarianship in a time of crisis is presented by Jennifer Rowley, professor of Information and Communications at Manchester Metropolitan University in Manchester, UK. Her conceptual chapter provides not only an extensive review of the literature, but also an overview of the value of collaborative initiatives that span organizational boundaries. She addresses choosing partners, building innovative networks, and how to successfully manage innovative and collaborative initiatives. Rowley also points out barriers that can arise in finding cross-organizational solutions to cost savings and other crises. She argues that library managers must think strategically about innovations, particularly with respect to managing collaborative initiatives.

My heartfelt thanks go to the authors who were so prompt and fully responsive to my editorial questions and suggestions. My thanks also go to members of the Editorial Advisory Board (EAB) for helping to shape this volume, for the time they spent reviewing submissions, and advising me about volumes in this series. The members are Barbara Genco, editor of Collection Management at *Library Journal*, New York, NY, Tula Giannini, dean of the School of Information and Library Science at Pratt Institute in Brooklyn, NY, Kenneth Haycock, professor Emeritus, Center for Research and Innovation, San Jose School of Library and Information Science, San Jose, CA, Maureen Mackenzie, associate professor of Management and Leadership at Dowling College, Oakdale, NY, Pat Molholt, Columbia University, New York, NY (retired), Marie Radford, associate professor at Rutgers University, Newark, NJ, and Robert A. Seal, dean of Libraries at Loyola University, Chicago, IL. Last but not least to be thanked is EAB member, W. David Penniman who will join me as Coeditor of Volume 35 — *Contexts for Assessment and Outcomes Evaluation in Librarianship*.

With this my third volume in the series, my appreciation is again extended to Diane Heath, Publisher of the LIS Division at Emerald and to members of her support team including Mary Miskin and more recently, Catriona Gelder.

References

American Library Association. (2011). *Add it up: Libraries make the difference in youth education*. Retrieved from http://www.ala.org/ala/issuesadvocacy/advocacy/advocacyuniversity/additup/index.cfm

Anstice, I. (2011, June 1). *Public library news: What's happening to your library*. [Web log post]. Retrieved from http://www.publiclibrariesnews.com/p/cuts-and-closures-by-local-authority.html

Blumenstein, L. (2010, July). Louisiana budget woes affect database funding, LSU, and LIS school. Retrieved from http://www.libraryjournal.com/lj/communityacademiclibraries/889587-265/university_of_washington_ischool_university.html.csp

Bosch, S., Henderson, K., & Klusendorf, H. (2011, April). Periodicals price survey 2011: Under pressure, times are changing. *Library Journal.com*. Retrieved from http://www.libraryjournal.com/lj/ljinprintcurrentissue/890009-403/periodicals_price_survey_2011_.html.csp

Clark, P. (2011). *State aid to libraries over the last 5 years*. Retrieved from http://www.thelibraryguy.com/2011/04/state-aid-to-libraries-over-last-5.html#comments

Diverse Staff. (2011, May). *U.S. higher education confronts historic financial challenges*. Retrieved from http://diverseeduction.com/article/15559/

Florida Library Association. (2011, March). Retrieved from http://www.wctv.tv/news/headlines/87360812.html

Global Reach. (2011, January/February). United Kingdom. *American Libraries*, *136*(1), 23.

Kelley, M. (2011a). Bottoming out? Severe cuts put big question marks on the future. *Library Journal 136*(1), 28–31.

Kelley, M. (2011b). University of Washington iSchool, University Libraries face budget pressures. Retrieved from http://www.libraryjournal.com/lj/communityacademicli braries/889587-265/university_of_washington_ischool_university.html.csp

Kniffel, L. (2009, May 14). *Cuts, freezes widespread in academic libraries.* Retrieved from http://www.americanlibrariesmagazine.org/news/05142009/cuts-freezes-widespread-academic-libraries

Marrs, A., & Ferguson, C. (Producers) & Ferguson, C. (Director). (2010). *Inside job* [Motion picture]. Sony Pictures Classics, USA.

National Network of Libraries of Medicine, Midcontinental region. (2011). Retrieved from http://nnlm.gov/mcr/evaluation/calculator.html

Oder, N., Barack, L., Blumenstein, L., Friedman, S., S. Hadro, J., and Witherell, M. (2010). OCLC report: Research libraries face risks. *Library Journal 135*(9), 14.

Research Information Network. (2010, March). *Challenges for academic libraries in difficult economic times: A guide for senior institutional managers and policy makers.* Retrieved from http://www.rin.ac.uk/challenges-for-libraries-FINAL-March 10[1].pdf

RLUK, Research Libraries UK. (2011). *The value of libraries for research and researchers.* Retrieved from http://www.rluk.ac.uk/content/value-libraries-research-and-researchers

Anne Woodsworth
Editor

Crises Cause Change

A Library "State of the State": Trends, Issues, and Myths

Keith Michael Fiels

American Library Association, Chicago, IL, USA

Abstract

The chapter provides a library "state of the state," discussing the issues, trends, and myths that shape the current library environment in the United States. It cites data from the American Library Association's *State of America's Libraries* (2010d) report. Issues discussed include library usage, library funding, the adaptation of new technologies, the profession of librarianship, the struggle to preserve public access to information, and the future prospects of libraries. The chapter discusses each of these issues in relation to public, academics, and school libraries, citing comparative data on funding and the adoption of new technologies for each type of library. Acknowledging that reality to libraries is not technological, but perceptual and political, discussion focuses on the growing role of advocacy and specific strategies that have proven successful in securing and/or preserving support for libraries. A number of commonly held myths are also examined, many of which are detrimental to libraries or inhibit our ability to respond to the issues and trends that are affecting libraries. The author concludes with some observations about the historic development of libraries, their continuing relevance in an era of rapid technological change, the need to look beyond short-term concerns and to closely examine and/or reject popular myths as we create libraries of the future.

Keywords: Libraries; Future trends; "Mega" issues; Funding; Advocacy

I. Introduction

In April, 2011, the American Library Association (ALA) released its fifth *State of America's Libraries* report (2011d). While the 70-page report is full of useful facts and figures, this chapter looks at what lies behind the numbers: What are the "mega" issues and "mega" trends that are affecting libraries? More importantly, how will our responses to these mega issues shape the future of libraries?

The chapter also discusses the author's views about a number of "myths,"—whether perpetuated by the media, the public, or by librarians themselves—which affect our response to these issues and trends.

LIBRARIANSHIP IN TIMES OF CRISIS
ADVANCES IN LIBRARIANSHIP, VOL. 34
© 2011 by Emerald Group Publishing Limited
ISSN: 0065-2830
DOI: 10.1108/S0065-2830(2011)0000034004

Myths are attractive because they serve as shorthand, allowing us to understand and characterize complex situations. At the same time, they are by definition not true representations of these complex situations. Often, they are downright wrong. The media love myths. They love to create them, and then they love to tear them down. In both instances, the public is entertained, papers are sold, and blogs attract followers. Library land is not exempt from myths. Some are useful, but many commonly held assumptions about libraries and what is happening in and to them, in fact turn out to be myths. Some of these library myths will be discussed here along with the ways in which they may be limiting thinking and/or the ability to respond to some of the mega issues faced by libraries and librarians.

So what are the mega issues that are affecting libraries? In my view, they are: the economy, the digital revolution, societal and demographic changes, building the librarian of the future, keeping information free, making the case for libraries, and a question: "can libraries even survive?". Each issue is discussed along with the myths and realities associated with them.

A. Exploring the Mega Issues

1. The Economy

Myth: Libraries are no longer used in an information age.
Reality: Libraries are more heavily used than ever.

The story here is both good news and bad news.

2. The Good News

The good news is that public library usage is at an historic high. In 2008 (the most recent year for which data are currently available), Americans visited their public libraries 1.5 billion times (an increase of 100 million visits over the previous year), and borrowed 2.3 billion items (Public Library Association, 2008). Since 2008 and the onset of the recession, data gathered by ALA show that library usage is up by 10% nationally, with some libraries reporting increases of 20 or even 30%.

The reasons for this appear to be twofold. First, people are using libraries more because they provide free reading materials, videos, and music at a time when nearly everyone's personal finances are stressed. Libraries are simply a great deal.

The second reason is that libraries are helping America get back to work. Data show that 20% of Americans, twice the unemployment rate, have been affected by a negative change in employment. This has led to unprecedented increases in library use by those looking for jobs, applying for jobs, and seeking to acquire new job skills. It has been estimated that over half of all major corporations now accept only online applications. This means that as many as half of the Americans who do not have home computers or laptops cannot apply for work.

According to a Pew Center on the States report, only 65% of Americans have broadband at home (2010, p. 1). In a recent study by Becker *et al.* (2010), one quarter of respondents reported that the library provides their only access to computers. Nationally, that would translate into approximately 75 million people who use their public library because they have no other access to computers. In two-third (67%) of American communities and 73% of rural communities, public libraries provide the only free public access to computers (ALA, 2010).

Public libraries also serve as a major resource for those seeking to establish new businesses. In Philadelphia, a study found that the library had helped start, sustain, or grow an estimated 8600 businesses, with a combined economic impact of almost $4 million (Diamond, Gillen, & Litman, 2010).

In colleges and universities across the country, many academic libraries have become "information commons," vibrant and crowded centers of campus learning and campus life. School libraries are rapidly becoming the school's "largest classroom," serving as 24/7 research and curriculum support centers, providing online services to students and teachers within, and beyond, the library and the school building.

3. The Bad News

The bad news is that funding for most libraries has been reduced or is static. Nineteen states in the United States reported decreases in funding for a majority of public libraries from 2010 to 2011. Seventy-two percent of libraries responding to a survey reported budget cuts, and 43% reported staff cuts (Kelley, 2011). Particularly hard hit have been urban libraries, with 86% reporting budget reductions and 90% reporting staff reductions, due in large part to decreases in state aid to libraries across the country. Seventeen states reported public library closures due to funding issues, with Pennsylvania and New Jersey leading the nation with between five and ten library closures in each state.

The data for academic libraries show a similar pattern with 42% of university libraries reporting budget cuts in 2010. Two-thirds reported that they will reduce funding for information resources, and one-third reported that they will be reducing staff expenditures (Nicholas, Rowlands, Jubb, & Jamali, 2010).

According to an annual survey by the American Association of School Librarians (AASL), school libraries also saw an overall 9½% nationwide decrease in funding in 2010. While elementary schools saw a welcome 8% increase in funding overall, this was offset by a 19% decline in funding for high school libraries. High poverty areas saw the largest decreases. Of even greater concern is the fact that the number of school libraries has declined for the first time nationwide, along with the number with certified media specialists.

At the state level, funding decreases are particularly dramatic, with one-quarter of states reporting decreases in funding for libraries and library programs of more than 10%. Overall, half the states reported decreases, and half reported that funding was stable.

Next year is expected to be even more difficult for the states. While 40 states have begun to see revenue increases, many are grappling with huge deficits, with federal stimulus funding for states ending in 2011. As noted above, these reductions in state funding have impacted major urban public libraries, urban school districts, and regional library systems, all of which depend to a larger degree on state funding.

Despite these trends, there was some good funding news: Library referenda across the country were overwhelmingly successful, with 87% of all funding referenda and 55% of all building referenda approved in 2010. Another piece of good news was the receipt of federal stimulus funds for increased broadband capacity by 27 states and 100 library systems.

B. The Digital Revolution

Myth: *Libraries are not changing with the times*
         Libraries are just about books
Reality: Libraries are actively embracing -and offering -digital content
         and e-books (and users are eating it up).

If there is one clear trend, it is that libraries of all types are eagerly embracing e-books and digital content. In this area, academic libraries lead the way, with public and school libraries not far behind. A survey by Polanka (2011) shows that 94% of academic libraries offer e-books, along with 72% of public and 33% of school libraries, and the number of libraries offering e-books is increasing rapidly. One in ten academic libraries circulates e-book reading devices, as do one in twenty in public and school libraries.

Digital resources now account for 57% of materials expenditures by academic libraries. Three hundred academic libraries manage institutional digital repositories, which offer access to research, databases, and other digital resources created by faculty and students.

School libraries increasingly provide remote access to digital resources for their faculty and students, with the average number of outside computers with access to the school library's resources increasing by 9% last year to 194.

Nearly every public library offers free public access to computers, and 85% of public libraries offer wireless access.

1. Changes in Publishing

In April, 2011, *USA Today* reported that the sale of e-books for the first time exceeded those for printed books, attesting to the speed with which digital publications are being adopted. The uncertainty surrounding what e-book formats and devices will ultimately prevail, how much e-books will end up costing, and what restrictions will be placed on the ability of libraries to circulate e-books is undoubtedly the most serious problem facing libraries at the moment, after funding issues.

While no one has a crystal ball, there are strong reasons to believe that the competitive market and the combined buying power of America's libraries will ultimately provide a solution that will include libraries as prominent players.

The size of the US book publishing industry is estimated to be around 24 to 40 billion US dollars. The total amount spent by libraries on published materials is thought to range from 1.7 to 4.5 billion US dollars. This means that libraries account for a significant portion of the revenue derived from their purchase of an estimated 288,000 titles in 2010. Given the size of the library market, it is extremely unlikely that libraries will not continue to play a major role in the new digital order.

2. Adapting to Social Networks

With two-thirds (61%) of adults using social networks (Zickuhr, 2011), use of social media by libraries is also growing rapidly. Eighty-five percent of public libraries reported using Facebook, half used Twitter, and 42% used blogs, primarily to promote library services (Rogers, 2010).

With 95% of Americans now owning cell phones (Zickuhr, 2011), and an increasing number having Internet-enabled devices, the race is on for libraries to develop handheld applications that will deliver library services to users, wherever they are.

C. Societal and Demographic Changes

America is changing, and changing rapidly. Current estimates are that the "minority" populations of America will be the majority in 20 years (US Department of Labor, 2010). These demographic changes pose a special challenge for libraries, because new immigrants often come from countries where public libraries do not exist or are used only by the elite.

A Harris survey (Harris Interactive, 2011) found that while 63% of whites and 64% of African Americans used their public library, the figure for Hispanics is just below half (49%).

Libraries have a long tradition, going back to the end of the 19th century, of reaching out to new immigrants. The challenge over the next decade will be to reach out to America's emerging minorities and to make them aware of the services and opportunities that libraries offer for everyone.

1. The Staffing Challenge

One of the key challenges is the library profession itself. Seeing a librarian who "looks" like the users and perhaps who speaks a little bit of their language, is a significant factor in making wary new library users more comfortable. The library profession as a whole has traditionally been far less diverse than the total population. In fact from 1990 to 2000, diversity in the library profession actually declined. In 1990, 85% of librarians were white, while in 2000 that figure rose to 86% despite significant increases in the overall number of African American, Asian/Pacific Islander, Native American, and Hispanic librarians (US Census Bureau, 2000).

Among the better known efforts to address this has been ALA's Spectrum program. Since its inception in 1997, the program has awarded scholarships to 700 African American, Hispanic, Asian/Pacific Islander, and Native American students. The Institute for Museum and Library Services has also undertaken a national effort to increase minority opportunities. With an estimated 5000 students graduating from library schools each year, however, these efforts represent only a small portion of all graduates. Clearly, more needs to be done. To that end, ALA embarked on a campaign to raise a million dollars for additional scholarships in 2010.

The 2010 census data on the profession will be available next year, and everyone is eagerly awaiting the results and what they will show about our efforts to help create a more inclusive profession that reflects the new users that libraries serve.

D. Building the Librarian of the Future

Myth: Librarians are shy, retiring people who like to read a lot
Reality: Librarians are outgoing, tech-savvy, "people" people
           (who like to read a lot)

The image of the librarian in the media may no longer involve the traditional glasses and bun, but old stereotypes die hard. Librarians today continue to battle their shy, retiring image.

The reality, of course, is that librarians have never been shy and retiring. The profession is known for its courageous stands against censorship and in support of intellectual freedom. More recently, its efforts to protect the right of library users to read what they want to without fear of government surveillance has led to opposition by ALA to provisions of the Patriot Act. While that repeal did not occur, we did come within one vote of repealing the provisions, and the many checks and balances have been placed on the broad powers granted under the legislation. In the process, librarians acquired a reputation as courageous fighters for freedom of speech rights.

Following Hurricane Katrina, ALA gained national media attention by being the first major association to hold a conference in New Orleans. Again, the courage of librarians was widely noted.

Our challenge is twofold: The first is to recruit and train a new generation of librarians, who are tech savvy and people-oriented. The second is to change public perception about the state of the profession.

In 2009, there were 27,000 degreed librarians in academic libraries, 48,000 in public libraries, 60,000 in public schools, and 15,000 in private schools, for a total of 150,000 librarians in the United States. An additional 192,000 other staff members worked in libraries, bringing the total number of library workers to 342,000 (ALA, 2011c).

Prior to the recession in 2008, library employment was growing at the rate of 2%, about the same as the population in general. Since the recession, there is strong evidence that the library workforce overall has decreased, perhaps by as much as 10%.

About 3% of librarians retire each year. At the same time, an estimated 5000 library students graduate each year (there are approximately 15,000 students currently enrolled in MLIS programs nationwide).

This brings us to next myth:

Myth: There will not be enough graduates to fill the place of those who will retire over the next decade.

This concern was prevalent a decade ago, when worries over the anticipated retirement of baby boomers were an issue. Ultimately, these concerns proved to be unfounded as the recession forced delays in retirements, and as the overall size of the labor force declined. This has led to the new myth:

Myth: There will be no jobs for graduates.

Reality: Somewhere between the two.

About 2900 librarians are now expected to retire each year, as baby boomers who have delayed their retirements finally leave the work force. When this is weighed in relation to graduates and others who leave the field for other reasons, the data

suggest that once the currently depressed employment market stabilizes, the ratio between graduates and jobs should be roughly in balance.
One final myth:

> Myth: *Younger librarians are not participating in associations.*
> Reality: Just the opposite.

Membership data at ALA show that overall, the association is younger than the profession as a whole, and that a larger proportion of younger librarians participate in the association than their older peers. Further, approximately two-third of library school students are ALA members.

E. Keeping Information Free

Librarians have dealt with censorship for many years, and it continues to be a major issue for libraries across the country. Each year, there are hundreds of documented attempts by individuals and groups to remove books and other materials from library collections, and many more go unreported. While censorship continues as a very visible attempt to restrict public access to information, many other threats exist.

1. Government Information

Free access to government information is constantly being threatened by budget cuts to dissemination programs, through elimination of government libraries, and through privatization of government information. One of the more dramatic examples of this occurred in 2006, with the administration's approval to close the Environmental Protection Agency's libraries throughout the United States. Staff were let go and collections were literally thrown into dumpsters. The library community fought back, with the result that Congress ordered the libraries to reopen.

Efforts to guarantee that Americans have access to federally funded research have prompted pilot programs and the introduction of legislation that mandates that federally funded research, once only available at extremely high cost through private publishers, would be made available through digital repositories at no cost to the public.

2. Copyright

Another threat to access is the global struggle over the future of copyright. On one hand, multinational corporations with budgets in billions are seeking to restrict the ability of libraries to provide access to e-information like they do in the print environment. Fair use is an abstract concept to most, but it is critically important in a digital environment where corporations are seeking to monetize every single bit of information.

These are not trivial issues. Enormous amounts of information are at stake, and libraries have found themselves at the center of the fray. Libraries are almost the only advocates for the public interest in this massive struggle for the future of access to information.

F. Making the Case for Libraries

Myth: *We can't do anything about library funding.*
Reality: We can.

Many librarians and quite a few people who really care about libraries feel that they can't "do" anything to affect the funding of libraries. The truth is that library supporters have tremendous influence – but only if they use it.

1. Advocacy

The concept of library advocacy is a relatively recent one in library thinking. ALA has been involved in advocacy at the federal level since the 1950s, but local advocacy is much more recent. Today, we know that advocacy involves certain time-tested strategies and skills. We also know that people can learn to be effective advocates.

The secrets of successful advocacy are rather straightforward:

- First, have a plan: How will the funds produce specific benefits to users and impact community members? How will cuts negatively affect community members? Ultimately, it is a vision – illustrated by specific examples—that drives funding.
- Second, do not be afraid to ask. No one has ever received additional support without asking. Public officials at every level are looking at ways to save money, and being silent is to become "low hanging fruit" for budget cutters.
- Third, enlist others to speak on your behalf. Library trustees, library friends, and library users who will benefit from improved services are all extremely effective advocates, as are those who will be negatively affected by cuts in funding and services. Community groups make for effective allies if they see library services as important. Members of the public will ultimately be the best advocates, as long as they understand the benefits that specific proposals will provide to them and the community.
- Last, advocates must be persistent. Not every new library building gets built right away, but experience shows that nearly all do get built eventually.

Experience also shows that librarians, trustees, and library supporters who are willing to take the time and effort to advocate for their libraries have a much higher success rate, and are more consistently able to secure funding than those who do not.

2. Public Perceptions

The good news here is that the Americans have very strong positive feelings about the value of libraries. A recent Harris Poll (Harris Interactive, 2011) showed that 94% of Americans agreed with the statement: "Because it provides free access to materials and resources, the public library plays an important role in giving everyone a chance to succeed" (p. 10). Ninety-one percent agreed that the library improves the quality of life in the community. Eighty-four percent agreed that it is important to their family's education, and 80% agreed it is critical to democracy. Seventy-nine percent agreed that their library "deserves more funding."

3. Research and the Value of Libraries

To make the case for library funding better, we also need to make better use of the growing body of research that documents the value and impact of libraries. For nearly a decade, a series of studies have analyzed the impact of school libraries on student achievement. Their findings have universally shown that students in schools with libraries, staffed by certified Library Media Specialists get better grades, score better on standard tests, and develop independent study skills that support lifelong learning and productivity.

Despite these compelling studies, educational establishments have ignored the benefits of libraries in their quest to improve student performance. As noted above, there has been a decrease in the number of schools with libraries, and elimination of trained school library media specialists as school budgets are cut.

This is simply folly. We need to go "head to head" with educational establishments and make the public aware of the value of school libraries and their librarians. Schools and students simply cannot be successful without libraries and the 21st century literacy skills that they teach. In public libraries, there is a growing body of studies that document their value, including a major statewide study in Florida Haas Center (2010). These studies consistently show that the public library returns between three and six dollars in direct economic benefit for every tax dollar they receive.

Diamond *et al.* (2010) demonstrated that the Philadelphia public library created more than $30 million in indirect economic benefits in addition to the materials it circulated and the information it provided to library users. As previously mentioned this included $4 million in benefits for 8600 small businesses and 1000 individuals who found work through the library. (Note that President Obama credits the New York Public Library with helping him find his first job). The Philadelphia study also indicated that homes within a quarter-mile of a branch library were worth on average $9600 more than homes further away.

A major study undertaken by the Association of College and Research Libraries (ACRL) (2010), a division of ALA, examined the value of academic libraries. The study discussed existing research that identifies library values in relationship to goals of colleges and universities. These goals may include:

- Student enrollment;
- Student retention and graduation;
- Student success, achievement, and learning;
- Student experience, attitude, and perception of quality;
- Faculty research productivity, grants, and teaching; and
- Institutional reputation and prestige.

4. Associations Can Help

While the body of research documenting the value of libraries is growing, the findings need to get into the hands of individual librarians, library supporters, and decision makers.

One example of how research can be deployed is ALA's *Add It Up: School Libraries Make the Difference* tool kit (ALA, 2011a). The online resource presents data from dozens of studies as a series of straightforward talking points for use by those looking to make the case for school libraries.

ALA has actively been engaged in building public support for libraries at the national, state, and local level for two decades. A recent merger with the National Friends of Libraries USA (FOLUSA) group brought thousands of friends groups nationwide into the Association's advocacy network. At the same time, ALA's *I Love Libraries* (ALA, 2011b) site with its stories about libraries saw three-quarter of a million visitors last year. The site is a high-profile platform for authors who support libraries and the value they provide.

The bottom line: We can secure increased funding for libraries, we can successfully fight budget cuts – but only if we are willing to be advocates and to support those who advocate for us.

G. The Biggest Issue of All: Can Libraries Even Survive?

Myth: With the Internet, everything is available for free and people no longer need libraries.

Reality: People need libraries more than ever.

No sooner was the Internet invented than certain pundits started to declaim that it would make libraries obsolete by providing everyone with all the reading material and information they need. Today's reality is quite different. Libraries are more heavily used than ever, and are being expanded to accommodate the influx of more users and more computers.

One of the reasons for this is that not everyone owns a personal computer, as discussed earlier in the chapter. While technology will certainly continue to advance, there is nothing that suggests that everyone will magically have state-of-the-art equipment and state-of-the-art skills to match. The reality is that there will always be "haves and have nots."

Second, valuable information is not free. Quite the contrary, the cost of information for serious researchers remains high. Libraries offer both free access and assistance with evaluation of information. Either way, the dream of unlimited free information has proven to be pipe dream.

Unfortunately, the myth of the vanishing library has been a convenient cover for those struggling to find easy targets in the current economic crisis. We have heard of the "library without walls" for many years and many politicians appear ready to hasten that trend by creating the "library without money."

Libraries and librarians remain surrounded by:

- Budget cutters looking for easy targets;
- Those who pay lip service to libraries but think they can be operated without financial support;
- Those who hate what libraries represent;
- Those who think they don't need libraries and can't imagine why others might; and
- Gurus, who tell us to "think outside the box."

Who can blame librarians if they become discouraged? All this author can say is: Don't believe them for a minute!

The simplest definition I can give of a library is: A collection of community-owned books and other resources designed to produce mutual benefit for the community and its members, and designed to produce collective benefits far greater than members could produce if each acted individually.

A library is a simple invention, as was the wheel. I would argue that they work equally well in a world of cuneiform tablets or a world of digital information. This brings us to the last myth:

Myth: Libraries came into existence magically and without any effort.
Reality: Libraries have always depended on the efforts of hard-working people who cared about the future of their communities and our nation.

The reality is that there never were any "good old days." The libraries we cherish today did not simply spring into existence; they were created brick by brick by people who had to struggle to create them at every step.

Libraries have made an enormous difference in our communities, our country, and the world. They have helped grow the economy and have fostered invention and innovation. They have helped forge millions of immigrants into a literate nation. They have nurtured a democracy that is the envy of the world.

These libraries are now ours to nurture, to support, and to lead into the future as strong and vibrant resources. They are not ours to give away. We talk about the future as if it is something that is happening to us, but reality is quite the opposite: We create the future.

II. Conclusion

Library perceptions and library realities do not always match.

Recent studies and data show that libraries are more heavily used than ever and that libraries are rapidly changing in response to societal and technological changes in America. At the same time, many library "myths," perpetuated by the media, the public, and librarians themselves, continue to plague the field. In some instances, myths threaten the very future of libraries at a time when they are most desperately needed—in the information age.

In the case of librarians, these myths can hamper critical work to transform libraries for the 21st century. The belief that libraries are powerless victims of societal and technological trends is a greater threat to them than any of the trends themselves.

In libraries of all types, librarians and library users are creatively responding to new technologies and changes. The vibrant libraries we have today were created by the hard work of people just like us, because they understood the value of libraries to individuals, communities, and democracy. Likewise, those who are now responsible for these libraries have the responsibility to create and sustain "libraries of the future."

Acknowledgement

This chapter was based on a paper delivered April 27, 2011 at the Massachusetts Library Conference, Danvers, MA

References

American Association of School Librarians. (2010). *School libraries count! National longitudinal survey of school library programs*. Retrieved from http://www.ala.org/ala/mgrps/divs/aasl/researchandstatistics/slcsurvey/2010/slc2010.cfm

American Library Association. (2010, Summer). Libraries connect communities: Public library funding & technology access study 2009–2010. *American Libraries* [Digital Supplement]. Chicago, IL: Author.

American Library Association. (2011a). Add it up: Libraries make the difference in youth education. Retrieved from http://www.ala.org/ala/issuesadvocacy/advocacy/advocacyuniversity/additup/index.cfm

American Library Association. (2011b). I love libraries. Retrieved from http://www.ilovelibraries.org/ourauthors/ourauthorsouradvocates/index.cfm

American Library Association. (2011c). Number employed in libraries: ALA library fact sheet 2. Retrieved from http://www.ala.org/ala/professionalresources/libfactsheets/alalibraryfactsheet02.cfm

American Library Association. (2011d). *The state of America's libraries: A report from the American Library Association.* Chicago, IL: Author. Retrieved from www.ala.org/ala/newspresscenter/mediapresscenter/americaslibraries2011/index.cfm

Association of College and Research Libraries. (2010). *Value of Academic Libraries: A Comprehensive Research Review and Report.* Researched by Megan Oakleaf. Chicago, IL: Author. Retrieved from http://www.ala.org/ala/mgrps/divs/acrl/issues/value/val_report.pdf

Becker, S., Crandall, M. D., Fisher, K. E., Kinney, B., Landry, D., & Rocha, A. (2010). *Opportunity for all: How the American public benefits from internet access at U.S. libraries* [IMLS-2010-RES-01]. Washington, DC: Institute of Museum and Library Services. Retrieved from http://impact.ischool.washington.edu/documents/OPP4ALL_FinalReport.pdf

Diamond, D., Gillen, K.C. & Litman, M. (2010). *The economic value of the Free Library of Philadelphia.* Philadelphia, PA: Fels Research & Consulting. Retrieved from http://www.freelibrary.org/about/FelsReport.pdf

Haas Center for Business Research and Economic Development. (2010) *Taxpayer return on investment in Florida public libraries.* Retrieved from http://haas.uwf.edu/librarystate.htm

Harris Interactive. (2011). *ALA January 2011 Harris poll quorum results.* Chicago, IL: American Library Association. Retrieved from http://www.ala.org/ala/research/librarystats/2011harrispoll.pdf

Kelley, M. (2011). *LJ's* budget survey: Bottoming out? Severe cuts today put big question marks on the future. Retrieved from http://www.libraryjournal.com/lj/communitymanaginglibraries/888434-273/ljs_2010_budget_survey_bottoming.html.csp

Nicholas, D., Rowlands, I., Jubb, M., & Jamali, H. R. (2010). The impact of the economic downturn on libraries: With special reference to university libraries. *Journal of Academic Librarianship, 36*(5), 376–382.

Pew Center on the States. (2010). *Bringing America up to speed: States' role in expanding broadband.* Washington, DC: The Pew Charitable Trusts. Retrieved from http://www.pewcenteronthestates.org/report_detail.aspx?id=59149

Polanka, S. (2011, February 9). *Library Journal* publishes library eBook survey results – Sample data here [Web log comment]. Retrieved from http://www.libraries.wright.edu/noshelfrequired/?p=1914

Public Library Association. (2008). *Public library data service report, 2008.*

Rogers, R. R. (2010, November). Social media, libraries, and web 2.0: How American libraries are using new tools for public relations and to attract new users – Third survey. Columbia, SC: South Carolina State Library. Retrieved from http://www.statelibrary.sc.gov/docs/pr/201012_pr_social_media_survey.pdf

U.S. Census Bureau (2000). *United States census 2000.* Retrieved from http://www.census.gov/population/www/cen2000/briefs/tablist.html

U.S. Department of Labor, Bureau of Labor Statistics. (2010). *Labor force characteristics by race and ethnicity 2009*. Washington, DC: Author. Retrieved from http://www.bls.gov/cps/race_ethnicity_2008_6.htm

Zickuhr, K. (2011). *Generations and their gadgets* [Pew Internet & American Life Project]. Washington, DC: Pew Research Center. Retrieved from http://pewinternet.org/Reports/2011/Generations-and-gadgets.aspx

The Role of Public Libraries, the Internet, and Economic Uncertainty

Kathryn Sigler, Paul T. Jaeger, John Carlo Bertot, Abigail J. McDermott, Elizabeth J. DeCoster and Lesley A. Langa
Information Policy & Access Center, College of Information Studies, University of Maryland, College Park, MD, USA

Abstract

Historically, library usage has increased during economic downturns. In the pre-Internet era, this meant increased usage of print materials and reference services. In the Internet era, however, the number of roles that public libraries can play in serving their communities has expanded greatly. This chapter provides insights into the ways in which American public libraries are using the Internet to meet patron, community, and government needs in this time of economic crisis. Drawing from the data and findings from the 2010–2011 *Public Library Funding and Technology Access* national survey, this chapter examines key issues at the intersection of public libraries, the Internet, and economic uncertainty and library/e-government partnerships that have resulted from the economic situation. In these difficult economic circumstances, US public libraries have been able to use the Internet to meet many vital patron and community needs, but they still face numerous economic difficulties in responding to these requests.

Keywords: Public Library Internet Roles; Public access; Digital Literacy; E-government; Employment assistance

I. Introduction

For more than 15 years, the *Public Library Funding and Technology Access*[1] studies have documented the rapid changes in Internet access and services in public libraries and the accompanying successes and challenges that the Internet has raised for libraries. Over these years, the presence of the Internet in public libraries has significantly shaped the social roles of public libraries

---

[1]Previously known as the *Public Libraries and the Internet* national survey. Previous study reports are available at http://www.plinternetsurvey.org

LIBRARIANSHIP IN TIMES OF CRISIS
ADVANCES IN LIBRARIANSHIP, VOL. 34
© 2011 by Emerald Group Publishing Limited
ISSN: 0065-2830
DOI: 10.1108/S0065-2830(2011)0000034005

and the expectations for public libraries by patrons, communities, and governments (Bertot, 2010; Jaeger, Bertot, & Fleischmann, 2010; McClure, Bertot, & Jaeger, 2010).

As a result of the early embrace of providing free public Internet access, public libraries have become centers of Internet access in society, with patrons, communities, employers, and governments relying on the availability of free public Internet access through public libraries (Bertot, 2009; Bertot, McClure, & Jaeger, 2008; McClure, Jaeger, & Bertot, 2007). While there are some critics of the Internet in public libraries, there is little dispute that the public library has become the primary community-based public access point for Internet services for people with no other means of access, for people with limited access, and for people who need help accessing information online. The studies show that the Internet both serves to augment existing library services and to establish new social roles, with e-government and emergency response being two of the most prominent new roles (Jaeger, 2008; Jaeger & Bertot, 2009).

More commonplace crises have also led to new ways that patrons rely on the public library. In the current economic downturn, use of public libraries and library computers for job-seeking activities, social services, e-mail access, entertainment, and other purposes has increased substantially. The huge increases in public library usage have gained the attention of many print, radio, and television media outlets (e.g., Carlton, 2009; CNN, 2009; Gwinn, 2009; Jackson, 2009; Van Sant, 2009). Further, as people reclassify home Internet access as a luxury that can be cut to save money in harsh economic times, library usage for information access and exchange is likely to continue to increase (Horrigan, 2008).

For all of the new responsibilities that libraries have taken on as a result of their role as guarantor of Internet access and training, the increased reliance on this access and training by patrons applying for jobs, seeking social support, and looking for free entertainment options in challenging economic times presents especially significant challenges for libraries. The same economic challenges that are increasing library and Internet need and usage are simultaneously draining library budgets, as state and local governments have been increasingly disinclined to invest in public libraries given the badly declining tax revenues and the financial uncertainties of the future.

A. Public Libraries and Economic Hardship

Libraries have long believed that economic downturns lead to increased usage of the library and its services, with references to this relationship dating back to as early as 1880 in library discourse (James, 1985). This relationship is now known as the "Librarian's Axiom" and has been demonstrated to be true through numerous studies (Davis, 2009, 2011; James, 1986; Lynch, 2002). During the Great Depression, the demand for library books and for reference services skyrocketed; the increased demand coupled with budget decreases left many libraries with decimated collections by the end of the Depression (Kramp, 2010). The needs of patrons during the Depression also led to expansions of services for unemployed adults and of children's services (Kramp, 2010). Subsequent recessions have increased demands for library services, though even in the best of economic times, libraries are a vital resource for individuals in economic distress (Berman, 1998; Nyquist, 1968).

This current prolonged downturn has been no exception. As 2008–2009 president of the American Library Association, Jim Rettig noted "public libraries have been America's first responders to the economic crisis" (2009, n.p.). Libraries in communities with long-term economic difficulties typically have more limited resources for patrons (Constantino, 2005). Yet, between 2006 and 2008, the number of Americans with library cards increased by 5%, in-person library visits increased by 10%, and library web site visits increased by 17% (Davis, 2009, 2011). "These increases in use translate into 25 million more in-person visits, 11 million more uses via computer, and about 4 million more uses by telephone" (Davis, 2009, p. 13). On average, circulation in libraries rose 5.6% between 2007 and 2008 alone (Hoffert, 2009). In 2009, more than 14 million people were considered regular users of library computers for Internet access (C. Hill, 2009).

In individual libraries, the impacts can be overwhelming, with some systems seeing a 25% increase in visits in one year or a 500% increase in computer usage in a three-year period (N. M. Hill, 2009). In 2010, 50% of the computer users in Wichita public libraries were using them for job and career purposes and more than 10% were using the computers to apply for unemployment benefits (Urban Libraries Council, 2010). The 2009–2010 president of the American Library Association, Camila Alire, stated that "while libraries have long been refuges for the down and out, anecdotal reports underscore that [libraries] are dealing with more people than ever before with mental health issues and basic needs such as food and shelter" (Nieves, 2010, n.p.).

The need for use of technology to access social services is particularly acute. In the United States, millions of people now rely on government-provided social services to meet basic needs: Medicaid (57.8 million people in 2006), food stamps (over 33 million in 2009), the Women Infant and Children (WIC) program (9 million in 2009), SSI (over 7 million in 2009), and many others (U.S. Centers for Medicare & Medicaid Services, n.d.; U.S.

Office of Retirement & Disability Policy, n.d.; U.S. Supplemental Nutrition Assistance Program, n.d.; U.S. Women & Infants & Children Program, n.d.). In addition to these federal services, each state provides a range of local services that cover health, family, employment, and other social services. With one in six Americans living in a household where there is difficulty feeding the members and nearly half of older adults facing poverty, many Americans who have never previously applied for social services now find themselves seeking government support (Chen, 2010; Reuters, 2010). However, most of these support services must now be applied for online (Bertot & Jaeger, in press).

With public libraries serving as the trusted social outlet for free public Internet access and assistance, people with no access, insufficient access, or insufficient digital literacy primarily turn to the library to apply for and access vital social services (Bertot, Jaeger, Langa, & McClure, 2006a, 2006b; Jaeger & Fleischmann, 2007). Because public libraries are so well positioned to offer e-government services, use of public library computers for this purpose is high, especially among users who have no other access to the Internet outside of the library (Becker et al., 2010).

In a typical library, this translates into increased usage of books, audio books, and DVDs for entertainment, particularly materials on job-seeking and resume-writing, and in Internet usage, with patrons primarily searching for employment, unemployment benefits, and social services (Holland & Verploeg, 2009; Martell, 2009). Such increases should not be surprising as jobs are scarce and, according to a 2009 survey, 63% of people have reduced their entertainment spending during the great recession (Gibbs, 2009). In addition, parents working longer hours and having less funds for after school activities equates to more children, tweens, and teens coming to the library for entertainment and a safe haven (Farrelly, 2009). People also see libraries as a place where patrons can get information from librarians on using the Internet to help save money (Porter & King, 2009). Thus, the economic downturn, by both exacerbating the digital divide and increasing the volume of applications for social services, is strongly driving public library computer and Internet usage (Bertot & Jaeger, in press; Gehner, 2010; Holt & Holt, 2010; Kinney, 2010).

B. Public Library Funding and Technology Access

The 2010–2011 *Public Library Funding and Technology Access* data clearly demonstrated that the funding choices made by governments in relation to the economic downturn have increased the difficulties public libraries face as the community provider of Internet access (Bertot, Jaeger, & McClure, 2010).

As Fig. 1 shows, the percentage of libraries reporting decreased hours jumped dramatically from 2.4% in 2007 to 15.9% in 2010, while the number of libraries reporting increases in hours dropped from 12.0% to 6.0% during the same time period (see Fig. 1). Fig. 2 reveals that, in trying to provide necessary services like help with employment information, 55.9% of libraries did not have enough staff to meet patron needs, 43.4% did not have staff with the necessary expertise, and 33.0% had too few workstations to meet demand. The lack of sufficient staff expertise (50.0%) was most dramatic in rural libraries, while lack of sufficient workstations (43.6%) was most pronounced among urban libraries. Over half of urban (52.6%), suburban (56.7%), and rural (56.3%) libraries report inadequate staffing levels as a significant barrier to meeting patron's employment-seeking needs.

On the other hand, the need for library services has dramatically increased because of the economic crisis, as patrons seek unemployment benefits and other social services, apply for jobs, and use the Internet for communication and entertainment purposes. In 64.5% of communities, the public library was the only provider of free public Internet and computer access in the community in 2010. As a result, in most communities, public libraries are the only place available for people to fulfill these increasing Internet needs.

Fig. 3 shows that, from 2009 to 2010, 69.8% of public libraries saw increases in the use of their public workstations, 75.3% saw increases in the use of their Wireless Internet, and almost half of public libraries saw increases in the use of electronic resources. These increases were most pronounced in urban and suburban areas, which had nearly identical increases in the wireless Internet and use of public workstations. This increased usage was heavily tied to increases in need for e-government resources for social support and online employment resources.

An increasing number of public libraries are providing access to a wide range of these types of job-seeking and e-government resources, and assisting patrons in their use. As is revealed in Fig. 4, 90.9% of libraries in 2010 offered access to jobs databases, 77.0% provided access to civil service exam materials, 74.5% offered resume assistance, and 71.9% helped patrons apply for jobs online. All of these numbers are increase over 2009. Similarly, Fig. 5 shows increase in all of the e-government services and assistance offered by public libraries. In 2010, 89.7% of libraries assisted patrons in using e-government websites, 80.7% helped patrons apply for e-government services, and 67.8% even helped patrons complete government forms online.

Ironically, public libraries have been viewed as easy targets for budget cuts by many, as evidenced by a Fox News Chicago editorial that asked: "With the Internet and e-books, do we really need millions for libraries?"

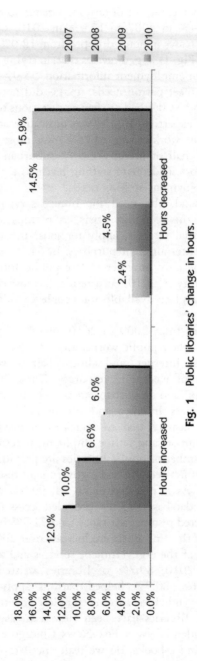

Fig. 1 Public libraries' change in hours.

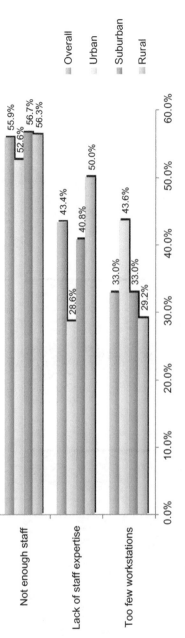

Fig. 2 Challenges affecting ability of public libraries to help patrons meet employment seeking needs.

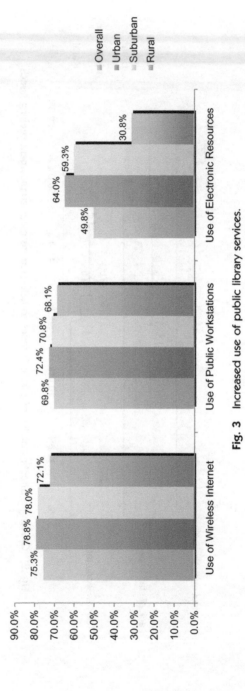

Fig. 3 Increased use of public library services.

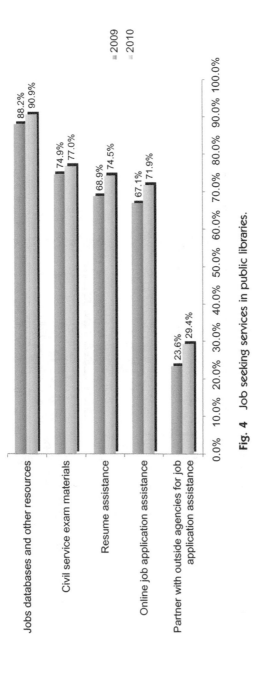

Fig. 4 Job seeking services in public libraries.

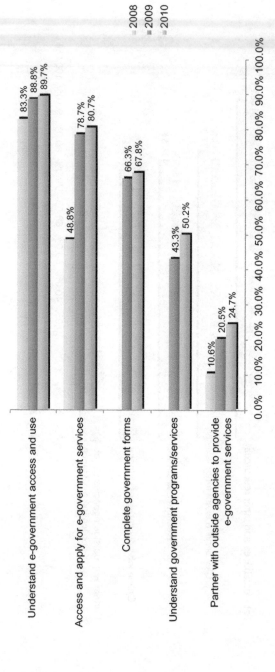

Fig. 5 E-government services in public libraries.

(Davlantes, 2010, n.p.). A similar sentiment was found in a Florida newspaper editorial, which asserted that the Internet, Google in particular, has made public libraries redundant and that "no serious research is carried on in the library stacks" (Elmore, 2008, n.p.)

C. Library Partnerships and the Economy

In 2010, 25.1% of public libraries reported partnering with government agencies, nonprofit organizations, and others to provide e-government services (Bertot et al., 2011). These types of partnerships can take many different forms and serve many different causes (Bertot & Jaeger, in press). Some partnerships involve a library and a government agency partnering to directly advance the overall work of the agency. Others are formed for very specific projects of interest to the agency. In any type of partnership between a public library and agovernment agency, library resources are being used to help fulfill the agency's mission. A number of these partnerships rely on the library's Internet capabilities to meet the economic needs of patrons, ranging from ensuring electronic access to social services, providing technical and digital skills for employment, connecting small businesses to the Internet, and bringing social services into the library (Bertot & Jaeger, in press; Urban Libraries Council, 2010).

1. Partnership Examples

An excellent example of the resources being developed by libraries to assist patrons in accessing e-government is Pasco County Public Library System's E-Government Tools page (Pasco County Library Cooperative, 2010). This page includes multiple video tutorials explaining the use of government websites, including unemployment, Medicaid, the Department of Veterans Affairs, and the Florida Department of Children and Families. The E-Government Tools pages feature special sections on important issues for those facing economic hardships: job seeking, with posts on career fairs, workshops, GED classes and other resources; healthcare; and finding doctors and health insurance. In addition to tutorials specifically related to government services, E-Government Tools also include video tutorials on basic digital literacy skills, including basic computer components, web browsing, and printing. In addition, Pasco County Public Library System loans patrons laptops to use in the library for e-government purposes. As of September, their staff had received 7529 queries about government services and 6015 laptop requests in 2010, including 1022 food stamp queries and 120 medical queries (Pasco County Library Cooperative, 2010).

In Alachua County, Florida, the Alachua County Library District (ACLD) has partnered with the Florida Department of Children and Families and two nonprofit contracted by the state to provide foster care and related services, the Partnership for Strong Families and the Casey Family Programs (Alachua County Library District, 2010; Blumenstein, 2009). Their collaboration, called The Library Partnership—A Neighborhood Resource Center, is a 7500 square foot facility that contains offices for child welfare agencies in addition to a full library branch. At The Library Partnership, the library staff works with other agencies to help patrons to fill out forms and access websites, and they also assist with programming. On the calendar for October were *Alachua County Housing Applications & Recertification, Child Care Information, Health Practices in Pregnancy & Beyond,* and *Parent to Parent.*

In Baltimore, Maryland, the City Health Department identified a problem and turned to the library for help in solving it (Baltimore City Health Department, 2010; Brewington, 2010). The problem was access to healthy food—many of the city's lower socioeconomic status (SES) neighborhoods are considered "food deserts" because they do not have grocery stores within walking distance. This forces residents, who frequently do not own cars, to rely on others or on public transportation to get fresh food, or to shop at the local corner stores and take-out restaurants, where there are few healthy options. The diet forced on residents by this lack of healthy food can have severe health consequences, including high rates of death caused by diet-related conditions such as heart disease, stroke, and diabetes. To help bring healthy foods into some of Baltimore's low SES neighborhoods, Health Department staff members are now at the libraries two days a week, helping people to order their groceries on laptops designated specifically for this program and taking payments, including with food stamps. The next day, or sometime even later that same day, patrons can return to the library to pick up their groceries. In this partnership, the library is directly helping the government agency to provide a social service through the use of its public access computers and Internet connection.

In San Francisco, California, the public library has partnered with the San Francisco Department of Public Health to help better serve their homeless patrons by hiring a full-time psychiatric social worker to work in the library (Knight, 2010; Nieves, 2010). In her first year she was able to direct more than 150 patrons to relevant social services. The library and Department of Health have also established a program that directly involves the library with those same social services agencies. After successfully completing a 12-week vocational rehabilitation program, those who had formerly been homeless can work at the library as "health and safety associates" up to 20 hours a week for $12 an hour, with duties including informing patrons of library policies and distributing flyers with information about social services.

II. Conclusion

The history of the *Public Library Funding and Technology Access* study parallels the years that governments have been developing e-government information, communication, and services. Between the mid-1990s and 2010, public libraries have moved through several relationships with Internet access and e-government information (Bertot, 2010). By the time e-government began to be a major emphasis of the federal government in the late 1990s, public libraries had already established the Internet infrastructure to serve as a main access point to e-government information, communication, and services (Jaeger & Bertot, 2010).

However, public libraries could not have expected that their roles in the provision of e-government would rapidly expand as government agencies increasingly offloaded access responsibilities onto public libraries—often directing people to public libraries for help. During this past decade, out of necessity, public libraries have moved from simply providing access to e-government to providing access, training, support, and even direct assistance for e-government (Jaeger & Bertot, 2011). Serving as an e-government center is now one of the largest roles of a public library in its community. With the range of e-government services that have been in greater demand during the economic downturn—applying for jobs, seeking unemployment benefits, applying for social services—the Internet access and assistance available in public libraries have been invaluable to countless individuals and communities.

As these individuals and communities seek to better their economic situations, and as governments continue to migrate their information, communication, and services online, there is increased pressure on libraries to serve as providers of employment and e-government services in their communities. Furthermore, governments and employers need libraries to serve as community-based public access technology venues that offer not only access to technologies, but also the individual assistance that governments or other organizations no longer provide, such as technology training, assistance completing forms, submitting applications, and much more.

These increased demands, however, come at a time when library budgets are being cut, leading to staff and hour reductions. The reality is that no one stakeholder—governments, employers, or libraries—can individually provide or meet the service and resource requirements of communities, particularly in circumstances of a severe economic crisis. But libraries are essential community providers of e-government access and employment services, and in doing so, serve "as a strong, constant thread in the community's tapestry" (Pearson, 2009, p. 22).

Whether explicitly acknowledged or not, libraries serve as a key partner in the delivery of e-government for every government agency that interacts with members of the public (Bertot & Jaeger, in press). When libraries and government agencies actively collaborate to meet community needs, they are able to address problems more effectively and can even tackle problems that the libraries and government agencies cannot address individually. As the findings discussed in this chapter show, this prolonged economic downturn has demonstrated the continuing central role of libraries in their communities, of the important contributions of libraries and their public access technology to supporting the economic needs of community members, and the significant potential of library/government agency partnerships in addressing economy-related issues for communities. The economic downturn of recent years has also created many new stresses of decreasing budgets and increasing usage for libraries as they meet vital community needs. Successfully reconciling these service needs and challenges will likely continue to be an issue for libraries long after this current economic crisis has subsided.

References

Alachua County Library District. (2010). *The library partnership\Alachua county library district*. Retrieved from http://www.aclib.us/library-partnership

Baltimore City Health Department. (2010, March 17). *Virtual supermarket program provides food access to underserved communities*. Retrieved from http://www.baltimorehealth.org/press/2010_03_17_VS_PR.pdf

Becker, S., Crandall, M. D., Fisher, K. E., Kinney, B., Landry, C., & Rocha, A. (2010). *Opportunity for all: How the American public benefits from internet access at U.S. libraries*. Retrieved from http://tascha.washington.edu/usimpact

Berman, S. (1998, March). On my mind – Libraries, class, and the poor people's policy. *American Libraries, 29*, p. 38.

Bertot, J. C. (2009). Public access technologies in public libraries: Impacts and implications. *Information Technology & Libraries, 28*(2), 84–95.

Bertot, J. C. (2010). Public libraries and the internet: A retrospective, challenges, and issues moving forward. In J. C. Bertot, P. T. Jaeger & C. R. McClure (Eds.), *Public libraries and the internet: Roles, perspectives, and implications* (pp. 15–35). Westport, CT: Libraries Unlimited.

Bertot, J. C., & Jaeger, P. T. (in press). Implementing and managing public library networks, connectivity, and partnerships to promote e-government access and education. In S. Aikins (Ed.), *Managing e-government projects: Concepts, issues and best practices*. Hershey, PA: IGI Global.

Bertot, J. C., Jaeger, P. T., Langa, L. A., & McClure, C. R. (2006a). Public access computing and Internet access in public libraries: The role of public libraries in e-government and emergency situations. *First Monday, 11*(9)Retrieved from http://www.firstmonday.org/issues/issue11_9/bertot/index.html

Bertot, J. C., Jaeger, P. T., Langa, L. A., & McClure, C. R. (2006b). Drafted: I want you to deliver e-government. *Library Journal, 131*(13), 34–39.

Bertot, J. C., Jaeger, P. T., & McClure, C. R. (2010). *Public libraries and the internet: Roles, perspectives, and implications*. Westport, CT: Libraries Unlimited.

Bertot, J. C., McClure, C. R., & Jaeger, P. T. (2008). The impacts of free public Internet access on public library patrons and communities. *Library Quarterly, 78*, 285–301.

Bertot, J. C., Sigler, K., Langa, L. A., DeCoster, E., McDermott, A. J., & Katz, S. (2011). *2010–2011 public library funding and technology access survey*. College Park, MD: Information Policy & Access Center. Retrieved from www.plinternetsurvey.org

Blumenstein, L. (2009, July 22). In Gainesville, FL, "The Library Partnership" Merges Branch, Social Services. *Library Journal*. Retrieved from http://www.libraryjournal.com/article/CA6672422.html

Brewington, K. (2010, March 18). Libraries help fill city nutrition gaps. *The Baltimore Sun*. Retrieved from http://articles.baltimoresun.com/2010-03-18/health/bal-md.hs.supermarket18mar18_1_food-deserts-healthful-grocery-stores

Carlton, J. (2009). Folks are flocking to the library, a cozy place to look for a job: Books, computers and wi-fi are free, but staffs are stressed by crowds, cutbacks. *Washington Post*, January 19, p. A1.

Chen, S. (2010). The new hungry: College-educated, middle-class cope with food insecurity. *CNN.com*. Retrieved from http://www.cnn.com/2010/LIVING/12/13/food.insecurities.holidays.middle.class/index.html

CNN. (2009). Hard economic times: A boon for public libraries. *CNN.com*. Retrieved from http://www.cnn.com/2009/US/02/28/recession.libraries/index.html

Constantino, R. (2005). Print environments between high and low socioeconomic status (SES) communities. *Teacher Librarian, 32*(3), 22–25.

Davis, D. M. (2009). Challenges to sustaining library technology. *Public Libraries, 48*(4), 12–17.

Davis, D. M. (2011). Public library funding: An overview and discussion. In J. C. Bertot, P. T. Jaeger & C. R. McClure (Eds.), *Public libraries and the internet: Roles, perspectives, and implications* (pp. 193–214). Westport, CT: Libraries Unlimited.

Davlantes, A. (2010). Are libraries necessary, or a waste of tax money? *Fox News Chicago*, June 28.

Elmore, G. (2008). Pull the plug on the library. *Gainesville Sun*, March 3.

Farrelly, M. G. (2009). Refuge in the library. *Public Libraries, 48*(4), 24–26.

Gehner, J. (2010). Libraries, low-income people, and social exclusion. *Public Library Quarterly, 29*(1), 39–47.

Gibbs, N. (2009). Thrift nation. *Time*, April 27, p. 24.

Gwinn, M. A. (2009). Library use jumps in Seattle area: Economy likely reason. *Seattle Times*, January 23.

Hill, C. (2009). Inside, outside, and online. *American Libraries, 40*(3), 39.

Hill, N. M. (2009). Three views. *Public Libraries, 48*(4), 8–11.

Hoffert, B. (2009). It's the economy. *Library Journal, 134*(3), 34–36.

Holland, S., & Verploeg, A. (2009). No easy targets: Six libraries in the economy's dark days. *Public Libraries, 48*(4), 27–38.

Holt, L. E., & Holt, G. E. (2010). *Public library services for the poor: Doing all we can*. Chicago, IL: American Library Association.

Horrigan, J. B. (2008). *Home broadband adoption 2008: Adoption stalls for low-income Americans even as many broadband users opt for premium services that give them more speed*. Washington, DC: Pew Internet and American Life Project.

Jackson, D. Z. (2009). The library-a recession sanctuary. *Boston Globe*, January 3, p. A11.

Jaeger, P. T. (2008). Building e-government into the library & information science curriculum: The future of government information and services. *Journal of Education for Library and Information Science, 49*, 167–179.

Jaeger, P. T., & Bertot, J. C. (2009). E-government education in public libraries: New service roles and expanding social responsibilities. *Journal of Education for Library and Information Science, 50*, 40–50.

Jaeger, P. T., & Bertot, J. C. (2010). Public libraries and e-government. In J. C. Bertot, P. T. Jaeger & C. R. McClure (Eds.), *Public libraries and the internet: Roles, perspectives, and implications* (pp. 39–57). Westport, CT: Libraries Unlimited.

Jaeger, P. T., & Bertot, J. C. (2011). Responsibility rolls down: Public libraries and the social and policy obligations of ensuring access to e-government and government information. *Public Library Quarterly, 30*(2), 91–116.

Jaeger, P. T., Bertot, J. C., & Fleischmann, K. R. (2010). Evolving relationships between information technology and public libraries. In J. C. Bertot, P. T. Jaeger & C. R. McClure (Eds.), *Public libraries and the internet: Roles, perspectives, and implications* (pp. 3–14). Westport, CT: Libraries Unlimited.

Jaeger, P. T., & Fleischmann, K. R. (2007). Public libraries, values, trust, and e-government. *Information Technology and Libraries, 26*(4), 35–43.

James, S. E. (1985). The relationship between local economic conditions and the use of public libraries. *Library Quarterly, 55*, 255–272.

James, S. E. (1986). Economic hard times and public library use: A close look at the Librarian's axiom. *Public Library Quarterly, 7*(3–4), 61–70.

Kinney, B. (2010). The internet, public libraries, and the digital divide. *Public Library Quarterly, 29*(2), 104–161.

Knight, H. (2010). Library adds social worker to assist homeless. *SFGate*, January 11. Retrieved from http://www.sfgate.com/cgi-bin/article.cgi?f=/c/a/2010/01/10/BAIT1BF6E3.DTL

Kramp, R. S. (2010). *The great depression: Its impact on forty-six large American public libraries*. Duluth, MN: Library Juice.

Lynch, M. J. (2002). Economic hard times and public library use revisited. *American Libraries, 33*(7), 62–63.

Martell, C. (2009). Hanging tough at our neighborhood libraries. *Public Library Quarterly, 28*, 336–343.

McClure, C. R., Bertot, J. C., & Jaeger, P. T. (2010). The ever changing impacts of internet access on libraries and their communities. In J. C. Bertot, P. T. Jaeger & C. R. McClure (Eds.), *Public libraries and the internet: Roles, perspectives, and implications* (pp. 261–281). Westport, CT: Libraries Unlimited.

McClure, C. R., Jaeger, P. T., & Bertot, J. C. (2007). The looming infrastructure plateau? Space, funding, connection speed, and the ability of public libraries to meet the demand for free internet access. *First Monday, 12*(12). Retrieved from http://www.uic.edu/htbin/cgiwrap/bin/ojs/index.php/fm/article/view/2017/1907

Nieves, E. (2010). Calif. Library reaches out to homeless patrons. *Boston Globe*, March 7. Retrieved from http://www.boston.com/news/nation/articles/2010/03/07/san_francisco_hires_social_worker_for_homeless_library_patrons/

Nyquist, E. B. (1968). Poverty, prejudice, and the public library. *Library Quarterly, 38*, 78–89.

Pasco County Library Cooperative. (2010). *Pasco County Library Cooperative – e-Government resources*. Retrieved from http://www.pascolibraries.org/egovtools.shtml

Pearson, P. (2009). Fundraising and advocacy in tough times. *Public Libraries*, 48(4), 21–23.

Porter, M., & King, D. L. (2009). Save money-use the web. *Public Libraries*, 48(4), 18–20.

Rettig, J. (2009). Once in a lifetime. *American Libraries*. Retrieved from http://americanlibrariesmagazine.org/junejuly-2009/once-lifetime

Reuters. (2010). Nearly half of elderly in U.S. will face poverty. *MSNBC.com*. Retrieved from http://www.msnbc.com

Urban Libraries Council. (2010). *Partners for the future: Public libraries and local governments creating sustainable communities*. Chicago, IL: Author.

U.S. Centers for Medicare and Medicaid Services. (n.d.). Table 145. Medicaid – Summary by state: 2000 and 2006. *Medicaid, Program Statistics, Medicaid Statistical Information System*. Retrieved from http://www.census.gov/compendia/statab/2010/tables/10s0145.pdf

U.S. Office of Retirement and Disability Policy. (n.d.). Table 2. Supplemental security income. *Social Security Administration, Supplemental Security Record*. Retrieved from http://www.ssa.gov/policy/docs/factsheets/cong_stats/2009/al.html

U.S. Supplemental Nutrition Assistance Program. (n.d.). Table of participation and benefits as of October 28, 2010. Retrieved from http://www.fns.usda.gov/pd/34SNAPmonthly.htm

U.S. Women, Infants and Children Program. (n.d.). *Table of WIC program: Total participation*. Retrieved from http://www.fns.usda.gov/pd/26wifypart.htm

Van Sant, W. (2009). Librarians now add social work to their resumes. *St. Petersburg Times*, June 8. Retrieved from http://www.tampabay.com/

Cutback Management in US Public Libraries: Deliberations, Decision Spaces, and Reflections

Jennifer Weil Arns[a] and Evelyn H. Daniel[b]

[a]School of Library and Information Science, University of South Carolina, Columbia, South Carolina, USA
[b]School of Information and Library Science, University of North Carolina at Chapel Hill, Chapel Hill, North Carolina, USA

Abstract

Public library management literature and public administration theory have been unduly influenced by economic thinking appropriate to the private sector but a poor fit to the public sector. In this chapter we attempt to explain that public sector interests are different and that decisions about their future should be made on a different basis. Specifically, this chapter addresses the problem of cutback management and compares decisions made by library managers in the Great Depression to those being made in current economic times. Questions are raised about the approach to cutbacks that typify current public management practices, and it is suggested that new models are needed to help public library managers and trustees deal equitably and efficiently with recurring economic fluctuations and the fundamental changes that these periods sometimes produce.

Keywords: Public libraries; cutback decisions; finance; leadership; research agenda; public administration; Great Depression

I. Introduction

Whether cyclical or episodic, periods of economic instability lead to difficult decisions in all types of organizations. In many cases, these involve termination of individuals and programs, sale of assets, and disruption of organizational hierarchies—all of which may be harmful to customers and to those who rely on these activities for income. In the private sector, economic gain is the goal: creating wealth, maximizing profit, and avoiding loss. In the public sector, by contrast, creating wealth may be defined as building a well-educated

LIBRARIANSHIP IN TIMES OF CRISIS
ADVANCES IN LIBRARIANSHIP, VOL. 34
© 2011 by Emerald Group Publishing Limited
ISSN: 0065-2830
DOI: 10.1108/S0065-2830(2011)0000034006

democratic society; maximizing profit can be seen as ensuring equality of conditions such that maximum human potential is realized.

Avoiding loss may be the point at which public sector interests most closely align with those of the private sector. Both sectors are likely to adopt a defensive stance that may foreclose new kinds of investments or public offerings. However, both sectors differ markedly in their definition of ownership: who should be protected from loss, for whom wealth should be created, and whose profit (however defined) should be maximized. The concept of "publicness" also raises issues concerning who "owns" public organizations and should rightfully expect to benefit from their assets and be protected from loss. How an organization achieves legitimacy is another important difference between public and private organizations.

Moore and Khagram (2004), in an insightful examination of business and public sector organizations, argue that business firms typically bring a "shareholder" view to corporate strategy looking at investors as "customers" and working to maximize the financial return on the shareholders' investments as the legitimate and legitimating concerns of the firm. In the public sector, by contrast, an alternative model of "stakeholder" takes a much broader view of ownership. In this case, employees, government policy makers, local communities, and the general public are key actors whose concerns and requirements need to be addressed to produce meaningful legitimacy.

In the case of public libraries, a "shareholder" view leads to renewed attention to those who serve on their governing boards and have legal and fiduciary responsibility for libraries (Moore, 2010; Reed & Kalonick, 2010). This suggests that these trustees are akin to investors for the public sector. The number of individuals serving on these boards in the United States at any time is uncertain, but it is reasonable to estimate that they number between 36 and 50,000 based on a membership of 5–11 for the 9221 public libraries (Henderson et al., 2010). According to recent data, the assets that public libraries hold in trust for their communities are considerable. The operating expenditures they guide surpass 10 billion dollars and the facilities are visited well over a billion times a year. With the exception of government appointees, board service is usually voluntary. The factors that motivate such service are diverse but are rooted in the concept of public service where civic obligations are seen as contributing to the welfare of the entire community. During times of economic uncertainty, public library trustees and those who provide library services generally strive to preserve services and minimize the risk of permanent damage to the assets and revenue streams with which they are entrusted.

The models that inform choices in such times are consequently of substantial interest, and their broader implications become clearer when they are considered within the context of economic history and public administration theory. This chapter addresses its topic from these two perspectives, as well as from public management models and strategies that public libraries have typically pursued during two periods: the Great Depression of the 1930s and the recent severe recession. It concludes by raising questions about the approach to cutbacks that typify current public management practices and suggests that new models and new decision spaces are needed to help public library managers and trustees deal equitably and effectively with recurring economic fluctuations and the fundamental changes that these periods sometimes produce.

II. The Power of Economic Cycles

To set the stage for examining cutback decisions made in the down cycle of the economy, a brief visit to economic theory and the impact of downturns on business will be useful. In his seminal work, *The Wealth of Nations*, Adam Smith (1902) lays the groundwork for current characterizations of the processes that propel economic growth and decline, including the classic factors of production—land, labor, and capital. During periods of prosperity, these are plentiful and relatively inexpensive, and activities that turn them into desirable commodities result in rising levels of income and even wealth. This in turn leads to healthy consumption and employment. However, the situation can erode for a variety of reasons. At the microeconomic level, market saturation can occur, a point at which commodities are no longer viewed by consumers as desirable or necessary. In these cases, production slows or stops, and if more desirable products are not developed, producers lose associated income, employment opportunities dwindle, and consumer demand for products becomes more fragile.

A second problem can occur when increases in the cost of production lead to overly expensive products that result in weak demand. In this case, businesses will eventually either cease production, look for ways to add value to renew product desirability, or develop strategies, such as automation or offshore fabrication, to bring prices back to a level that consumers find attractive. In a third case, scarcity of land, labor, and/or capital (the classic factors of production) may have a similar effect. When the capital needed for production becomes less available or disappears, businesses typically allow production to decline or simply close down. As this occurs, income and purchasing power decline, debtors are unable to meet their obligations, the value of bank assets is weakened, pessimism grows, spending is delayed, and employment opportunities disappear.

It is sometimes difficult to ascribe an economic downturn to a single incident or agent. In the case of the Great Depression, writers point to a complex set of conditions, including unstable banking and capital markets (Bernanke, 1995), uncertainty concerning future income (Romer, 1988), irrational and overoptimistic investment behavior, and highly vulnerable market situations (Galbraith, 1955).

The current economic downturn has also been associated with a variety of causes (Weisberg, 2010). According to some economists, it was caused by regulatory failures that encouraged development of unpredictable financial products. Others point to an overinflated housing market that encouraged insupportable debt levels. The results have been somewhat easier to distinguish than the causes. In 2009 and 2010 many firms, including large ones such as Microsoft and IBM, resorted to employee cutbacks (McDougall, 2009; Sum & McLaughlin, 2010; Wingfield, 2010). Thirty percent of the employers responding to a Kaiser survey indicated that they either reduced the scope of health benefits provided to workers or increased cost-sharing by workers in response to the poor economy. Twenty-three percent of employers indicated that they had devolved a greater share of premium costs for insurance to workers (Kaiser, 2010). According to the U.S. Department of Labor's Bureau of Labor Statistics (2010), retail trade employment fell by 28,000 in November 2010, with department stores and furniture and home furnishings stores accounting for about half of these losses. For example, for the current downturn, public charities and foundations also experienced difficulties, with 40% of those surveyed indicating that donations had dropped between January 1 and May 31, 2010 (GuideStar, 2010). And, just as private firms felt the need to cut back benefits to employees and to take other steps to manage the down cycle, so, too, the public sector has had to respond.

III. Public Management Cutback Strategies

Government organizations have proved to be vulnerable to recessions and subject to the problems associated with organizational decline (Horwitz, 2009; Levine, 1978, 1979; Miller & Svara, 2009). Shrinking revenues have led to reorganizations, jobs have been eliminated, and the employees providing public services have experienced the anxiety that accompanies potential or eventual loss of income. Those who depend on public services for transportation, water treatment, and the like have experienced a sense of loss, as the quality of services slowly decline or disappeared.

46%	Increased existing fees for services	44%	Eliminated or significantly reduced travel budget	52%	Implemented *targeted* cuts in expenditures
23%	Added new fees for services	11%	Implemented furloughs for staff/ reducing the number of hours worked	19%	Laid off staff
35%	Reduced services	43%	Frozen salaries	60%	Deferred capital projects
14%	Eliminated services	7%	Reduced salaries	13%	Revised union contracts to reduce pay or benefits
66%	Left vacant positions unfilled	28%	Eliminated or significantly reduced professional development budget	12%	Other (Please describe)
40%	Eliminated positions	30%	Implemented *across-the-board* cuts in expenditures		

Fig. 1 Measures implemented by local governments to address fiscal crises (Moulder, 2009).

Recent reports suggest that many public organizations have been attracted to decision-making models similar to those used by the private sector. This is evident in terms of workforce reduction, product modification, discontinuation of services, and acceptance of declining service quality. A study of county service agents by Packard, Patti, Daly, Tucker-Tatlow, and Farrell (2008) indicated that modifying levels and types of services, developing alternative sources of revenue, and helping employees move to other jobs figured prominently among downturn strategies. Lewis & Mello's (2009) investigation of the coping strategies employed by the largest city in each state yielded similar efforts to cut costs with the more prominent being hiring freezes, benefit cuts, and wage freezes. Similar results are seen in recent reports by Hoene (2009) and Moulder (2009). They point to other practices, including deferment of capital projects, reduction of services, and increases in fees. Fig. 1 summarizes the measures that responding local governments used to meet shortfalls in incoming revenue streams.

A. The Great Depression

The literature indicates that public libraries resorted to similar strategies when faced with the widespread economic hardships in the Great Depression.

Kramp (1975) notes that the 46 large American public libraries in his study tended to respond sequentially as finances worsened, beginning with economies related to supplies and maintenance, then book funds, and lastly to salaries. Kramp also found that other measures were used such as the introduction of new and/or increased fees, improvements in filing systems, as well as finding new revenue streams, including state and federal aid. Luyt (2007) also points to libraries' efforts to obtain external funding. Duffus (1933), in contrast, provides a poignant contemporary view of a variety of efforts undertaken by what he considers to be "starving libraries." Many of these actions correspond to the measures reflected in Moulder's (2009) contemporary study, namely, reduced hours, reduced collection expenditures, across the board budget cuts, unfilled staff vacancies, reduced and frozen salaries, and service cutbacks.

Novotny's (2010) account of Chicago Public Library in the Depression is similar. Branch hours were reduced, book buying was suspended for 4 years, and about one-fifth of the staff was released. Writing closer to the onset of the Depression, Herdman (1943) noted that "Between the years of 1930 and 1935, public libraries in the United States reacted somewhat uniformly to the combined influences of smaller appropriations and larger demands" (p. 310). Decisions made by the leaders of the 150 libraries in her sample resulted in a decrease in salary expenditures of about 10% and a decrease in book expenditures of about 30%. Periodical and binding expenditures and miscellaneous maintenance expenditures also declined, but to a lesser degree.

The annual reports of individual public libraries provide a more detailed picture of the impact of the Great Depression.

1. District of Columbia Public Library

In the case of the District of Columbia Public Library (DCPL), the 1929 *Annual Report of the Board of Trustees* was optimistic, noting that the growth of the Library was sound and sure and that the Trustees looked forward with confidence to the Library's further wholesome development (DCPL, 1929, p. 1). In 1930, the trustees still looked forward to a level of expansion that would meet the needs of the two-thirds of the city's population who lacked convenient library facilities (DCPL, 1930). By 1931, however, the trustees noted that "it seems particularly unfortunate with the increased leisure of government employees and at a time when there is much unemployment that the Library had been compelled to shorten hours." They also noted difficulties created by the inability to increase staff or fill vacant positions (DCPL, 1931, p. 19).

In 1932, it is clear that the situation had worsened, as the Trustees reported that plans for additional branches and expanding the main library have been "retarded," while

> demands of hundreds of new readers, some who desire to improve their equipment in order to hold their present position or prepare for better ones, and others who wish to forget their troubles by reading diverting books or tone up their morale by calling on the 'literature of power,' fairly swamp every library agency. (DCPL, 1932, p. 19)

Under these discouraging circumstances, "efficient, loyal, and devoted" staff valiantly attempted to carry on. By 1933, the Trustees reported a "deplorable situation" in which the Library faced unprecedented demands for service as its appropriations continued to be cut (DCPL, 1933, p. 57). Remaining staff members bore a service burden that greatly exceeded capacity, the seven buildings still open were badly in need of repair, and the book fund had been severely cut.

2. Boston Public Library

The Annual Reports of the Director and the Trustees of the Boston Public Library (BPL) reflect similar experiences. In 1928, the Trustees were optimistic and reported steady progress in renewing and repairing equipment and repairs to the Central Library. Mention was made of new Reader's advisory services and popular concerts (Trustees, 1928). The 1929 report noted that circulation to children had risen, and it included the usual request for bequests and increased funding to meet the rising demand (Trustees, 1929). Although no mention of the Depression is made in the 1932 report, statistics indicate reductions in the city appropriations, trust fund income, book expenditures, and the number of volumes added, along with increases in the number of books borrowed, a growing number of cardholders, and the opening of three new branches (Trustees, 1932).

City appropriations, trust fund income, book expenditures, and the number of volumes added were lower again in 1933. In the 4 years up to this point, the report noted a circulation increase of 53% and a decrease in expenditures of 46%. Reflecting on these changes, the Director noted that

> The added leisure time of a great mass of adult readers due to shorter hours of labor or involuntary unemployment have added greatly to the use of the library as a study and reading center. Its very quiet is inviting to the disturbed and distressed in this period of anxiety and complexity. This natural effect of today's conditions of depression increases demands on the staff in performing its duty, and has correspondingly increased the responsibilities of the Director and his assistants (Trustees, 1933, p. 23).

B. The Current Recession

In April 2010, the American Library Association (ALA) indicated that 41% of states in the United States reported declines in state funding for public libraries (*Survey*). Preliminary analysis of public library data from the Institute of Museum and Library Services (2010) suggests that close to two-thirds of the public libraries serving more than 400,000 people experienced a decline in total revenue between 2008 and 2009. Another 9% experienced an increase in total revenue of less than 1%, and approximately 80% experienced a decline in state funding. While the responses of libraries facing situations such as these have naturally varied, they are characterized by a recent sample of *Library Journal* headlines:

- *Proposed budget in Texas nearly zeros out key state library funds* (Kelley, 2011b)
- *Camden Free Library to close doors* (Blumenstein, 2011a)
- *Gary Public Library faces steep budget cuts* (Warburton, 2010)
- *Budget cuts force Houston library to shorten hours* (Budget Cuts, 2010)
- *To close budget gap, Queens Library to lay off 46* (Oder, 2010)
- *Reading PL plans to close all branches* (Oder, 2009d)
- *DCPL reduces hours* (DCPL, 2009)
- *Omaha closed branch, lays off 25% of FTE for the year* (Oder, 2009c)
- *Dallas cuts would slam budget* (Dallas, 2009)
- *Hawaii proposes minimum of 2-day closures per month* (Oder, 2009a)
- *Indiana system to close three of four branches* (Indiana, 2009)
- *Indiana tax cuts hurt PLs* (Blumenstein, 2008)
- *Memphis Mayor: Close five libraries* (Oder, 2008)

Looking at public library cutback decisions, they can be grouped into three major categories: reductions in staff and/or in compensation, reductions in service hours, and reductions in collection development funds.

1. Staff and Compensation Reductions

An initial review of the literature indicates that compensation and salary-related expenditures were often considered when major expenditure reductions were needed, although these decisions were typically not called for immediately (Oder, 2009a). By 2010, more than 40% of the libraries responding to the *Library Journal Budget Survey* indicated that they had frozen salaries and reduced staff. Libraries serving one million or more were hardest hit, losing, on average, 50 employees (*Service*, 2010). In 2011, 72% of the libraries surveyed indicated that their budgets had been cut, and 43% had cut staff positions (Kelley, 2011a).

At the local level, there were numerous reports of compensation-related considerations, including the elimination of 41 positions at the Cuyahoga County Public Library (Flagg, 2009), 155 jobs at the Dallas Public Library, TX (Watson, 2010), and one-third of the staff at the Charlotte Mecklenburg Public Library system, NC (Frazier, 2010). At the Queens Borough Public Library, 14 nonunion positions from various administrative departments were considered for elimination, including 25% of the senior management staff (Oder, 2010). Citing an unprecedented financial crisis, cuts amounting to about 20% were recently considered in Detroit (Blumenstein, 2011b). Similar measures were considered for the Miami-Dade Public Library where 32 part-time positions were slated for elimination (Miami-Dade, 2010), and at the Jefferson County Public Library, CO, where freezing salaries was considered and 25 positions eliminated through attrition (Colorado lib., 2010).

2. Reductions in Service Hours

According to a recent national poll, nearly 4 in 10 mayors report cutting library services (U.S. Mayors, 2010). Local reports provide specific examples of situations where economic pressures led to considerations related to services. Examples include the Ferguson Library's plan to stagger branch hours in response to a $1.2 million budget cut (Sadowska, 2010) and the Montclair Public Library's consideration of closing a branch in response to an $800,000 reduction in funding (Emling, 2011). A number of other libraries considered significant service reductions (Budget Cuts, 2010; Colorado lib., 2010; Cranberry, 2011; Des Moines, 2009; Philadelphia, 2009; Plumley, 2010; Residents meet, 2007; San José, 2010; Sugar Grove, 2007); and in an "unprecedented" move, the Charlotte Mecklenburg Library recently considered relying on volunteers to maintain decreased service hours (Volunteers, 2010). The D.C. Public Library also reported that it was considering cuts that would affect service hours every day of the week at its main and neighborhood libraries, would look to volunteers to make up for budget shortages, and would discontinue its youth outreach program (DCPL, 2009).

3. Reductions in Collection Development Expenditures

As the second largest component of many library budgets, collection expenditures are also frequently targeted. The Dallas Public Library considered reducing collection expenditures to $900,000 in 2009 from $3.7 million in 2008 (Dallas, 2009). An overall 10% budget cut in Fort Worth, TX, led to a 20% collections budget decrease (Blumenstein, 2010b). An 8% reduction for materials was considered at the Jefferson County Public

Library, CO, in 2010 (Colorado lib., 2010), while the Houston Public Library considered a similar 6% reduction (Budget Cuts, 2010). Other strategies have involved reductions in capital expenditures, and in equipment and building maintenance.

Branch closings also figure in these decisions, with reports suggesting that these have been considered in a number of large cities, including Boston, MA, where 10 neighborhood branches were initially slated for closing. Accompanied by the prospect of laying off one-quarter of the library staff, these actions were described by one columnist as "cuts that would irrevocably alter America's oldest municipally funded library system" (Ryan, 2010). A New York interest group also recently noted that if "the city subsidy for the libraries remains at the level proposed by the Mayor for the fiscal year that begins July 1, more than three dozen branch libraries may be closed" (Maher & Turetsky, 2011). Similar considerations have been reported in Portland, ME, and Indianapolis, IN (More branch closures, 2010).

C. Implications

In situations such as these, necessary decisions are rarely welcome, and they deserve careful consideration for several reasons. Each has to do with the concept of *publicness,* once captured in a possibly apocryphal quip, often attributed to Herbert Simon that "Public organizations are a lot like private organizations in a lot of unimportant ways," and more recently in Rainey's rhetorical question, "If there is no real difference between public and private organizations, can we nationalize all industrial firms, or privatize all government agencies?" (p. 66). Both of these remarks speak to the serious contention that there are fundamental differences between public and private organizations and that these gain importance as we try to understand the nature of their resources and the impact of their decisions (Bozeman, 2010; Bozeman & Bretschneider, 1994; Moulton, 2009). In the case of public libraries that face growing service demands accompanied by austere financial prospects, this observation raises questions about the use of private sector strategies.

1. Staff and Compensation Reductions

This approach to cutbacks poses at least one obvious problem. At a deep level, the "motivational landscape" of public sector employment tends to be shaped by the strong "pull" of public service values. Once staff cuts are made, those who remain are likely to try to maintain service levels (Rayner, Williams, Lawton, & Allinson, 2011) and will usually be disappointed and disheartened as the quality of the services they provide eventually decline. The social contract in the public sector also provides an expectation of reasonable job security, employee benefits, and equitable treatment (Durant, Girth, & Johnston, 2009; Houston, 2000; Kelman, 2006; Perry, 2000) in return for commitment to the public interest and lower salary expectations. As Pandey (2010) notes, violations of this contract are likely to pose more severe motivational problems among public sector employees than might be the case in the private sector and, perhaps even more important, may hurt prospects for attracting future public sector employees. In the case of public libraries, where professional salaries tend to be lower than private sector salaries, these decisions could have far-reaching institutional implications that need to be considered at the national level.

2. Reductions in Service Hours

Cutbacks in services and hours raise fundamental questions about the objectives of public library services. From an economic perspective, the demand for public library services may be thought of as relatively inelastic, particularly in times of economic distress. In fact, history shows that the demand for public library services goes up as downward economic cycles worsen, a fact clearly demonstrated in the library reports from the Great Depression and recent discussions. For this reason, cutbacks in hours of service during periods of hardship create the obvious potential for socially disproportionate shortages from two publicness perspectives. People who have the least will feel the loss of service most severely. Those who are most politically attuned and financially capable will be able to avoid the pain of service loss most readily. In the case of public libraries, these problems speak to the issues of legitimacy and equity. As Pandey (2010) notes, "If we accept that a key role for government is to provide for and take care of those least able to take care of themselves, what are the ethical and practical implications of letting opportunism prevail?" (p. 568).

3. Reductions in Collection Development Expenditures

Capital expenditures and capital depletion raise another publicness issue—the long-term impact of strategies and choices. Levine (1978) addresses this in relation to hiring freezes when he notes that although these measures relieve some degree of managerial stress, they also "take control over the decision of whom and where to cut ... and thereby reduce the possibility of intelligent long range cutback planning" (p. 322). Service cutbacks also raise long-term issues related to political capital. This issue is placed in perspective by Keele

(2007) who notes that "trust is not a manifestation of how the public views political leaders but a result of how much the public engages in civic life and the attendant attitudes of trust and reciprocity that develop in civic activity" (p. 3).

More traditional capital assets are generally held in trust for the benefit of the community in perpetuity. The public library trustees who hold them are by definition charged with their continuing operation, the preservation of property, and the equitable distribution of the benefits of these investments to all of the intended beneficiaries (McClarren & Thompson, 1995; for examples, see Dixon, 2009; *Kentucky Public Library Trustee Manual* (2009); and Ohio Laws and Rules Chapter (2011)).

Fiduciary duty requires trustees to exercise the highest levels of "good faith, trust, confidence [,] candor [,] honesty and loyalty" in their official actions. As they do so, they are expected to act in the best interest of "the other person" (Garner, 1990, p. 523). Hutchings (1982) includes obedience, diligence, and loyalty, as components of fiduciary duty. Smith (1995) interprets the fiduciary duty of a trustee as a "special kind of moral responsibility" (pp. 5–16) that is triadic in nature. The parties to the triad are the initiator of the trust, the trustee, and the beneficiary of the trust. The initiator of the trust defines the purpose of the trust, and trustees must remain loyal to that purpose, just as they must remain loyal to the best interest of the beneficiaries.

When branches are closed or allowed to deteriorate, the effect on beneficiaries is necessarily felt unevenly within the community. Koontz, Jue, and Bishop (2009) suggest that in the past, branch closings have been more likely to occur in communities where the percentages of owner-occupied housing and white-occupied homes are lower than the national averages. If this pattern were to become a characteristic of cutback decisions, it would raise public sector equity issues and questions about fiduciary responsibility that do not arise in the private sector. Economic externalities also come to play in these decisions. Authorities on reading development describe a number of contexts and activities needed for children and adults to become fluent readers (Fisher, 2005; Report, 2000). Access to reading materials is fundamental to these experiences, and public libraries have traditionally provided an important opportunity for reading development to those who are not encouraged to read at home or are unable to develop reading skills in the classroom environment (Celano & Neuman, 2001; Durrance & Fisher, 2005; Tate & Lange, 1974). As literacy skills develop the entire community benefits.

Reductions in collection budgets raise other questions in terms of the long-term effect of these decisions. Although the presence and frequency of statutory limitations on public library board powers have traditionally varied from state to state and community to community (Bostwick, 1920; Garceau, 1949; McClarren & Thompson, 1995; Scheppke, 1991), public library trustees and directors, unlike those at private institutions, are generally tasked with investment decisions which assume that their organizations will continue to exist (Miller, 1997; Smith, 1995). As recessions recede, their libraries are likely to return to previous operating patterns, at which point human resources can be added. The opportunity costs associated with prior collection decisions raise a more difficult set of issues—the benefits of materials foregone, the likelihood that they will be added during periods of continuing austerity, and the eventual impact of these decisions on library use and circulation.

Other dangers become apparent when we look at questions related to social capital. As Pollitt (2010) notes, public services are "the most visible and far-reaching part of the state, as far as most citizens are concerned" and consequently "a prime site at which attitudes and opinions concerning government are formed" (p. 3). This point is particularly relevant to public libraries. They are among the most visible of public services, and while most people in a given community never encounter those who provide road maintenance, for example, they often recognize members of the library service staff when they are seen outside their libraries. Those who argue that public library services are not critical ignore this fact - that public library services are not only a bargain, typically providing a return on investment of four to eight dollars. ([Buffalo, 2007; Griffiths, King, & Lynch, 2005; Imholz & Arns, 2007; NorthStar, 2008; OCLC, 2011; Pennsylvania, 2011; State of Vermont, 2008; Steffen, Lietzau, Lance, Rybin, & Molliconi, 2009; Utah, 2008) but are also a transaction rich environment that fosters friendships as well as civic engagement (Alstead & Curry, 2003; Audunson, Vårheim, Aabø, & Holm, 2007). For these reasons, it is not surprising that service cuts often encounter client opposition and that advocates speak passionately about, and for, their public libraries.

IV. Reflections and Conclusion

Today, we would all agree that times have changed, as has our understanding of value. The expectation of immediate service 24/7 and the ubiquity of the Internet suggest that a return to "normalcy" in public library service delivery may not happen or even be desirable. Competition for reference and advisory services is keen, whereas the public library had no real competitor in the decades following the Great Depression. E-books and e-journals have long been predicted to take the place of print books and journals. Although they have not yet replaced print collections, people are learning to read in different formats, and where economies are possible, a continuing trend of print replacement by electronic media will no doubt strengthen. The expectation that the print collections in public libraries and the space allocated to these materials will follow yesterday's trends is not realistic, but the opportunities that come with change will occur more rapidly in some communities than in others, and their reception is likely to follow a similarly uneven pattern.

Decision-makers have also changed in some situations. Whereas in the past the boards of trustees provided a strong public voice in decisions about how funds should be allocated and what and how to cutback when economic exigency requires, this dialog appears to be less certain today. Government organizations in small towns as well as in cities are more likely today to be centralized under a professional government manager. A professional library director typically serves as the head of one of several more-or-less coequal public service departments reporting to the city, town, or county manager. In place of recession-related and other budgetary decisions being made by the library's board of trustees, these decisions are today more often made by the government manager with input from the library director while the trustees act in little more than a broadly advisory capacity. When this occurs, the strength gained from the progressive tradition of popular governance is minimized, mistakes become likely, and public organizations verge upon the values of profit driven organizations. Box, Marshall, Reed, and Reed (2001) raise this issue when they speak of substantive democracy and the actions that redirect public interest to community wide needs, such as those that emerge during recessionary periods.

Perhaps more than anything else, a radical change in the conception of public library administration may be necessary. Even a cursory review of public library literature suggests that "New Public Management" ideas impelled partly by technology and partly by efforts to make governments conform to the market economy of the private sector still persist, although a number of authors have questioned the extent to which casting the citizen as a customer is appropriate for government (Box et al., 2001; Dunleavy, Margetts, Bastow, & &Tinkler, 2006; Terry, 2005). Fabian (2010) notes that

> The private and public sectors operate within different circumstances. The field of operation of the former is market and proprietorship, and of the latter, democracy and the rule of law ... The goal of the two systems is fundamentally different: the aim of the private sector is profit-maximization beside cost-minimization, and the aim of the public sector is to manage public tasks at the same level, if possible, for all the clients. (pp. 42–43).

This issue directly addresses our understanding of the relationship between citizen and state. Denhardt and Denhardt (2011) describe the values that they believe should be represented in public service: giving primacy to serving citizens rather than customers, seeking the public interest, valuing citizenship over entrepreneurship, and valuing people over productivity. They note that "The New Public Management encourages public administrators to act and think as entrepreneurs of a business enterprise" when they are not the owners of their agencies or programs (pp. 556–557). While this is clearly the case, recognition of this fact sometimes seems to be missing from the public library literature as well as in the decision spaces where cutback decisions are made when communities are characterized as markets, public library trustees are not active in the decision process, and members of the community are viewed as customers rather than beneficiaries.

Sorting out these issues and doing this well will require a commitment to public library research that has not always been readily apparent (Hersberger, 2001) and is likely to seem more difficult under persistent funding constraints. Scorsone and Plerhoples (2010) point to a significant need for studies that (1) examine the implications of alternative public sector decisions, (2) determine whether improved models are emerging, and (3) identify the steps that public organizations can take to prepare for future downward cycles. In the case of public libraries, a research undertaking of this scope will require collaborative effort and funding beyond the local level. Improved models appear to merit this investment.

The research agenda for these issues needs to start with an important set of questions:

- What are the core aspects of library service and how can these be sustained and promoted during periods of economic turmoil?
- Who are the "stakeholders" of public libraries and how are their interests preserved and maximized?
- What are the legitimating features of public libraries today?
- Is there a difference between the period of public library retrenchment in the Great Depression and the more recent recession? Should public libraries pursue the same strategies now that were followed previously?

In the period following the Great Depression, public libraries tended to return to more stable funding, while hours, services, collections, and staffing returned incrementally to their former levels and began to expand following the plans for expansion articulated by trustees in the earlier period.

- Should this be our current model? or
- Should we be moving into new territory where our previous assumptions will prove to be less valuable than\expected?

The answers to these questions will eventually become apparent, but they are more likely to result in advances if they are pursued within a publicness framework. This may mean foregoing private sector strategies that create profit and political support by providing specialized services to small, but well-defined market segments. It may also mean reconceptualizing the relationships we build with those who own and use our libraries. As we do this, it will be useful to keep in mind Denhardt and Denhardt's observation that, "Public organizations and the networks in which they participate are more likely to succeed in the long run if they are operated through processes of collaboration and shared leadership" (p. 56). This implies a public service model in which decision spaces are open and public library trustees bring the voice of the community to decisions about reductions.

References

Alstead, C., & Curry, A. (2003). Public space, public discourse, and public libraries. *Libres, 14*, 1. Retrieved from http://libres.curtin.edu.au/libres13n1/pub_space.htm

Audunson, R., Vårheim, A., Aabø, S., & Holm, E. D. (2007). Public libraries, social capital, and low intensive meeting places. *Information Research, 12*(4). Retrieved from http://InformationR.net/ir/12-4/colis/colis20.html

Bernanke, B. (1995). The macroeconomics of the great depression: A comparative approach. *Journal of Money, Credit and Banking, 27*(1), 1–28.

Blumenstein, L. (2008, April 15). Indiana tax cuts hurt pls. *Library Journal.* Retrieved from http://www.libraryjournal.com/article/CA6547068.html

Blumenstein, L. (2010, August 20). Forth Worth Library, TX, plans to close three branches. *Library Journal.* Retrieved from http://www.libraryjournal.com/lj/home/886478-264/fort_worth_library_tx_plans.html.csp

Blumenstein, L. (2011a, January 6). Camden Free Public Library to close doors. *Library Journal.* Retrieved from http://www.libraryjournal.com/lj/home/888684-264/camden_free_public_library_to.html.csp

Blumenstein, L. (2011b, February 3). Detroit PL working on aggressive budget reduction plan. *Library Journal.* Retrieved from http://www.libraryjournal.com/lj/home/889124-264/detroit_pl_working_on_aggressive.html.csp

Bostwick, A. (1920). *Administration of a public library.* Chicago, IL: American Library Association.

Box, R. C., Marshall, G. S., Reed, B. J., & Reed, C. M. (2001). New public management and substantive democracy. *Public Administration Review, 61*(5), 608–619.

Bozeman, B. (2010, July/August). Hard lessons from hard times: Reconsidering and reorienting the "managing decline" literature. *Public Administration Review, 70*(4), 557–563.

Bozeman, B., & Bretschneider, S. I. (1994). The "publicness puzzle" in organization theory: A test of alternative explanations of differences between public and private organizations. *Journal of Public Administration Research and Theory, 4*(2), 197–224.

Budget Cuts Force Houston Library to Shorten Hours. (2010, April 7). *Houston KTRK.* Retrieved from http://abclocal.go.com/ktrk/story?section=news/local&id=7372922

Buffalo & Erie County Public Library. (2007). *Erie County taxpayers: Your return on investment in the library.* Retrieved from http://www.buffalolib.org/aboutthelibrary/ect.asp

Celano, D., & Neuman, S. B. (2001). *The role of public libraries in children's literacy development: An evaluation report.* Harrisburg, PA: Pennsylvania Department of Education, Office of Commonwealth Libraries.

Colorado Lib.: Perfect storm. (2010, September 15). *Library Journal,* 12.

Cranberry Public Library Budget Cuts. (2011, January 18). *Cranberry township Pennsylvania.* Retrieved from http://www.twp.cranberry.pa.us/index.aspx?NID=1598

Dallas cuts would slam budget. (2009, August). *Library Journal,* 12.

DCPL reduces hours. (2009, October 15). *Library Journal,* 14.

Denhardt, J. V., & Denhardt, R. B. (2011). *The new public service: Serving, not steering* (3rd ed.). Armonk, NY: M.E. Sharpe.

Des Moines PL: One-week furlough to save jobs. (2009, March 1). *Library Journal,* 14.

District of Columbia Public Library. (1929). *Thirty-second annual report of the Board of Trustees and thirty-first annual report of the Librarian of the Public Library of the district of Columbia.* Washington, DC: Government Printing Office.

District of Columbia Public Library. (1930). *Thirty-third annual report of the Board of Trustees and thirty-second annual report of the Librarian of the Public Library of the district of Columbia.* Washington, DC: Government Printing Office.

District of Columbia Public Library. (1931). *Thirty-fourth annual report of the Board of Trustees and thirty-third annual report of the Librarian of the Public Library of the district of Columbia.* Washington, DC: Government Printing Office.

District of Columbia Public Library. (1932). *Thirty-fifth annual report of the Board of Trustees and thirty-fourth annual report of the Librarian of the Public Library of the district of Columbia.* Washington, DC: Government Printing Office.

District of Columbia Public Library. (1933). *Thirty-sixth annual report of the Board of Trustees and thirty-fifth annual report of the Librarian of the Public Library of the district of Columbia.* Washington, DC: Government Printing Office.

Dixon, S. (Ed.). (2009). *Iowa library trustee's handbook.* Library Development, State Library of Iowa. Retrieved from http://www.statelibraryofiowa.org/ld/t-z/Trustees/trustee-handbook

Duffus, R. L. (1933). *Our starving libraries: Studies in ten American communities during the depression years.* Boston, MA: Houghton Mifflin.

Dunleavy, P., Margetts, H., Bastow, S., & Tinkler, J. (2006). New public management is dead-long live digital-era governance. *Journal of Public Administration Research & Theory,* 16(3), 467–494.

Durant, R. F., Girth, A. M., & Johnston, J. M. (2009, September). American exceptionalism, human resource management, and the contract state. *Review of Public Personnel Administration,* 29(3), 207–229.

Durrance, J., & Fisher, K. (2005). *How libraries and librarians help: A guide to identifying user-centered outcomes.* Chicago, IL: American Library Association.

Emling, S. (2011). Grassroots group plans to protest Bellevue Library Branch closing tonight. *Montclair Patch.* Retrieved from http://montclair.patch.com/articles/with-the-bellevue-branch-closed-the-library-board-explains-its-budget-decisions

Fabian, A. (2010). New public management and what comes after. *Issues of Business and Law,* 2. Retrieved from http://versita.metapress.com/content/952217224131u5w5/fulltext.pdf

Fisher, R. (2005). Teacher-child interaction in the teaching of reading: A review of research perspectives over twenty-five years. *Journal of Research in Reading, 28*(1), 15–27.

Flagg, G. (2009, August/September). State budgets hammer libraries nationwide. *American Libraries*, 19–21.

Frazier, E. (2010, March 18). Library system will close branches, lay off staff. *Charlotte Observer*. Retrieved from www.charlotteobserver.com/2011/01/31/2025471/observer-to-cut-20-jobs.html

Galbraith, J. K. (1955). *The great crash, 1929.* Boston, MA: Houghton Mifflin Co.

Garceau, O. (1949). *The public library in the political process.* New York, NY: Columbia University Press.

Garner, B. A. (1990). *A dictionary of modern legal usage.* New York, NY: Oxford University Press.

Griffiths, J.-M., King, D.W., & Lynch, T. (2005). *Florida's public libraries build strong economies: A taxpayer return on investment report.* Tallahassee, FL: Florida Department of State, State Library and Archives of Florida. Retrieved from http://dlis.dos.state.fl.us/bld/roi/pdfs/2005_SLAF_ROI_report.pdf

GuideStar. (2010). *The effect of the economy on the nonprofit sector: A June 2010 survey.* Retrieved from http://www2.guidestar.org/rxg/news/publications/nonprofits-and-economy-june-2010.aspx

Henderson, E., Miller, K., Craig, T., Dorinski, S., Freeman, M., Isaac, N., ... Schilling, P. (2010). *Public libraries survey: Fiscal year 2008* [IMLS-2010–PLS-02].Washington, DC: Institute of Museum and Library Services. Retrieved from http://harvester.census.gov/imls/pubs/Publications/pls2008.pdf

Herdman, M. M. (1943). The public library in depression. *Library Quarterly, 13*(4), 310–334.

Hersberger, J. (2001). The current state of public library research in select peer-reviewed journals: 1996–2000. *North Carolina Libraries, 59*(1), 10–14.

Hoene, C. W. (2009, December). City budget shortfalls and responses: Projections for 2010–2012. *Research Brief on America's Cities*, (4). Washington, DC: National League of Cities. Retrieved from http://www.awcnet.org/documents/NLCBudgetShortFallsResponsesResearchBrief.pdf

Horwitz, L. (2009, September 22). Layoffs, furloughs, and union concessions: The prolonged and painful process of balancing city budgets. *The Pew Charitable Trust: The Philadelphia Research Initiative.* Retrieved from http://www.pewtrusts.org/uploadedFiles/wwwpewtrustsorg/Reports/Philadelphia-area_grantmaking/Layoffs,%20Furloughs%20and%20Union%20Concessions%20FINAL.pdf?n=7888

Houston, D. J. (2000). Public-service motivation: A multivariate test. *Journal of Public Administration Research & Theory, 10*(4), 713–727.

Hutchings, M. M. (1982). The legal liability of library trustees. *Journal of Library Administration, 3*(2), 5–13.

Imholz, S., & Arns, J. (2007). *Worth their weight: An assessment of the evolving field of library valuation.* New York: Americans for Libraries Council. Retrieved from http://www.ila.org/advocacy/pdf/WorthTheirWeight.pdf

Indiana system to close three of four branches. (2009, March 15). *Library Journal*, 14.

Institute of Museum and Library Services. (2010). *Library statistics: Compare public libraries.* Washington, DC. Retrieved from http://harvester.census.gov/imls/compare/index.asp

Kaiser Family Foundation and Health Research and Educational Trust. (2010). *Employer health benefits: 2010 summary of findings.* Retrieved from http://ehbs.kff.org/pdf/2010/8086.pdf

Keele, L. (2007). Social capital and the dynamics of trust in government. *American Journal of Political Science, 51,* 241–254.

Kelley, M. (2011a, January 15). LJ's 2010 budget survey: Bottoming out? *Library Journal.* Retrieved from http://www.libraryjournal.com/lj/home/888434-264/ljs_2010_budget_survey_bottoming.html.csp

Kelley, M. (2011b, January 21). Proposed budget in Texas nearly zeros out key state library funds. *Library Journal.* Retrieved from http://www.libraryjournal.com/lj/home/888925-264/proposed_budget_in_texas_nearly.html.csp

Kelman, S. (2006). Downsizing, competition, and organizational change in government: Is necessity the mother of invention? *Journal of Policy Analysis and Management, 25*(4), 875–895.

Kentucky, Department for Libraries and Archives. (2009). *Kentucky public library trustee manual.* Retrieved from http://kdla.ky.gov/librarians/Documents/trusteemanual.pdf

Koontz, C. M., Jue, D. K., & Bishop, B. W. (2009). Public library facility closure: An investigation of reasons for closure and effects on geographic market areas. *Library & Information Science Research, 31,* 84–91.

Kramp, R. S. (1975). *The great depression: Its impact on forty-six large American public libraries.* Duluth, MN: Library Juice Press.

Levine, C. H. (1978). Organizational decline and cutback management. *Public Administration Review, 38*(4), 316–325.

Levine, C. H. (1979). More on cutback management: Hard questions for hard times. *Public Administration Review, 39*(2), 179–183.

Lewis, C. W., & Mello, J. (2009). Coping with crises: Budgeting in recession by large U.S. cities. *Government Finance Review, 25*(6), 35–40.

Luyt, B. (2007). The ALA, public libraries, and the great depression. *Library History, 23*(2), 85–96.

Maher, K., and Turetsky, D. (2011, April 13). *Funding cuts could shelve many library branches* [Web log comment]. Retrieved from http://ibo.nyc.ny.us/cgi-park/?p=288

McClarren, R. R., & Thompson, R. (1995). The trustee and the law. In V. G. Young (Ed.), *The library trustee: A practical guidebook* (5th ed., pp. 61–70). Chicago, IL: American Library Association.

McDougall, P. (2009, March 26). IBM layoffs include wide ranging U.S. job cuts. *Information Week.* Retrieved from http://www.informationweek.com/news/global-cio/outsourcing/showArticle.jhtml?articleID=216400346

Miami-Dade cut, but steady. (2010, November 1). *Library Journal.* Retrieved from http://www.libraryjournal.com/lj/ljinprintcurrentissue/887162-403/newsdesk_november_1_2010.html.csp

Miller, G. J., & Svara, J. H. (Eds.). (2009, January). *Navigating the fiscal crises: Tested strategies for local leaders.* White Paper prepared for the International City/County Management Association by Alliance for Innovation. Retrieved from http://www.co.washoe.nv.us/repository/files/1/fiscal_crisis.pdf

Miller, J. (1997). Representation in government boards and commissions. *Public Administration Review, 57*(2), 160–168.

Moore, M., & Khagram, S. (2004). *On creating public value: What business might learn about government about strategic management.* Corporate Social Responsibility Initiative Working Paper No. 3. Harvard University, John F. Kennedy School of Government, Cambridge, MA. Retrieved from http://www.hks.harvard.edu/m-rcbg/CSRI/publications/workingpaper_3_moore_khagram.pdf

Moore, M. Y. (2010). *The successful library trustee handbook.* Chicago, IL: American Library Association.

More branch closures possible in Indianapolis and Portland, ME: Proposals are part of budgets for fiscal year starting in July. (2010, April 26). *Library Journal.* Retrieved from http://www.libraryjournal.com/article/CA6725481.html

Moulder, E. (2009). *ICMA state of the profession survey.* Washington, DC: International City/County Management Association. Retrieved from http://icma.org/en/icma/knowledge_network/documents/kn/Document/100267/ICMA_2009_State_of_the_Profession_Survey

Moulton, S. (2009). Putting together the publicness puzzle: A framework for realized publicness. *Public Administration Review, 69*(5), 889–900.

NorthStar Economics. (2008). *The economic contribution of Wisconsin public libraries to the economy of Wisconsin.* Madison, WI. Retrieved from http://dpi.wi.gov/pld/econimpact.html

Novotny, E. (2010, April 7). Hard choices in hard times: Lessons from the great depression. *RUSQ, 49*(3), 222–224. Retrieved from http://www.rusq.org/2010/04/07/hard-choices-in-hard-times/

OCLC. (2011). *Public libraries: Return on information.* Retrieved from http://www.oclc.org/roi/

Oder, N. (2008, April 15). Memphis mayor: Close 5 libraries. *Library Journal.* Retrieved from http://www.libraryjournal.com/article/CA6547070.html

Oder, N. (2009a, August 27). Hawaii proposes minimum of two-day closures each month. *Library Journal.* Retrieved from http://www.libraryjournal.com/lj/communityfunding/855642-268/story.csp

Oder, N. (2009b, January 15). Libraries are either tightening budgets or preparing to do so. *Library Journal.* Retrieved from http://www.libraryjournal.com/article/CA6625159.html

Oder, N. (2009c, September 1). Squeezed by mayoral directive, Omaha PL closes branch, lays off more than 25% FTE. *Library Journal.* Retrieved from http://www.libraryjournal.com/article/CA6676640.html?desc=topstory

Oder, N. (2009d, October 26). Stung by state and city cuts, Reading (PA) PL plans to close all branches. *Library Journal.* Retrieved from http://www.libraryjournal.com/article/CA6703788.html

Oder, N. (2010, July 23). To close budget gap, queens library to lay off 46. *Library Journal.* Retrieved from http://ala-apa.org/newsletter/2010/08/11/to-close-budget-gap-queens-library-to-lay-off-46/

Ohio Laws and Rules. Chapter 3375: Libraries. (2011). *LAWriter.* Retrieved from http://codes.ohio.gov/orc/3375

Packard, T., Patti, R., Daly, D., Tucker-Tatlow, J., & Farrell, C. (2008). Cutback management strategies: Experiences in nine county human service agencies. *Administration in Social Work, 32*(1), 55–75.

Pandey, S. K. (2010). Cutback management and the paradox of publicness. *Public Administration Review, 70*(4), 564–571.

Pennsylvania Library Association. (2011). *Return on investment (ROI) materials*. Retrieved from http://www.palibraries.org/displaycommon.cfm?an=1&subarticlenbr=23

Perry, J. (2000). Bringing society in: Toward a theory of public-service motivation. *Journal of Public Administration Research & Theory, 10*(2), 471–488.

Philadelphia libraries remain open, but staff cuts mean fewer days. (2009, January 6). *Library Journal*. Retrieved from http://www.libraryjournal.com/article/CA6626723.html

Plumley, A. (2010, December 29). Libraries to close 4 days to save. *The Wichita Eagle*. Retrieved from http://www.kansas.com/2010/12/29/1651007/libraries-to-close-4-days-to-save.html

Pollitt, C. (2010). *Cuts and reforms—Public services as we wove into a new era*. Retrieved from http://www.pa-knowledge.org/documents/IIASPORTALPAPER.pdf

Rainey, H. G. (2009). *Understanding and managing public organizations*. San Francisco, CA: Jossey-Bass.

Rayner, J., Williams, H. M., Lawton, A., & Allinson, C. W. (2011). Public service ethos: Developing a generic measure. *Journal of Public Administration Research and Theory, 21*(1), 27–51.

Reed, S., & Kalonick, J. (2010). *The complete library trustee handbook*. New York, NY: Neal-Schuman.

Report of the National Reading Panel: Teaching Children to Read: An evidence-based assessment of the scientific research literature on reading and its implications for reading instruction. (2000). Washington, DC: National Institute of Child Health and Human Development, National Institutes of Health.

Residents meet to save Bowling Green branch. (2007, August). *American Libraries*, 20.

Romer, C. D. (1988). *The great crash and the onset of the great depression*. NBER Working Paper No. 2639. Retrieved from http://emlab.berkeley.edu/users/cromer/CRomerQJE1990.pdf

Ryan, A. (2010). Library may cut 10 of its branches: Boston weighs layoff of quarter of staff. Retrieved from http://www.boston.com/news/local/massachusetts/articles/2010/02/18/library_may_cut_10_of_its_branches/

Sadowska, C. (2010). Ferguson library perseveres through budget cuts. *Stamford Patch*. Retrieved from http://stamford.patch.com/users/caroline-sadowska

San José could lose 35%. (2010, April 15). *Library Journal*, 16.

Scheppke, J. (1991, September-October). The governance of public libraries: Findings of the PLA governance of public libraries committee. *Public Libraries, 30*(5), 88–94.

Scorsone, E. A., & Plerhoples, C. (2010). Fiscal stress and cutback management amongst state and local governments: What have we learned and what remains to be learned? *State and Local Government Review, 42*(2), 176–187.

Smith, A. (1902). *The wealth of nations*. New York, NY: P.F. Collier and Son.

Smith, D. H. (1995). *Entrusted: The moral responsibilities of trusteeship*. Bloomington, IN: Indiana University Press.

State of Vermont, Department of Libraries. (2008). *The economic value of Vermont's public libraries: 2006–2007*. Montpelier, VT. Retrieved from http://libraries.vermont.gov/sites/libraries/files/misc/plvalue06-07.pdf

Steffen, N., Lietzau, Z., Lance, K. C., Rybin, A., & Molliconi, C. (2009). *Public libraries—A wise investment: A return on investment study of Colorado libraries*. Retrieved from http://www.lrs.org/documents/closer_look/roi.pdf

Sugar Grove Library to cut hours. (2007, February). *ILA Reporter*, 28.

Sum, A., & McLaughlin, J. (2010). Massive shedding of jobs in America. *Challenge*, *53*(6), 62–76.

Survey reveals a decline in public library state funding. (2010, April). *American Libraries*, 10.

Tate, B. L., and Lange, P. C. (1974). The role of the public library as an alternative force in early childhood education. Commissioned Papers Project (No. 3). New York, NY: Columbia University Teachers College.

Terry, L. D. (2005). The thinning of administrative institutions in the hollow. *State Administration & Society*, *37*(4), 426–444.

Trustees of the Public Library of the City of Boston. (1928). *Seventy-seventh annual report of the trustees of the Public Library of the City of Boston*. Boston, MA: Author Retrieved from http://www.archive.org/stream/annualreport1928bost#page/n9/mode/2up

Trustees of the Public Library of the City of Boston. (1929). *Seventy-eighth annual report of the trustees of the Public Library of the City of Boston*. Boston, MA: Author. Retrieved from http://www.archive.org/stream/annualreport1929bost#page/n9/mode/2up

Trustees of the Public Library of the City of Boston. (1932). *Eighty-first annual report of the trustees of the public library of the city of Boston*. Boston, MA: Author. Retrieved from http://www.archive.org/stream/annualreport1932bost#page/n9/mode/2up

Trustees of the Public Library of the City of Boston. (1933). *Eighty-first annual report of the trustees of the Public Library of the City of Boston*. Boston, MA: Author. Retrieved from http://www.archive.org/stream/annualreport1933bost#page/n9/mode/2up

U.S. Department of Labor. (2010, December 3). *Bureau of labor statistics news release*. Retrieved from http://www.bls.gov/news.release/archives/empsit_12032010.pdf

U.S. mayors cutting road repairs, police departments, parks, libraries to cope with economic downturn, according to new Harris/Reader's Digest poll. (2010, November 23). *PRNewswire*. Retrieved from http://www.prnewswire.com/news-releases/us-mayors-cutting-road-repairs-police-departments-parks-libraries-to-cope-with-econom ic-downturn-according-to-new-harrisreaders-digest-poll-110127959.html

Utah State Library Division. (2008). *Return on investment of public library services to Utah's economy*. Retrieved from http://library.utah.gov/documents/library_value/utah_roi.pdf

Volunteers add hours in Charlotte, raise questions. (2010, September 15). *Library Journal*, 13.

Warburton, B. (2010, December 29). Gary public library faces steep budget cut. *Library Journal*. Retrieved from http://www.libraryjournal.com/lj/mobilemhome/888581-422/gary_public_library_faces_steep.html.csp

Watson, B. (2010, July 15). Local news: Dallas libraries bracing for more cuts in budget crunch. *WFAA.com*. Retrieved from http://www.wfaa.com/news/local/Dallas-libraries-bracing-for-more-cuts-in-budget-crunch-98570859.html

Weisberg, J. (2010, January 9). What caused the economic crises? The 15 best explanations for the great recession. *Slate*. Retrieved from http://www.slate.com/id/2240858/

Wingfield, N. (2010, July 6). Microsoft planning small job cuts. *Wall Street Journal*. Retrieved from http://online.wsj.com/article/SB10001424052748704862404575351772843530454.htm

Forced Advocacy: How Communities Respond to Library Budget Cuts

Lisa K. Hussey[a] and Diane L. Velasquez[b]

[a]Graduate School of Library and Information Science, Simmons College, Boston, MA, USA
[b]Independent Scholar, Westmont, IL, USA

Abstract

This chapter provides in-depth case studies of two large urban public libraries in the United States and how communities and libraries respond to reductions mandated by their funding agencies. Boston Public Library (BPL) and Los Angeles Public Library (LAPL) are both in communities that faced, and are still facing, recessionary budget pressures that began in 2007. Each community and library system has responded in different ways. In the recent past, in both Boston and Los Angeles, the Mayors and City Councils have supported libraries that have come to define the great cultural heritage and heart of these cities in the past. In 2010, however, both cities faced unheard of budget pressures. In Boston, there was a budget shortfall of $3.6 million. In Los Angeles, the budget shortfall began in 2007 due to huge increases in pension payments to city workers, particularly in the police and fire departments (City of Los Angeles Web site, 2011). In Boston, the community was told there could be branch closures. In Los Angeles, the budget shortfall created severe personnel, material, and service cuts. How each library and their leaders responded to those challenges differed. The level of support that their communities provided and the manner in which it was provided also differed. The two cases describe what can happen when budget crises occur and how libraries and their communities deal, or do not deal with them. The cases also reflect how the two library systems serve metropolitan areas with very distinct characteristics.

Keywords: Boston Public Library; Los Angeles Public Library; Public libraries; Budget reduction; Advocacy; Recession

I. Introduction

Since the current recession began in 2008, many US public libraries have made reductions in staff, materials, technology, service hours, and closed branches. While this is not a new phenomenon during recessions, the breadth and depth of current cuts have not been faced since the Great Depression in the 1930s. There have been sweeping proclamations from mayors, city and state governments about the need to cut budgets, and in some instances, the calls are affecting systems that previously have not had to face major cuts such as Boston, Chicago, and Los Angeles. Smaller systems, such as Prescott, Arizona, and Oak Brook, Illinois, have proposed passing more of the costs onto users through service fees.

The timing of these reductions coincided with a large influx of patrons flooding public libraries looking for job search assistance using free Internet access and getting training. Library budget reductions have, in many instances, forced advocacy by communities in order to maintain hours and services. Part of this advocacy is expected to focus on innovations that include how the library is funded and staffed, as well as how materials are procured. Many of the ways that public libraries are currently managed are not creative. Some management styles date back to the mid 20th century and are generally mired in bureaucratic principles. Therefore, communities and city managers are asking for changes in the ways that libraries look at their stakeholders and manage their employees, materials, resources, and processes.

There are other systems that have either been threatened with branch closings or actually closed branches due to shortfalls in city budgets. The Boston Public Library (BPL) President and the Library's Board of Trustees originally announced a plan in February 2010 to close 10 of its 26 branches due to budget problems. The community was outraged. The original proposal was scaled back and in the end the President recommended that only four branches be closed. This option was accepted by the city's Mayor but still met with opposition from the community. It also resulted in political pressure from the State Legislature that threatened to withhold more funding if any more branches were closed.

The result of cuts and reductions in library service has brought outcries in many communities. When the original cuts were first announced in Boston, families and community groups held impromptu meetings and demonstrations to show support for the BPL system. The Oak Brook, IL public library made news with a story about a public meeting and the library supportive reaction of members of the crowd (Smith, 2009). These are just two examples of how library communities have responded to announced budget cuts. Community reactions highlight some questions concerning the expectations of support of the library. In short, two dominant questions emerge: to what degree are announcements made in order to force the library community to advocate for their library's existence? As the recession continues, how much more support is expected to be passed onto the community?

Literature on the subject of advocacy and budget cuts comes mainly from practitioners who focus on highly practical aspects of reductions. These articles range from anecdotal narratives (Alire, 2010; Battistella, 2010), to "how to" stories (Duckor, 2009; Feldman, 2010), survey data on library referendums (Dempsey, 2009, 2010), the role of trustees in the process (Battiste, 2006), and literature about the Great Depression (Novotny, 2010). While the literature provides some good practical examples and suggestions, scholarly research in this area seems to be lacking.

The ability to advocate is something many library school students are told is necessary to keep the library visible and viable in the community. A short study of the Websites of 56 library and information science school course titles and/or descriptions showed that only two of them had courses with advocacy in the title. Fifteen had courses with marketing in the title. These courses were electives and tracked under management specializations. The University of Western Ontario was the only school with both marketing and advocacy courses (Table 1).

Specific courses are not the only way Masters of Library and Information Science (MLIS) students get exposure to advocacy and marketing. Many courses, such as foundations, general and specialized reference and management, will cover advocacy and marketing but only as part of an overview of librarianship. The need for constant marketing and advocacy is often downplayed or minimized when presented within the larger context of librarianship.

While the American Library Association (ALA) and the Public Library Association (PLA) have conference programs and Websites that discuss advocacy and budgets, there is no place that specifically teaches best practices. Since there is a gap in scholarly literature on advocacy, this chapter provides one small step toward filling it.

Table 1
ALA Accredited Library Programs with Specific Courses

	Classes	Percent
Marketing	15	26.8%
Advocacy	2	3.6%

The research in this chapter focuses on two library systems: Boston Public Library (BPL) and Los Angeles Public Library (LAPL). Both systems faced major budget reductions in 2010, but they had different ways of dealing with the problems and how they communicated with their respective communities. One used forced advocacy to stave off reductions and the other sought public support through a citywide vote amending to the city's charter.

A. Defining Forced Advocacy and Public Good

Forced advocacy—When governments threaten to reduce funding for services like a library, community members either choose, and/or are encouraged, to advocate for and protest such cuts.

Public good—This is "a very special class of goods that cannot practically be withheld from one consumer without withholding them from all and for which the marginal cost of an additional person consuming them, once they have been produced, is zero" (Johnson, 2005). Library services are considered a public good, funded through tax receipts such as property taxes, sales taxes, or other sources.

II. Boston Public Library

A. Introduction

In the context of the current financial crisis, focusing on the BPL system is significant for several reasons. BPL is the oldest public library system in the United States with a long history as an important part of Boston's cultural community. BPL serves more than residents of Boston. Boston, Cambridge, and nearby suburbs are home to 79 colleges and universities (NCES, 2011) and BPL is a secondary resource for various student bodies. BPL also provides online services to any resident of Massachusetts and is the Library of Last Recourse for the Commonwealth of Massachusetts.

BPL serves a very diverse community. Boston has traditionally been a city of neighborhoods defined by their ethnic make-up, such as Chinatown, the heavily Irish South Boston and the Italian North End. The 2005–2009 American Community Survey (ACS) estimated the population of Boston to be at 625,304, a 6% increase in population from the 2000 Census (U.S. Census Bureau, 2009a). There were slight shifts in the different ethnic populations, with the most significant increase in the Hispanic or Latino population, growing from 14.4% to 15.7% of the overall population (U.S. Census Bureau, 2009a).

BPL provides services at the Central Library in Copley Square and in 26 branch libraries throughout Boston neighborhoods with a long service hours. Branch libraries stay open until 8:00 p.m. on Mondays and Thursdays and until 6:00 p.m. on Tuesdays and Wednesdays. The Central Library is open until 9:00 p.m. Monday through Thursday. All libraries close at 5:00 p.m. on Fridays. All but one branch provide services on Saturdays, with hours ranging from 9:00 a.m. to 2:00 p.m. or 5:00 p.m. The Central Library is open from 9:00 a.m. to 5:00 p.m. on Saturdays and 1:00 p.m. until 5:00 p.m. on Sundays from October until May (BPL, 2011).

BPL's role is not seen as being limited to an information center or a place to check out books. It is viewed as part of the cultural foundation of the city, and is highlighted on the City's Website as one of the cultural spots of the city. The research for this case study covers the period of January 19, 2010 to April 12, 2010.

B. Public Discussion and Involvement

While budget cuts are often public, discussions about what to cut and how to deal with less money are not. However, when dealing with a significant shortfall for fiscal year 2010/2011 (FY11), BPL and its administrators created opportunities for a public conversation about the budget, major problems created by the shortfall, and potential solutions for FY11 and the future. Beginning with the initial budget announcement, BPL provided a consistent flow of information to the public. The following were made available on BPL's Website:

- Minutes of Board of Trustees' meetings,
- copy of the proposed budget,
- a schedule for community meetings,
- details and definitions of measurements used for deciding branch closures,
- a monthly newsletter, including a very public request for financial support.

The public's discussions were determined, incendiary, and conciliatory. Official statements from BPL and the Mayor's office generally tried to present a positive attitude and focused on using the financial crisis as an opportunity to evaluate and strengthen the BPL and develop a plan for the future. The tenor of newspaper articles ranged from supportive of the ideas presented by BPL to cynicism and an outright attack on both current plans for dealing with the budget and strategic plans with goals for 2015. There were calls for a return to previous times when money was more readily available and for board members who were more politically savvy. Comments from library patrons and supporters were both belligerent and panicked, while at the same time supportive of the BPL as a cultural, community, and educational institution.

BPL's President, Amy Ryan, announced a budget shortfall of $3.6 million in a Board of Trustees meeting on January 19, 2010. In the months following, President Ryan and the Board used strong proactive actions by openly discussing the budget issues, holding public forums to solicit public opinion about possible cuts in services and potential branch closures. On April 9, 2010, the Board of Trustees voted to accept a proposal to close four branch libraries. Although the conversation continued after this vote, this three-month period illustrates the influence of official information and public advocacy in a budget crisis.

C. The Chronology of Events

Although the initial announcement was upsetting and surprising, public reaction was not immediately panicked. There was some confidence in the ability of BPL's leadership to handle the crisis well. President Ryan had been previously praised in *The Boston Globe* for not complaining and whining about money issues and her focus on becoming "more nimble," working within the reality of less money and heavier use (Anonymous, October 6, 2009). Prior the January 19, 2010 announcement, President Ryan had been dealing with an unsustainable model of staffing that was stretched too thin to provide consistently high levels of service across all branches (BPL, 2010a). Causes of the shortfall were presented, including a $6.3 million (a 73% decrease over two years by the state for BPL to serve as the Library of Last Recourse). At the January 19th meeting, there was little discussion beyond presentation of the current budget and highlighting an imminent $3.6 million shortfall from the city.

1. February 17, 2010

Real discussion about the cuts began at the February 17th Board of Trustees meeting. From the beginning, politics played a strong role in discussions. Before addressing plans for dealing with the cuts, the Board made a statement of support for Mayor Menino and his continued commitment to BPL by pointing out that he "has done much better by the BPL, much better than Mayor Bloomberg has done by the New York Public Library" (BPL, 2010b, para 12). The Board also addressed the drop in funding from the State, stating that the "Commonwealth has hit the BPL hard with respect to the Library of Last Recourse funding, but there is no point in recriminating and nobody on Beacon Hill was moved by bad faith or a generalize hostility to literacy" (BPL, 2010b, para 15). The language, while mild and somewhat conciliatory, was clearly laying blame for some of the budget woes with the State.

Despite the political commentary, focus of the February meeting was to present two possible options for dealing with the budget shortfall. President Ryan highlighted the current state of operations at BPL, focusing on problems with staffing levels and maintaining hours and services, issues that had existed prior to current budget woes. Even without cuts, the current system was unsustainable, due to unfilled vacancies and the need for staff from different libraries to cover gaps at other locations. Discussion focused on using the current budget problems as an opportunity to find innovative way to establish a sustainable model of operations and set up the library of tomorrow. Their goal was to have BPL become a library that "touches every Bostonian in one of three ways—online, in libraries, and in the community and a leader in delivering core services" by 2015 (BPL, 2010b). President Ryan stressed that decisions would be made using empirical data and input from the community. Within this context, Ryan and the Board presented two options for the FY11 budget. Both options required a reduction of about 100 positions, including existing and vacant positions, across the system. *Public Service Option 1* would maintain the existing structure and number of branches but with severely shortened hours and services. This model would necessitate staff working at more than one branch, possibly up to three separate locations, to cover loss of employees. *Public Service Option 2* would close between 8 and 10 branches and consolidate service points at the Central Library in Copley Square. After presentation and discussion of these options, President Ryan suggested that BPL move forward with Public Service Option 2 and begin collecting data to determine how to streamline services and which branches to close. The importance of technology and online services was stressed throughout the discussion, with President Ryan pointing out that if online services were its own "branch," it would be the sixth busiest branch in the system.

At this point, the language used was intense and statements were meant to get attention. Discussion about closing branches was more incendiary than those about cutting hours. The introduction of politics and using subtly charged language about fiscal support from State and City governments aimed at placing pressure on the State and maintaining good relations with the City. There was strong focus on the future, in terms of sustainability and in relation to the growing importance of technology to library services and users expectations. Not surprisingly, there was immediate reaction, both at the meeting and in the press. Several articles and editorials about budget issues and the cultural importance of BPL appeared between the February and March Board meetings.

At the February meeting, several individuals commented on alternatives to cuts in service, namely improving fundraising, encouraging community input, and the potential human impact of layoffs. One person requested that the Board resign due to its lack of political savvy to be replaced by members who "know how to have a strong presence at the State Legislature, Congressional, and Foundational level, as well as in the neighborhoods of Boston" (BPL, 2010b, para 54). Concepts such as the importance of the library as place, the historical significance of BPL, and BPL's role in assisting and educating children, seniors, and immigrants were repeated throughout public discussion. While much of what was presented was not strongly supportive of Public Service Option 2, speakers tried to present issues in a positive framework rather than assigning blame or strongly criticize BPL's administration.

The day after the February meeting, *The Boston Globe* highlighted the potential cuts, loss of staff, and strong reactions from the community, such as distance difficulties and culture in relation to the users of the branch libraries. While not explicit, the comments introduced issues of class and socio-economic status of library users. One patron described BPL as "miniature cultural arts centers for so many people who can't afford to go downtown to the theatre . . . [e]ach branch is a safety center for children and a cultural gem for those who cannot afford the culture world of the wealthy" (Ryan, 2010a, p. B1). Socioeconomic issues were also touched on with respect to transportation issues. "When you shut something down, you foreclose an option for a young person or an elderly person . . . who will not walk to the branch in the next neighborhood." These sentiments were echoed in an editorial printed a week later. In it McGrory (2010) describes the library as a "treasure island," a place of potential wonder and learning. He wrote "The reality is, a library is isn't merely a building with books, but a place where all things are possible . . . [t]his city, any city, can beat down ambition, but the library, with all that literature creates endless potential" (p. B1). McGrory also mildly criticized focus on technology by stressing the importance of the library's physical space, calling it the "great equalizer [where] you don't need a home computer, you don't need broadband, and you don't need an e-reader." In other words, the library was viewed as a space where anyone could find important resources, especially in the actual physical space. This sentiment was echoed in Tuft University's *Tufts Daily* that discussed the potential cuts and how they might affect access to resources for faculty and students. White (2010, para 25) mentioned the importance of libraries to the community and directly addressed the role of technology stating that "just because you have the Internet doesn't mean you don't need libraries." These comments were some of the first to publicly push back at the heavy stress on technology in BPL's future.

Not all the published discussions were supportive or uncritical. In one editorial in *The Boston Globe* meeting, a writer criticized the library's Board for their lack of "fundraising acumen" and called for a heavier financial contribution from the private sector in Boston (Anonymous, 2010a, para A10). While Anonymous understood the possible need to cut services and close branches, s/he also pointed out the need "to have confidence that the trustees have done everything in their power to mitigate the losses." The author also suggested that BPL's unions provide concessions about using volunteers in place of staff. This suggestion was strongly criticized by the President of Local 1526 of the American Federation of State, County and Municipal Employees (AFSCME). Cadillac stated that the Union does not "support the misguided notion that volunteers can replace the important, modest-wage jobs our members do to keep the library running smoothly" (Cadillac, 2010, p. A16). She also pointed out that AFSCME members had already accepted a wage freeze from October 3, 2009 until September 30, 2010 without any retroactive pay or wage increase and had seen insurance costs increase to ease the budget gap. Cadillac was defensive and attempted to shift focus away from the union and back to City and State officials. Both editorials were critical and outspoken, focusing on shortcomings of Board members and beginning a public argument about blame, solutions, and the role of the Union in the process.

2. March 9, 2010

At this Board meeting, the main topic was the measures for determining that branches to close. The meeting began with an acknowledgement from Ryan that "we are all in this together" and stressed that although many aspects of library service and user expectations had evolved, the driving vision and mission was unchanged from the past and that the importance of service to the community was still central (BPL, 2010c). The minutes noted that up until 1990, libraries essentially offered the same type of services for over a century and that within the last 20 years the rapid growth and change has been exponential. The change discussed was primarily in reference to technology and President Ryan used this focus on service to reinforce the importance of sustainability for BPL. She said "We owe it to the people of Boston to re-imagine the BPL into one that truly provides tomorrow's services today" (para 19).

It was within this context that President Ryan introduced "Draft BPL Measures and Other Definitions" to be used to collect data in making decisions about branch closings. The measures were broken down into *Public Use Measures, Operational Measures, Geographic Measures,* and *Other Considerations* (BPL, 2010c). The definitions and details of the measures were posted to BPL's Website along with notes from the Board meetings and other budget related documents.

Traditional library services, such as book circulation, story times, and programming were defined as core services, but there was a strong concentration on technology. President Ryan emphasized the need to transform the boundaries of library service beyond the walls of buildings, such as community outreach as well as online services. Sean Nelson, the Chief Financial Officer (CFO), further supported the need to address technology in the budget process by highlighting an increasing demand for services that included circulation, Web visits, public wireless sessions, and digital downloads. President Ryan pointed out that BPL owes it "to our employees to build a financially sustainable and stable workplace and we also owe it to the citizens of Boston to deliver a stronger, better public library" (BPL, 2010c, para 36). It was clear throughout the meeting that service, sustainability, and the increasing importance of technology were central to the administration's plans for dealing with a shrinking budget.

Political wrangling continued. A representative from the Mayor's Office reported on ongoing initiatives to try to improve economic support for BPL and encouraged contact with State legislative representatives, urging Friends of the Library (FOL) groups to put pressure on the State to increase funding for public libraries. As in earlier meetings, funding cuts by the state was again a focus for discussion. This time, however, it was accompanied by an explicit request for community action. Ten days later, BPL released a schedule for four community meetings and an online chat session to collect feedback on the budget process. An announcement also stressed that no decisions would be made at the March 24, 2010 Board meeting at which discussion and FY11 budget review would continue.

Once again there was strong public reaction to comments by President Ryan and the Board. This time reaction was more intense, with a critical edge while still being supportive. There were suggestions for fundraisers, particularly targeting the wealthier residents of Boston, and a plea to advocate for BPL as a whole rather than focusing on individual branches. A few audience members asked those present to remember where BPL's funds comes from and that there are limitations as to how much can be funded. Two speakers mentioned that no libraries had closed during the Great Depression and suggested that the Board do some research into how budget issues were managed at that time. Some participants openly questioned plans to partner with local community groups to make up for the loss of a branch library since the City of Boston was cutting funding to these programs as well. There was open concern about competition between neighborhoods to keep their libraries open. "Boston is still a city of turfs and closing branching would pit each neighborhood against one another" (BPL, 2010c, para 65). Apprehensions about socioeconomic and class issues were raised again. One participant stated concern that "reducing branch hours is an attack on the poor and adversely affect the neighborhood financially" (BPL, 2010c, para 61). Others requested that data collection include an analysis of what the communities would be losing, as well as using the proximity of the library to housing projects and schools as part of the measurement.

While not panicked, tenor of conversations was beginning to change at this point. There was more willingness to question President Ryan and the Board, as well as some preparation to fight for specific branches, either because they were a home branch or in lower income neighborhoods.

Reaction in the press was also more critical and questioned motives behind decision making. *The Boston Globe* echoed many of the concerns and harsh comments at the Board meeting. Some were openly critical of Mayor Menino, accusing him of pitting neighborhoods against each other. Another questioned the "real" motivation for closing branches by asking if "the underlying issue is really about money ... if you got your $3.6 million, would you still be looking to close branches?" (Ryan, 2010b, p. B1). He also questioned the proposed options and the strong focus on technology by highlighting the importance of the library as place rather than an outlet for technology. "Not the computers, not the high-tech, not the downloadables, libraries are about books and librarians. I didn't hear anything about that in your vision" (Ryan, 2010b, p. B1).

Another article in *The Boston Globe* mirrored many of the same issues, questions, and concerns expressed at the March 9 Board meeting. Walker (2010a) questioned some of the public statements, as well as the motivations, particularly in relation to money and the ultimate goal.

> Some suspect that this crisis is not entirely about money, and they're probably right ... No, the other issue – carefully couched – is consolidation. That means closing underused branches or those in lousy facilities, instead of spending the money to make them marginally better. Of course, to say that publically would be terrible politics, even if has the benefit of a certain cold logic. (p. B1)

Walker also expressed concern over potential problems in 2010 and 2011 as a result of the pursuit of goals expected to be achieved in 2015. Nostalgia for "better times" also entered the conversation in a call for the days of more politically adept and better connected Board members, such as Bill Bulger, who could "have pried $3.5 million out of the Legislature with a couple of phone calls" (Walker, 2010b, p. B1). As was the trend at this point in March, the language was more critical and openly questioned the motivations and decisions of President Ryan, Board members, and Mayor Menino.

Criticism, however, was not limited to the BPL administration and Boston's city government. A discussion thread following the article raised questions about the role of State legislators. The most telling remark pointed out that "any councilor who loses even on library loses his support in that neighborhood" (Bosdem, 2010). This is one of the first open statements from the community criticizing the State Legislature rather than just BPL and Mayor Menino.

Yet, even at this point, not all public dialogue focused on criticism. There was also discussion of how the community had begun to rally and raise support for branch libraries. Slack (2010) reported on a staged read-in to show support for a branch library, and advised having a public conversation on options for improved funding, such as tax increases and fundraising. According to Slack, the President of the Friends of the BPL spoke asking the community to accept some of the responsibility for maintaining services, stating "we've been mainlining on outside resources for too long. We've got fund our own resources here" (p. B10). Although the importance of community support had been a constant theme from the beginning, this was one of the first explicit public requests for community advocacy.

Much of the March discussion included a review of issues, questions, and proposals presented in earlier meetings. These included problems with the status quo of operations management, and working beyond the library's walls to meet community needs. The meeting also reviewed the financial picture, highlighting both the shortfall of funds and the cut in State funding. President Ryan and the Board also acknowledged the significant public engagement beyond just participation at Board meetings. As of this meeting, BPL had received 650 e-mail messages and 600 comments from the community. More community meetings were scheduled with weekend sessions and Spanish language translation at some to encourage wider participation. President Ryan also announced an agreement with unions to a wage freeze in order to save positions. The day after the meeting, BPL's Website held detailed definitions for data collection measures and a budget page.

Participants' comments at the meeting included both praise regarding the process and concern about the potential cuts. Several in the audience thanked the Board and President Ryan for their willingness to have open discussion and encouraging community participation. The FOL group expressed readiness to help with fundraising and to sustain services. There was concern about the heavily quantitative nature of the measures, worry that healthy branches would not suffer because of poorly supported or rarely used branches and that the plan was using the budget crisis as an opportunity to transform the library. One participant urged that decisions about changes or transformations be delayed for at least a year. On the whole, comments were more focused on support for the Board and President Ryan and encouragement for public participation in the process. The public discussion was clearly encouraging good public advocacy for BPL and for its users.

Articles following the meeting were also more low-key and thoughtful. *The Boston Globe* covered two community events. Both events were characterized as calm and civil, and noted that participants are "lovers of libraries, the kind of people who opt for intellectual strategy, not inflammatory scenes, to fight" (Wen, 2010, p. B1). Strong loyalties to specific branches were noted and apprehensions over potential turf wars were reiterated. Additionally, not everyone felt that the discussion about the cuts was influencing decisions, as was illustrated by one comment that "[e]verything has been coming from above the masses" (Teehan, 2010, p. B10). There was also concern that there was not enough effort being put into finding alternative solutions, commenting that administrators should "stop saying 'I can't' and start saying 'I'll try'" (p. B10). Geographic issues were also mentioned, noting that Boston is "not a car culture ... [i]t's not as easy as saying oh, I'll just drive another mile and park in the parking lot," which limits access even to libraries only a few miles away (Ryan, 2010c, p. B1).

While not incendiary, language used by members of the community at this point was intense and more combative. Criticisms in early April were about the entire process, not just the budget proposals or the administration's actions. Communities seemed to be preparing to fight for their own branch library rather than the BPL system as a whole. Yet, in spite of the criticism, the public was clearly willing to advocate for BPL. The public dialogue was helping to fuel enthusiasm and participation in the process.

3. April 7, 2010

The April meeting began with a review of feedback from the four community meetings, highlighting common themes including "the importance of the library in the lives of children, seniors, and new

Bostonians; the appreciation for libraries that are within walking distance of
people's homes; the significance of libraries in people's personal histories ... ;
the idea that bigger branches are not always better; and messages of
appreciation for BPL staff" (BPL, 2010d). The importance of this feedback to
the decision process was heavily stressed relative to the impending budget
vote on April 9.

In addition to information about the branch libraries, President Ryan
also emphasized analysis of the administration of the Central Library in
Copley Square to identify unnecessary redundancies and other areas to
minimize costs. Using this feedback and analysis as a framework, President
Ryan reviewed the two Public Service Options: keeping all the branches open
with severely reduced hours and closing 8–10 branch libraries.

She introduced a new option (now listed as Option 2), of closing only
four branches and keeping 22 open. The four potential closures were
identified as the Faneuil Branch in Allston/Brighton, Lower Mills in
Dorchester, Orient Heights in East Boston, and Washington Village in
South Boston. The rationale for each closure was discussed and included
limitations on technological expansion, American with Disabilities Act
compliance, aging building repairs, and low levels of programming and
program attendance. After long discussion, President Ryan endorsed
Option 2 as the plan to move BPL forward. She described it as the "most
prudent option that preserves as many branches as possible, fills critical
vacancies, and allows for improvements that do not require staff to work at
more than one location and to build critical partnerships with the
community" (BPL, 2010d).

As is evident from President Ryan's comments and Trustee statements,
official language was trying to present a middle-ground solution to a very
time-sensitive problem. While public feedback had been collected and
publicly lauded as helpful and important, the hard decisions needed to be
made soon. President Ryan and the Board were presenting an option that
they expected would be accepted as the best solution and one that had been
determined not just by the administration but also by community
advocacy.

Not surprisingly, many public participants expressed concern over any
branch closings. Some were upset over the closings due to "the unlikely
possibility of the affected branches to ever reopen" and out of fear for
future branch closings "in light of the aging facilities that are in critical
need of repair" (para 69). Petitions were presented from across the city
with 1817 signatures in support of branch libraries. Concerns were also
expressed about the entire process being too rushed and requested a State
of Emergency for more time to make a fully informed decision. However,

not all of the comments were negative. Some participants emphasized the need to prepare the affected communities and to set up outreach programs prior to any closures. Another suggestion was to have BPL use the strong public advocacy movement to help develop a strategic fundraising plan. Another recommended that all libraries remain open since this reflected the "wishes of the community expressed at the community meetings" (BPL, 2010, para 78).

As in previous meetings, comments were both supportive and critical. Some recognized a middle-ground solution, while others felt the voices of the community had not been clearly heard. Once again, there was a clear statement about the importance of community advocacy and the role of the community in the continued survival the public library system.

The Boston Globe published a summary of the April 7 meeting the following day. The newly proposed option of closing four branches was described as "the middle ground" (Ryan, 2010d) between previous proposals. The main criticism was aimed at Mayor Menino's office, despite an announcement on April 6th (BPL, 2010d) the City of Boston add about $280,000 back into the budget. One city councilor questioned Mayor Menino's decision asking "it is important that the [$3.3 million budget shortfall] comes from the library and not other departments" (Ryan, 2010d). City residents also questioned the decisions, especially in light of community support. Ryan quoted one such comment "I'm outraged at what the city is trying to do, closing community libraries. We've got a big fundraiser coming up ... We're not going to let this die" (p. B1). With the announcement of actual closures, language was getting more panicked and combative, particularly by those more closely connected to the targeted libraries.

4. April 9, 2010

At the opening of this meeting, the legal requirement to approve the FY11 budget by that date was reiterated (BPL, 2010e). After a final review of the three options, the Board voted to proceed with Option 2: that 22 branches remain open with four to be closed. President Ryan also presented a plan and a tentative timeline to work with the affected communities to identify organizations with which to partner, to continue services as best as possible, to encourage community involvement in the delivery of services, and to identify possible partnerships throughout Boston to help minimize the loss of services.

That same day Mayor Menino's office issued a press release announcing the budget decision. Its focus was on the fact that 22 libraries in the BPL system would remain open rather than on the closures. The Mayor's office stressed the importance of sustainability, especially in light of the increasing demand on services. The language was optimistic, presenting information as a good solution to a bad problem, and placing it in the context of ongoing money woes and increased expectations of service. The press release also noted strong public participation through e-mails and letters and contributions of the community members in public meetings.

Community reaction to the vote continued many of the themes from previous discussions. Comments were both supportive and critical. Criticism was not limited to BPL's administration, but included politicians at both city and state levels. Many were concerned about long-term effects on neighborhoods and on the city of Boston. Some spoke of the loss of cultural institutions, while others focused on the potential negative impacts on education and learning. In all of it, there was still support for BPL and some acceptance and tentative approval for the decision to close four branches.

Prior to the final budget vote on April 9, attendees were invited to speak. Comments were intense, focusing on influencing the vote rather than attacking President Ryan and the Board. Several speakers stressed the importance of the library as a place, particularly for new Bostonians, immigrants, and children. Speakers referred to the closings as a "catastrophe" and worried about the "dire impact it would have on children who learn the love of books and to read for the first time in the neighborhood branches" (BPL, 2010e, para 54). Others had concerns about the measurements used to identify the four targeted branches, noting that the Washington Village branch, while small, has "one of the highest usages per square foot," and Lower Mills branch's "excellent circulation usage." The one clearly critical remark was aimed at the Boston State Legislature representatives. Given that a large part of the funding problems stemmed from State cuts, one participant felt "dismay regarding the lack of State Boston Representatives attending the public discourses" (BPL, 2010e, para 65).

In the days immediately following the vote, there was strong reaction in the press. *The Boston Globe* on April 10, 2010 provided an overview of issues and concerns about branch closings, and a frank discussion about money issues. The importance of the library to the community was evident, describing Boston as a city "full of readers and [libraries] are their sacred spaces" (Walker, 2010b, p. B1). The decision was described as both inevitable and as a manipulative political ploy. "The city had threatened to close even more branches, which is a time-honored Menino tactic for cushioning bad news—if you threatened to close 10 branches, but only shutter four, you can pretend to have made the best of a bad situation" (p. B1). At the same time,

Walker noted that some of the library branches are "more popular when they are under siege than on a daily basis" and acknowledged that BPL's operational problems were "ripe for an overhaul" (p. B1). Ultimately, in spite of concerns about the speed of the process and apprehensions over losing these branches forever, Walker ended the article by stating that "making no choices simply is not a choice right now" (p. B1).

The Boston Globe also covered the Board meeting. While Ryan's article commented about the library as place and as a cultural center, he stressed the significance of the budget shortfall and quoted Mayor Menino comments "As mayor and chief executive of this city, I have to make decisions with the resources available" (Ryan, 2010d, p. B1). However, Ryan conveyed a strong sense of moving forward from this point. Criticisms of the speed of the entire process were evident, but so were calls for further support. "It's important these kids have an outlet ... [and] today is not the end of the process" (Ryan, 2010d, p. B1).

D. Conclusions or a New Beginning?

The struggle with the FY11 budget continued calendar year 2011. Despite the struggle in Boston, there were some successes particularly with respect to public influence and advocacy for BPL. BPL continued its advocacy work and held four roundtable meetings with BPL's CFO early in 2011. As of the deadline for this chapter, BPL faced another budget crisis based on further reductions in State funding. In response, BPL and its administration continue its open communication policy and building on relationships established during the 2010/2011 budget debate. Its Website continues to provide up-to-date information about the budget, potential new cuts such as reducing or eliminating Sunday hours, reducing collection budgets, and continuing to leave critical vacancies open (Nelson, 2010).

The influence of public opinion and actions had strong political implications beyond the City of Boston. In May 2010, the 18 State Legislators from Boston succeeded in approving an amendment to the FY11 State budget stating that if BPL closes any branch library, or eliminates any positions from the Central Library, the library would lose the remainder of its State funding. On July 1, 2010, Governor Duvall Patrick signed the FY11 State budget requiring BPL to maintain services at 2009 levels without any additional funding.

While not conceding the need to close the branches, Mayor Menino announced in July 2010 that the four targeted branches would remain open until the city could draw up plans to repurpose the buildings for future use.

Table 2
BPL Budget Summary FY 2008–09 Through FY 2010–2011

Funding Source	FY 2008–2009	FY 2009–2010	FY 2010–2011
City of Boston	$31.2M	$29.7M	$30.4M
State Funding (Library of Last Recourse, State Aid, Boston Regional Library System)	$8.9M	$4.0M	$2.4M
Other Sources (Trust Funds, Gifts, Grants, Federal Erate, MetroBoston Library Network	$8.0M	$7.4M	$6.8M
Total all sources	$48.0M	$41.1M	$39.6M

In September 2010, Mayor Menino appointed State Representative Byron Rushing to the BPL Board of Trustees. This appointment can be seen two ways. First, to better connect the fiscal needs of BPL with State decision makers and second to force forcing State Representatives to deal with their actions. Rushing was one of those who backed the amendment to the State budget.

In the end, BPL had to deal with $1.5 reduction between FY10 and FY11 with the only increases coming from the City of Boston (see Table 2 for complete breakdown). On March 23, 2011, the Board of Trustees approved a $39.34 million budget for 2011–2012. This budget has a $1.5 million shortfall based on estimated expenses. Once again, BPL provided detailed information to the community and continued to obtain strong advocacy support for BPL and its services. Table 2 shows the decline of BPL's budget from 2008 through FY 2011.

E. Boston to Los Angeles

The situation in Boston had community and city government support. BPL President Ryan, while still relatively new, established a strong base of support and was able to act from a position of strength to lead BPL through its budget crisis. In Los Angeles, the situation was vastly different. There the Mayor Antonio Villaraigosa and City Council had done their best to decimate the library system from 2007 through 2010 when the position of City Librarian position had been held by three different people. LAPL budget problems progressed quickly without community involvement.

III. Los Angeles Public Library

The LAPL is the second largest urban public library in the United States based upon expenditures (Miller, 2011). According to the 2010 Census, the population of Los Angeles was 3,792.621. The ACS (in 2009) estimated the population of Los Angeles to be 3,796,840 (U.S. Census Bureau, 2009b). When looking at the different ethnicities, all were down according to ACS except for Caucasian and Hispanic/Latino populations with the latter population having the largest increase.

LAPL has 8 regional libraries, 64 community branches, and 1 central library. Prior to 2007, all libraries were open seven days a week with evening hours four days a week except for Friday through Sunday. All of that changed with the recession from 2007 until 2011. As of 2011, all libraries are closed Sundays and Mondays. The regional and branch libraries are open Tuesdays and Thursdays from 12:30 to 8:00 p.m., and Wednesdays, Fridays, and Saturdays from 10:00 a.m. to 5:30 p.m. The Central Library is open Tuesdays and Thursdays from 10 a.m. to 8:00 p.m., and Wednesdays, Fridays, and Saturdays from 10:00 a.m. to 5:30 p.m. As the recession deepened, many families lost jobs, houses, and met other hardships. Due to loss of tax revenue, the recession has hit municipalities, counties, states, and the federal government hard. Tax revenue, particularly property tax, funds many of the services that get taken for granted in the good financial times.

This case study looks at the LAPL system as whole over the fiscal years (FY) of 2008 through 2010. The research was done through analyzing the Board of Library Commissioners of Los Angeles Minutes for 2008, 2009, and 2010, the City's adopted budgets for fiscal years 2007–2008, 2008–2009, 2009–2010, and 2010–2011, and the proposed Library Department budget for 2011–2012. It also drew newspaper articles from the *Los Angeles Times*, *LA Weekly*, and other newspapers on the Internet, online blogs, and Websites commenting on the LAPL and the City of Los Angeles management, LAPL's Website, a conversation with City Librarian, Martín Gómez, City of Los Angeles Website, and the Honorable Mayor Antonio Villaraigosa's Website. There is some discussion about what is beginning to occur for FY 2011–2012 budget cycle.

A. Governance of Los Angeles Public Library System

LAPL's governance system is simple. There is a City Librarian appointed by the Mayor, confirmed by the City Council, who serves at the Mayor's request. The Board of Library Commissioners has five Los Angeles residents appointed for five-year terms by the Mayor and confirmed by City Council.

They serve at the pleasure of the Mayor. The Board has fiduciary responsibility for LAPL regions and branches and supervises the Library Foundation, various FOL groups, and any other matters in which it chooses to get involved. The Board approves policies for the library system. The Board does not always agree with the Mayor and City Council on decisions that they have made regarding financial or personnel issues. Employees of LAPL are represented by the Librarian's Guild.

B. Property Taxes Fund Public Libraries

California is the state that passed Proposition 13 in the late 1970s that holds property tax increases to 1% per year unless the property is sold. In the year it is sold, the property can be revalued at the selling price and then revert to having property tax increases held to 1% per year. LAPL is a little different. The City Charter for Los Angeles has minimum funding requirements for the public library written into its bylaws. This, in effect, can tie the hands of the mayoral administration that controls the budget. The current charter in effect since April 1, 2009 states:

> ... the financial support of the Library Department, there shall be appropriated an annual sum of not less than 0.0175% of assessed value of all property in the City as assessed for City taxes (Los Angeles City Charter, 2009, p. 84).

Property includes residential, commercial, and any other property that is taxed by the city of Los Angeles. The Mayor, however, has been able to avoid meeting that required funding level. Any additional funds needed by the library would come out of the city's General Fund subject to mayoral approval.

C. LAPL Budgets—2008–2011

The City of Los Angeles has been in a precarious budget situation since 2007. The City spends approximately 73% of the budget on police and fire. The remaining 27% is divided among the remaining city departments. The Library Department, as LAPL is called, has not had a great time financially during the recession between 2007 and 2011. The overarching problems that led to fiscal disaster include changes at the top, paying the city back for operating costs, and loss of free Time Warner wireless Internet connectivity.

During this time period, one City Librarian retired, there was an interim city librarian, and a new one was hired on July 1, 2009. This led to lack of continuity at LAPL and, no doubt, some loss of strong ties to the city administration.

1. Paybacks for Operating Costs

Beginning in fiscal year 2008–2009, the Mayor required the Library Department to start repaying the city's general fund for some of its operating costs. Prior to July 2008, they were covered in full by the city. Operating costs include items such as utilities, custodial costs building maintenance, fuel, and fleet costs. Payback of operating expenses began as an incremental step process with the amount increasing every year. During FY 2008–2009, the payback amount was $6,147,994 and in FY 2009–2010 it was $17,080,317 (LA Budgets, 2008, 2009). It is roughly $20 million per year in 2010–2011.

2. General Budget Climate

The LAPL system endured tough cuts to services, employees, and hours. No one line item has been left untouched. The Library Department has not been alone in the unprecedented budget reductions. The Parks and Recreation Department was also hit hard as during this time period. The City Librarian and the City Council members have noted that police and fire departments have been untouched during this difficult financial period.

The budgets for the fiscal years ending 2005–2006, 2006–2007, and 2007–2008 are listed by revenue and expenditures in Table 3.

Table 3
LAPL Revenue and Expenditures, FY 2005–2006 Through FY 2007–2008

	FY 2005–2006	FY 2006–2007	FY 2007–2008
Revenue			
City of LA	$61,429,673	$65,732,558	$65,525,712
Other revenue	8,752,569	6,866,945	7,738,579
Total revenue	$70,182,242	$72,599,403	$73,264,291
Expenditures			
Salaries	$53,567,746	$56,925,907	$59,079,920
Expenses	3,757,332	4,162,143	4,108,815
Library materials	10,842,608	11,430,111	9,830,111
Total expenditures	$68,920,900	$72,599,401	$73,264,291
Related costs	45,003,824	46,346,829	48,686,791
Total LAPL costs	$113,924,724	$118,946,230	$121,951,082
No. of employees	1,141	1,129	1,131

Source: City of Los Angeles, Budgets FY 2005-06, 2006-07, 2007-08.

3. FY 2008–2009 Budget

For the fiscal year (FY) 2008–2009 budget, the Mayor and City Council requested a number of reductions in the Library Department budget:

1. Reduce the book budget of $9.9 million by $2.2 million to $7.7 million;
2. Close the eight regional libraries on Sundays; and
3. Demand mandatory furlough days for civilian city employees (Board Minutes, 2008a, p. 2).

The Board was not pleased when the City Librarian informed them in April, 2008 of what was to be cut. Through advocacy by the Librarian's Guild, employees, patrons, and the Library Board of Commissioners, none of the requested reductions occurred. The Mayor had as part of his goals, to increase literacy and to stop gang activity. Many of the Board members used these goals to point out that 22 branches had literacy programs and that cutting library hours would be detrimental to the Mayor's goals.

The then City Librarian Fontayne Holmes subsequently reported that City Council approved restoration of funding for Sunday service hours for regional branches, and added $2.2 million to the library book funds (Board Minutes, 2008b, p. 4) for a total FY 2008–2009 budget of $129 million and 1100 employees by the end of June, 2009.

4. FY 2009–2010

Because of decreasing property values, the amount of revenue coming to the city was less than expected. Nevertheless, the Library Department was to receive 0.0175% of all of the assessed value or properties per the City Charter. The proposed budget for this fiscal year was negotiated by an Interim City Librarian, Kris Morita. The first situation Morita had to deal with was a "no growth" budget for FY 2009–2010 mandated by the Mayor (Board Minutes, 2008c, p. 2).

The Library Department, in an attempt to maintain the previous year's service levels, pointed out that with 18 million people visiting the library in FY 2008–2009, and that LAPL was the most frequently used of the City's services (Board Minutes, 2008c, p. 3). Morita came up with two proposals for FY 2009–2010. Proposal one maintained the materials budget at $9.7 million and offered to make 45 temporary positions into regular full-time ones.

Proposal two would do the same but also included replacement of computers and printers that were seven or more years old. It included $35,000 in funds to pay for a wireless Wi-Fi and Internet service previously supplied free by Time Warner. The total requested for the second proposal was $87.6 million that would have shown slight budget growth as opposed to the Mayor's flat budget.

After the Interim City Librarian had submitted these two proposals, the Mayor asked for an additional 9% reduction from the final FY 2009–2010 budget that would mean a $6.4 million reduction (Board Minutes, 2009a, p. 6). There were three places from which the 9% reduction could occur: people, materials, and service hours. Morita stated, "... that for the Library Department 9% equates to $6.4 million, which is a tremendous hit because more than 80% of the Library budget is comprised of salaries, thus requiring the elimination of 90 positions" (Board Minutes, 2008c, p. 5). The $6.4 million equated to reduction of approximately 115 FT positions that in turn would decrease in service hours for branches and reduce material expenditures.

In the end, the materials budget was reduced from $9.7 million to $6.8 million, a 30% decrease (Board Minutes, 2009b). All city departments then received an additional request for a 10% decrease in salary accounts from the Mayor, which meant another $6.4 million for the Library Department. Twenty-five vacant positions that were eliminated were not included in the 115 positions remained to be cut. It was determined by the Board that a decrease in salary expenditures would have to be through retirements, furloughs, layoffs, or a combination thereof.

LAPL also complied with City's decision to close offices on the second and fourth Fridays of each month beginning July 1, 2009 and LAPL (Board Minutes, 2009b, p. 5). All full-time civil service employees were to work a 72 hour pay period for 26 biweekly pay periods during the 2009–2010 fiscal year work furlough program (Board Minutes, 2009c, p. 9). In essence, every full-time employee in the Library Department received a pay cut of 10% per pay period.

During September 2009, the city began planning for an Early Retirement Incentive Program (ERIP) for 2,400 employees citywide in an effort to save payroll costs and reduce the need for layoffs and furloughs (Board Minutes, 2009d, p. 6). A cap was included because departments could not fill the positions vacated through early retirement. At the time ERIP went into effect, LAPL had a shrunken full-time staff complement of 929 employees.

By December 2009, 145 LAPL employees had applied. Of the 145, there were 40 librarians in a class that was capped at 20 and 18 were senior librarians in a class capped at 14. The City's Human Resources department was to determine who of the 145 would be eligible (Board Minutes, 2010a).

On top of 110 open positions that had been caught in a hiring freeze, and the 145 library employees who wanted to take early retirement, the

Mayor and Council wanted another 100 positions eliminated at LAPL. With all these positions potentially being eliminated, LAPL would have a complement of approximately 793 employees. This would mean a 30% reduction in force. It should be noted that at times of full employment, the library had had 1132 positions. A 30% reduction in force meant that service hours at the branches would be severely affected.

With 110 vacant positions and 107 projected early retirements, the Interim City Librarian requested eliminating all Sunday hours and reducing evening hours to two days a week from four. The new hours would have the regional and branch libraries opened for 44 hours a week and the central library open 52 hours a week. At the end of FY 2009–2010, the Library Department had a staff complement of 992 along with 140 vacant and frozen positions. It had budget of $134.6 million as of June 30, 2010. While the budget increased slightly, this was offset by the need to pay back operating costs.

5. Budget for FY 2010–2011 Grows Smaller Still

Beginning July 1, 2009, a new City Librarian, Martín Gómez, had been given the reins of the LAPL system. No one had informed him of the budget situation or the devastation to come during his first year in the position.

When the initial budget discussions began, City Librarian, Martín Gómez, reported to the Board that the City would be facing significant downturn in revenue of over $200 million (Board Minutes, 2010b). Because of the decreased revenues, all city departments had been given instructions to prepare for further workforce reductions. The Library Department had been told to plan for elimination of 100 positions. These would be in addition to early retirements and the 115 positions unfilled due to the hiring freeze (Board Minutes, 2010b). The staff reduction could be as high as a 30%.

The FY2010–2011 budget saw a slight increase of 0.36% or $131,732,200 (Board Minutes, 2010c). The city included a $22 million general fund reimbursement for utilities and employee benefits and $1.9 million the first payment of two for early retirement payouts (Board Minutes, 2010d). This budget was where the reduction in forces would be felt. In the end, a total of 328 positions were eliminated (Table 4).

The 328 positions that were lost caused the loss of yet another day of service in all branches. The total payroll savings in salaries and benefits were $16.2 million. The one upside to losing the 328 positions was that, while most of the other departments in the city would lose one day per pay

Table 4
Number of Eliminated Positions at LAPL by FY 2011

97	Vacancies
107	Early retirements
100	Layoffs full-time equivalent positions
24	Eliminated positions
328	Total

period to furloughs, the library system would not (Board Minutes, 2010d). The layoffs included 60 part-time messenger clerks so the library system actually laid off 120 of the messenger clerks in order to achieve 100 FTE positions.

The materials budget was maintained at the same level as the FY2009–2010 at $6.8 million—one of the lowest materials cost per capita in the country for an urban library and for the size of population served.

6. Special Meeting of the Board, June 16, 2010

A special meeting of the Board of Library Commissioners meeting was called on June 16, 2010 to discuss placing a ballot for a parcel tax measure on the November 2, 2010 State General Election to maintain and restore Library services and reduce its dependency on the City's General Fund (Minutes, 2010e, p. 1).

A survey of registered voters indicated that a $39.00 parcel tax would pass by 68% of those surveyed. The parcel tax paid would give the library $30 million in addition to the city chartered amount. The ballot measure for the library would need 66 2/3% (also called a super majority) of eligible voters approving the parcel tax, as required by California law (CA State Code Chapter 6 Art. 1 § 95.2).

After a lengthy discussion, the Library Board voted unanimously to approve placing the tax measure on the November ballot. Hopes were dashed, however, when the City Council and Mayor voted it down because it would have cost the City $4.2 million to add it as a stand-alone item in a state general election.

D. Community Engagement

Where was the community during the budgeting process at LAPL? Why weren't communities involved in helping to set schedules at branches? When asked about it, Martín Gómez, City Librarian stated "The move to cut hours happened pretty quickly. People were so numb with what was happening in the economy and their life. People were more concerned with personal well being" (M.J. Gómez, personal communication, January 6, 2011). There were not many articles in the Los Angeles press until after the budget had passed and been implemented.

After layoffs had occurred and early retirements took effect, reality sank in. Patrick McDonald wrote an article entitled "City of Airheads: Villaraigosa dismantles L.A.'s Vaunted Library System" in *LA Weekly*. The most controversial item mentioned was the library closings on Mondays. He questioned where kids would go after school to do homework and use computers. "Now, with most Los Angeles Unified School District (LAUSD) schools starting class this week, teachers are assigning homework to hundreds of thousands of students, many of whom don't have the necessary Internet access" (McDonald, 2010a, p. 2). Because of the lack of public Internet access computers being unavailable to complete homework and without Monday access for school children, the cut in funds at LAUSD and LAPL has, and continues to make, completion of homework difficult for K-12 students.

Bloggers on the *LA Weekly* (2010) site commenting on the article had a wide range of opinions. Many of them felt that the City of Los Angeles was not handling funds correctly. As someone said "The problem here is not the lack of funds to keep the libraries open, but rather misallocation and misuse of funds by the City of LA" (Anonymous, 2010b).

Some of the bloggers commented on the number of people who were in, and using the libraries during the summer. Marilyn stated " . . . All summer long, the library was PACKED with kids and their parents and grandparents and siblings, reading on the rugs, reading on the benches, reading, reading, reading. The computers were full. It was (is) really the 'people's university'" (2010). Marilyn's statement actually backs up some of LAPL's own statistics that visits to the libraries were up. In 2009, the 72 branches and central library had over 18 million visitors (LAPL Fact Sheet, 2010).

The ability of the LAPL system to actually handle more visitors and have higher use rates than ever with budget cut and a decimated staff was a tribute to management of the Library Department. Garnering public support after cuts occurred might be too late. The purpose of advocacy is to build support through community groups such as FOL so that when libraries are threatened, there is a built-in support system that will go to work on their behalf, putting pressure on government funding sources. This did not happen in LAPL's case.

E. Charter Amendment

Once branches were open only two nights a week and closed Sunday and Monday, City Council members were inundated with phone calls, e-mails, and letters (M. J. Gómez, personal communication, January 6, 2011). Gómez was approached by the chair of the City Council budget committee to prepare an amendment to the City Charter. At the November 4, 2010 Library Board meeting, the City Librarian mentioned that a motion had been made by two City Councilmen to review the Charter formula and how it applies to the LAPL system (Board Minutes, 2010f). If an amendment were placed on ballots for the March 8, 2011 municipal election, it could increase the percentage of the Library Department receives from property taxes assessments. Unlike the parcel tax proposed in June 2010, this would not increase property taxes. In essence by asking for an increase from 1.75% to 3.0% of the total property taxes collected, the City would have to find the 1.25% increase elsewhere in its budget. To pass a charter amendment takes a simple majority of voters at 50% plus one, unlike the parcel tax's super majority. If it passed, funding increases would rise from 0.0175% to 0.0300% incrementally over a four-year period, as follows. If the charter amendment is passed funding would increase as follows (Table 5).

When the charter amendment, called Measure L, was presented to City Council, it passed unanimously, 15-0 (Board Minutes, 2010g).

The one provision of the charter amendment was that the measure would ensure that at least 45% of the incremental amount of the increase from 0.0175% to 0.0300% would have to be used for the increased library services, programs, or hours. The charter amendment is written in such a way that it is to the library systems advantage (see appendix). A caveat in the Amendment was that the Library Department will pay for all of its operating costs by FY 2014–2015 (Gómez, 2011).

Table 5
Measure L Proposed Funding Increase

Fiscal Year	Percentage	Estimated Funding Increase
2011–2012	0.0206	$11,787,569
2012–2013	0.0237	25,098,360
2013–2014	0.0269	38,366,625
2014–2015	0.0300	51,677,416

Source: Santana, 2010.

Table 6
LAPL Budget 2008–2009 Through 2010–2011

Fiscal Year	Approved Budget
2008–2009	$129,000,000
2009–2010	$134,630,453
2010–2011	$131,732,200

Source: City of Los Angeles, Budgets, FY 2008-09, 2009-10, 2010-11.

Prior to the election, there was some news coverage in the local Los Angeles papers. The *Los Angeles Times* had an editorial against passing Measure L (2011). The editorial said that if the City of Los Angeles, including the Mayor and City Council, wanted to fund the library adequately, it should do so without having the vote to change the City Charter (Vote no., 2011). The irony of Measure L is that the Mayor and 13 of 15 Council members endorsed Measure L after going through several years of painful budget negotiations and reductions in the Library Department. The police and fire departments were also against Measure L because they felt the funds would come from their budgets. In FY 2010–2011, the police and fire department budgets were $1.18 billion and $495 million, respectively. In the *LA Weekly* article, the police union came out sharply against Measure L (McDonald & Meinicoff, 2011).

McDonald and Meinicoff (2011) supported Measure L and took the Mayor and the City Council to task for the size and cost of their office staff. Between them, they had a larger staff than the President of the USA, with 477 staff members and a budget of $50.6 million.

On March 8, 2011, Measure L passed in the City of Los Angeles with a *Yes* vote of 63%. This means that over the next four years the budget of LAPL will be increased by $11.7 to $51.7 million as shown in Table 4. Passage of Measure L would allow the eight regional libraries plus the Central Library to be open seven days a week and the branches to be open six days a week. LAPL would also be able to hire 123 staff members to cover additional days and hours of opening.

F. Total Budget Ups and Downs, FY 2008–2009 Through 2010–2011

The City of Los Angeles and the Library Department have seen budget ups and downs over the last four years. With passage of Measure L, the City Librarian and LAPL will have some breathing room.

There are other implications for LAPL from passing Measure L. LAPL will be responsible for 100% of their operating costs by FY 2014. In Table 6 the column entitled "Various Special" is where operating cost reimbursement funds sit.

IV. Conclusion

A. Differences

BPL and LAPL have some stark differences that need to be pointed out (Table 7).

Both case studies point to long-range effects that are still permeating through their communities. Every year both library systems and their city managements will go through negotiations about library budgets. With a long-term recession that still has its claws in the economy and shrinking tax revenues that fund municipalities and state governments, it is likely that BPL, LAPL, and their sister libraries will continue to go through this kind of dogfight every year into the foreseeable future.

The glaring difference between the two library systems was that Boston was effective in using a highly transparent budget process and forced advocacy to avoid radical reductions in its budget. In Los Angeles, however, the process was not transparent and there was little public advocacy until after the impact of budget reductions was felt at the local level. Another

Table 7
Basic Data About Boston and Los Angeles

Item	Boston	Los Angeles
Population at 2010 Census	617,594	3,792,621
% Increase over 2000 Census	4.8	2.6
% Latino/Hispanic increases	26.8	7.0
Number of libraries in system	27	73
Best transportation mode	Walking or public transit	Driving (car is king)
City density	Concentrated and dense	Sprawling
Case study time frame	January through April 2010	2008 through 2011

Source: U.S. Census Bureau, 2000a, 2000b, 2010a, 2010b.

difference was that LAPL used an election to effect funding improvements whereas Boston did not. In Boston, government officials at the city and state levels began, and are still, negotiating the state's subvention to BPL for serving as the Library of Last Recourse.

1. Community Advocacy

The difference between the two cities in advocacy is marked. In Boston, the community was involved and vocal from the beginning when President Ryan and the BPL Board of Trustees began conversations about closing branches. Boston community members and other stakeholders immediately began getting involved in the budget process. Boston citizens came to Board- and community-centered meetings to have their say. News stories and blogs publicized meetings, and the largest paper in the region, *The Boston Globe*, covered the story from the beginning, printing many articles and editorials about budget issues and community responses.

In Los Angeles, the community was never part of the conversation. The Los Angeles Mayor, City Council, and LAPL management made all the decisions without input from their stakeholders. Once Martín Gómez became City Librarian, he contacted the Library Guild's President who then began attending Board meetings. The only articles in the press appeared after the Mayor and City Council had decimated the budget. The articles were not in the *Los Angeles Times*, the largest paper in the city, but in an online and print newspaper, the *LA Weekly*.

The Los Angeles community at large did not really start reacting until hours of opening had been cut in branches. When the libraries were open only five days a week, the press commented that it was one of only two library systems in the country to do this (McDonald, 2010b). Why did it take so long for the community to recognize the situation? Sometimes it takes losing something and recognizing the loss to mourn it. Council members e-mail and phones were extremely busy with complaints about the cuts in service hours after they went into effect (M.J. Gómez, personal conversation, January 6, 2011).

B. Lessons for the Future

Could both problems in Los Angeles and Boston have been avoided? Given the wide-ranging impact of the recession, budget problems were inevitable. However, the way in which they were introduced by the different funding bodies could have been better. Improved communication between the parties could have gone a long way toward finding reasonable solutions before unrealistic budget cuts and ultimatums were issued. Unfortunately, politicians just do not always work that way. They pressurize agencies to decrease budgets and wait to see if they make the reductions, and then they wait to gauge community reaction to loss of services. While reactions in Boston and Los Angeles were different, the importance of the community was clear. In Boston, the community stepped up from the start and began advocating for BPL and its services. In Los Angeles, it took time for services to disappear and only then there was strong community reaction. In the end, the community showed their support by easily approving Measure L and guaranteeing continued and stronger support for LAPL. Both systems found a way not only to survive but also to continue or reinstate quality services through outreach and advocacy, even if it began as a forced process.

Appendix: Public Library Funding. Charter Amendment L

Shall the Charter be amended to incrementally increase the amount the City is required to appropriate annually from its General Fund to the Library Department to an amount equal to .0300% of the assessed value of all property in the City, and incrementally increase the Library Department's responsibility for its direct and indirect costs until it pays for all of its direct and indirect costs, in order to provide Los Angeles public libraries with additional funding to help restore library service hours, purchase books, and support library programs?

References

Alire, C. (2010). Crisis in Colton libraries. *American Libraries*, 41(1/2), 6.

Anonymous. (2009). More library for less money. *The Boston Globe*, October 6, p. A10.

Anonymous. (2010a). In crisis, libraries need better boar, more private funds. *The Boston Globe*, February 19, p. A10.

Anonymous. (2010b). The problem here is not the lack of funds to keep the libraries open. *LA Weekly*, September 21. Retrieved from http://blogs.laweekly.com

Battiste, C. A. (2006). Advocacy and the Canadian public library trustee. *Feliciter*, 52(3), 107–108.

Battistella, E. (2010). What a library closure taught me. *Library Journal*, 135(4), 42.

Bosdem. (2010, March 10). *Even without funding cuts, the Boston Public Library might still cut branches, chairman says* [Web log comment]. *Universal Hub*. Retrieved from http://www.universalhub.com/2010/even-without-cuts-boston-public-library-might-stil

Boston Public Library (BPL), Trustees of the Public Library of the City of
    Boston. (2010a, January 19). *Meeting of the corporation and administrative
    agency.* Retrieved from http://www.bpl.org/general/trustees/trusteeagenda
    011910.htm
BPL, Trustees of the Public Library of the City of Boston. (2010b, February 17).
    Meeting of the corporation and administrative agency. Retrieved from http://
    www.bpl.org/general/trustees/trusteeagenda021710.htm
BPL, Trustees of the Public Library of the City of Boston. (2010c, March 9). *Meeting
    of the corporation and administrative agency.* Retrieved from http://www.bpl.org/
    general/trustees/trusteeagenda030910.htm
BPL, Trustees of the Public Library of the City of Boston. (2010d, April 7). *Meeting
    of the corporation and administrative agency.* Retrieved from http://www.bpl.org/
    general/trustees/trusteeagenda040710.htm
BPL, Trustees of the Public Library of the City of Boston. (2010e, April 9). *Meeting
    of the corporation and administrative agency.* Retrieved from http://www.bpl.org/
    general/trustees/trusteeagenda040910.htm
BPL. (2011). *Main page.* Retrieved from http://www.bpl.org
Cadillac, E. C. (2010). Unfair to portray union library workers as obstructionist. *The
    Boston Globe*, February 26, p. A16.
California State Code. (n.d.). *Revenue and taxation code, Section 95.2.* Retrieved from http://
    www.leginfo.ca.gov/cgi-bin/displaycode?section=rtc&group=00001-01000&file=
    95-95.4
City of Los Angeles. (2009). *City Charter.* Retrieved from http://www.amlegal.com/
    nxt/gateway.dll?f=templates&fn=default.htm&vid=amlegal:laac_ca
City of Los Angeles. (2011). Retrieved from http://www.lacity.org
City of Los Angeles, Board of Library Commissioners. (2008a, April 25). *Minutes.*
City of Los Angeles, Board of Library Commissioners. (2008b, May 22). *Minutes.*
City of Los Angeles, Board of Library Commissioners. (2008c, November 20).
    Minutes.
City of Los Angeles, Board of Library Commissioners. (2009a, April 29). *Minutes.*
    Retrieved from http://www.lapl.org/about/blc_docs.html
City of Los Angeles, Board of Library Commissioners. (2009b, May 14). *Minutes.*
    Retrieved from http://www.lapl.org/about/blc_docs.html
City of Los Angeles, Board of Library Commissioners. (2009c, June 11). *Minutes.*
    Retrieved from http://www.lapl.org/about/blc_docs.html
City of Los Angeles, Board of Library Commissioners. (2009d, September 10).
    Minutes. Retrieved from http://www.lapl.org/about/blc_docs.html
City of Los Angeles, Board of Library Commissioners. (2010a, January 14). *Minutes.*
    Retrieved from http://www.lapl.org/about/blc_docs.html
City of Los Angeles, Board of Library Commissioners. (2010b, January 28). *Minutes.*
    Retrieved from http://www.lapl.org/about/blc_docs.html
City of Los Angeles, Board of Library Commissioners. (2010c, May 27). *Minutes.*
    Retrieved from http://www.lapl.org/about/blc_docs.html
City of Los Angeles, Board of Library Commissioners. (2010d, June 16). *Minutes.*
    Retrieved from http://www.lapl.org/about/blc_docs.html
City of Los Angeles, Board of Library Commissioners. (2010e, June 16). *Minutes,
    Special Meeting.* Retrieved from http://www.lapl.org/about/blc_docs.html

City of Los Angeles, Board of Library Commissioners. (2010f, November 4). *Minutes.* Retrieved from http://www.lapl.org/about/blc_docs.html

City of Los Angeles, Board of Library Commissioners. (2010g, November 18). *Minutes.* Retrieved from http://www.lapl.org/about/blc_docs.html

City of Los Angeles, Controller's Office. (2005). *Budget, fiscal year 2005–2006.* Retrieved from http://controller.lacity.org/stellent/groups/ElectedOfficials/@CTR_Contributor/documents/Contributor_Web_Content/LACITYP_008021.pdf

City of Los Angeles, Controller's Office. (2006). *Budget, fiscal year 2006–2007.* Retrieved from http://controller.lacity.org/stellent/groups/ElectedOfficials/@CTR_Contributor/documents/Contributor_Web_Content/LACITYP_008022.pdf

City of Los Angeles, Controller's Office. (2007). *Budget, fiscal year 2007–2008.* Retrieved from http://controller.lacity.org/stellent/groups/ElectedOfficials/@CTR_Contributor/documents/Contributor_Web_Content/LACITYP_008023.pdf

City of Los Angeles, Controller's Office. (2008). *Budget, fiscal year 2008–2009.* Retrieved from http://controller.lacity.org/stellent/groups/ElectedOfficials/@CTR_Contributor/documents/Contributor_Web_Content/LACITYP_008024.pdf

City of Los Angeles, Controller's Office. (2009). *Budget, fiscal year 2009–2010.* Retrieved from http://controller.lacity.org/stellent/groups/ElectedOfficials/@CTR_Contributor/documents/Contributor_Web_Content/LACITYP_008025.pdf

City of Los Angeles, Controller's Office. (2010). *Budget, fiscal year 2010–2011.* Retrieved from http://controller.lacity.org/stellent/groups/ElectedOfficials/@CTR_Contributor/documents/Contributor_Web_Content/LACITYP_012825.pdf

Dempsey, B. (2009). Libraries build the case for voter support. *Library Journal,* 135(5), 68–71.

Dempsey, B. (2010). Voters step up. *Library Journal,* 135(5), 62–66.

Duckor, A. (2009). From awareness to funding. *American Libraries,* 40(1/2), 45–47.

Feldman, S. (2010). Unleash the power of the library. *Public Libraries,* 49(2), 4–5.

Gómez, M. J. (2011). *Budget submittal, FY 2011–2012* (Retrieved from http://www.lapl.org/about/blc_docs.html). Los Angeles, CA: Library Department

Johnson, P. M. (2005). *A glossary of political economy terms.* Retrieved from http://www.auburn.edu/~johnspm/gloss/public_goods

LA Weekly blogs. (2010, September). Blog content. *LA Weekly.* Retrieved from http://blogs.laweekly.com

Los Angeles Public Library. (2010). *Los Angeles public library facts* [for Fiscal Year 2008–2009]. Retrieved from http://www.lapl.org/

Los Angeles Times. (2011). *Vote no. on Measure L.* [Editorial], *Los Angeles Times,* February 14. Retrieved from http://articles.latimes.com/print/2011/feb/14/opinion/la-ed-measurel-20110214

Marilyn. (2010). I work as a volunteer reading to kids at my local library on Tuesday. *LA Weekly,* September 20. Retrieved from http://blogs.laweekly.com

McDonald, P. R. (2010a). City of airheads: Villaraigosa dismantles L.A.'s vaunted library system: Mayor mirrors Detroit's disastrous choice. *LA Weekly,* September 16. Retrieved from http://www.laweekly.com/content/ . . . /1058321/

McDonald, P. R. (2010b). *LA Weekly* readers sound off on Mayor Antonio Villaraigosa's dismantling of public libraries. *LA Weekly,* September 17. Retrieved from http://blogs.laweekly.com/

McDonald, P. R., & Meinicoff, M. (2011). L.A.'s library Measure L: There's lots of hidden city hall fat to fuel the 73 shuttered libraries. *LA Weekly*, February 24. Retrieved from http://www.laweekly.com/2011-02-24/news/l-a-s-library-measure-1/2/

McGrory, B. (2010). Treasure islands at risk. *The Boston Globe*, February 26, p. B1.

Miller, K. (2011). *Top 50 urban public libraries based on expenditures*. Washington, DC: Institute for Museum and Library Services.

National Center for Educational Statistics. (2011). *Search for school, college, and libraries*. Retrieved from http://nces.ed.gov/globallocator/index.asp?search = 1&State= &city=&zipcode=02115&miles=10&itemname=&sortby=name&College=1& CS=F013E342

Nelson, S. (2010, September 30). *BPL fiscal overview*. Retrieved from http://www.bpl.org/ general/trustees/fy12_bpl_budget_trustee_presentation_2011march23.pdf

Novotny, E. (2010). Hard choices in hard times: Lessons from the great depression. *Reference User Services Quarterly*, 49(3), 222–224.

Ryan, A. (2010a). Library may cut 10 of its branches: Boston weighs layoff of quarter of staff. *The Boston Globe*, February 18, p. B1.

Ryan, A. (2010b). The passions run high as libraries' fates debated. *The Boston Globe*, March 10, p. B1.

Ryan, A. (2010c). Library releases data on traffic at branches: Statistics will shape plans for cutbacks. *The Boston Globe*, April 1, p. B1.

Ryan, A. (2010d). Close 4 branches, library chief says: In plan, 94 jobs also would be cut to end $3.3 gap. *The Boston Globe*, April 8, p. B1.

Santana, M. A. (2010, November 16). *Fiscal impact of proposed charter amendment for library funding* [Interdepartmental correspondence]. Retrieved from http:// clkrep.lacity.org/onlinedocs/2011/11-1100-S2_rpt_cao_11-16-10.pdf

Slack, D. (2010). Supporters not ready to close book on libraries: Will push tax increases to help fund branches. *The Boston Globe*, March 14, p. B1.

Smith, G. (2009). Oak Brook tries to live with scaled down library: Falling sales tax revenue means budget cuts. *Chicago Tribune*, November 9. Retrieved from http:// articles.chicagotribune.com/2009-11-09/news/0911080190_1_village-library-residents-have-library-cards-librarians/2

Teehan, S. (2010). More than 100 fight for library branches. *The Boston Globe*, April 4, p. B10.

U.S. Census Bureau. (2000a). *Boston City, Massachusetts profile of general demographic characteristics: 2000*. Retrieved from http://factfinder.census.gov

U.S. Census Bureau. (2000b). *Los Angeles City, California profile of general demographic characteristics: 2000*. Retrieved from http://factfinder.census.gov

U.S. Census Bureau. (2009a). *Boston City, Massachusetts demographic and housing estimates: 2005–2009*. Retrieved from http://factfinder.census.gov

U.S. Census Bureau. (2009b). *Los Angeles City, California ACS demographic and housing estimates: 2005–2009*. Retrieved from http://factfinder.census.gov

U.S. Census Bureau. (2010a). *Boston City, Massachusetts P2: Hispanic or Latino and Not Hispanic 2010 Census Redistricting Data*. Retrieved from http://factfinder2. census.gov

U.S. Census Bureau. (2010b). *Los Angeles City, California P2: Hispanic or Latino and Not Hispanic 2010 Census Redistricting Data*. Retrieved from http://factfinder2. census.gov

Walker, A. (2010a). Make book on these cuts. *The Boston Globe*, March 13, p. B1.

Walker, A. (2010b). Take a stand on branches. *The Boston Globe*, April 10, p. B1.

Wen, P. (2010). Disquiet outside Boston Public Library: Branch-closing fears lead to tactful protest. *The Boston Globe*, March 29, p. B1.

White, J. (2010). Boston Public Library considers branch closures, service cuts. *Tufts Daily*, March 2. Retrieved from http://www.tuftsdaily.com/boston-public-library-considers-branch-closures-service-cuts-1.2175796

Survival Tactics

Survival Facts

Changing Organizations: Three Case Studies

W. David Penniman

Consultant, Columbus, OH, USA

Abstract

Three case studies in change involving both corporate and academic institutions are described in detail and analyzed in a systematic manner including an "autopsy" of the change strategies and results. In each case, the environment at the outset, the strategies for change, the concluding environment, and the autopsy are presented. Some generalized conclusions from the three cases are presented as well.

Keywords: Change strategies; Corporate library; Informatics school; Library Network; Consortium

I. Introduction

Veteran organizational change agents will tell you that success is often hard to come by and a "batting average" of over 300 (as in baseball) is exceptional (Kotter, 1995). Where "culture change" is involved, the success rate drops even lower (Smith, 2002). It has been argued, in fact, that it is fruitless to attempt to change a culture as it will always trump strategy (Schneider, 1999). This may be true but the author leaves it to readers to make their own judgment based on the following cases, all three of which represent some short-term successes, but with final outcomes for at least two that can only be characterized as strike outs.

As in many other instances, the failures have as many lessons embedded as do successes. Taking the time to evaluate cases of both success and failure is worthwhile, and a careful autopsy of a failure is often most informative. This chapter takes a frank look at three instances in which dramatic change was attempted within deeply entrenched organizational cultures known for stability—or at least highly resistant to change from forces both within and without.

LIBRARIANSHIP IN TIMES OF CRISIS
ADVANCES IN LIBRARIANSHIP, VOL. 34
© 2011 by Emerald Group Publishing Limited
ISSN: 0065-2830
DOI: 10.1108/S0065-2830(2011)0000034008

The three cases are drawn from both industry and academe. They involve the laboratory, the classroom, the library, and administrative offices. They convey both strategies for change and barriers to change. Most importantly they present the outcomes for each case in an analytical manner with an associated "autopsy."

The cases span several decades, different environments, and organizations of different sizes. The most common thread running through them is the dynamic of change and how it was resisted, embraced, or ignored. The cases describe the consequences that ensued from each situation.

The chapter begins with an evaluation of the Library Network operating within AT&T just after divestiture. It then moves on to the development of the School of Informatics at the University at Buffalo, a State University of New York (SUNY) institution. Finally, the operation and transformation of a statewide collaborative network serving public, academic, and school libraries in New York State is evaluated. The opinions expressed are solely those of the author, and others involved in the organizations may see these situations differently. The only claim made is that the author was not only there, but in charge of the organizations being analyzed. For better or for worse, this provided a unique perspective to each situation.

II. AT&T Bell Labs, 1984–1991

On January 1, 1984, the monopoly known as AT&T was officially broken up following a ruling of the US District Court for the District of Columbia when presiding Judge Harold H. Greene accepted a settlement proposed by the US Department of Justice and AT&T. It had taken nearly eight years for that antitrust decision to be reached. The decision to break up the largest single employer next to the federal government was an extremely difficult one to adjust to on the part of the employees of the behemoth. Their reaction was reminiscent of the five stages of grief articulated by Kübler-Ross (1969)—denial, anger, bargaining, depression, and acceptance. For many, the first stage persisted right up to the point of their departure from AT&T.

From 1984 to 1991, the author directed information services for AT&T Bell Laboratories starting with a staff of over 200 and a budget in excess of $20 million that subsequently grew to a staff of 300 and a budget of $30 million through absorption of additional organizations. As of January 1984, information offerings to members of technical staff (MTS) included database services, management information systems, telecommunications, technical libraries, and physical delivery services. *The primary challenge was to convert this traditional technical information support system into an online-oriented, corporate-wide information network providing computerized technical, business, and marketplace information to individuals and groups throughout AT&T, and to do so at a competitive cost.* This was done in an evolving environment (postdivestiture) where a monopoly oriented culture was no longer viable. Despite the necessity of this change in culture apparent to those outside of AT&T, within there remained many who said "not on my watch" or "not until I retire will changes be made".

A. Environment upon Arrival

I arrived in early January 1984, just one week after divestiture was implemented. What I found is listed below in terms of the overall situation and specific issues related to staff, management, funding, and vendor relationships.

- Situation: 200 employees serving Bell Labs scientists via information services including 23 libraries, an archive, database services, and other miscellaneous information support activities (e.g., executive information service).
- Culture (see Schein, 2004) was one of internal promotion and growth with almost all managers being "homegrown." Many employees were second generation, some were even third generation. Employees proudly spoke of being "Bell shaped."
- The culture of library management was to remain aloof from staff (e.g., they did not sit with nonsupervisory staff at the same table in dining areas).
- Staff, particularly technical staff, were never fired. Instead, they were "stimulated" to resign.
- Funding for information activities was automatic and incrementally increased.
- Vendor relations were long standing and renewal of contracts was virtually automatic. For example, the company providing binding services for journals was "offended" when asked for a competitive bid.
- Automation existed only in the backroom. There was no OPAC in use for library users. In fact, they used a bound book catalog that was updated quarterly. I had never seen one of these previously, but was assured that the members of technical staff (Bell Labs scientists, also called MTS) liked having this "desktop access."
- MTS were accustomed to high-touch personalized services and enjoyed long-standing personal relations with the library staff, many of whom shared a background in science or engineering.
- There was a general denial of divestiture in the ranks and a belief among some that all would return to "normal" once the federal government realized its error and overturned Judge Greene's ruling.

B. Strategies for Change

It was clear that radical change was required, not just within the library organization, but throughout administrative service units of the laboratories. Under new leadership at the very top level, an entrepreneurial business within a business approach was imposed on all units previously viewed as "overhead operations." The libraries were no exception. This made the changes I planned much easier to introduce since they were consistent with organizational change efforts being attempted throughout the enterprise.

Strategies included the following:

- Treat each library or information service as a business that must stand on its own in terms of self-sufficiency. Activities that supported individual units such as centralized cataloging had their costs prorated across the libraries they served.
- Target-specific change activities focused on the culture that encouraged greater risk-taking and entrepreneurial approaches. It was clear that the culture would always trump any strategy that was in conflict with it. Therefore, the culture had to change.
- This meant that we needed to "change" the people or else change the "people." See below for more related actions.
- A high visibility venture involving the design, construction, and display of a prototype "information access station" as a centerpiece exhibit for the 1985 NFAIS Conference helped to find the true risk takers who, over a relatively short period of time, were promoted into key management positions.
- Reassign or "stimulate" retirement of managers who were unable or unwilling to make the transition. This was akin to the situational leadership model described by Hersey (1984) where individuals both unable and unwilling to participate need special treatment. Also, some staff members were encouraged to find other positions when it became clear they were unable to adapt to the new environment.
- Clear mission and vision statements were developed involving all Library Network staff. This also included new "corporate branding" which identified every unit as part of the AT&T Library Network. The statements that were developed and accepted by the staff were:
  ○ Mission: Provide technical, business and marketplace information to individuals and groups throughout the enterprise at a competitive cost.
  ○ Vision: Be recognized for contributing to the success of the enterprise by furnishing information that gains the organization a competitive advantage in the marketplace.
- Many planning sessions and open discussions were held regarding driving forces, limits on the ability to grow via new services, and enhancement of current services. These meetings helped us all learn that I could not lead unless others were willing to follow and sometimes this meant compromise both on my part and on the part of others.

C. Environment at Departure

Seven years later, the Bell Labs situation was quite different and included the following:

- The organization known as the AT&T Library Network had over 300 employees and had added responsibility for mail and other information service delivery systems and a growing role in management information systems.
- Many smaller libraries were closed bringing the total down to 16 installations from 23, but with the introduction of information access stations developed under the NFAIS project mentioned above. These access stations served as a transition to a dominant desktop focus. For a description of

design of these access stations see Penniman, (1987). Note that this concept was more than a mechanism to find risk takers, it also provided a transition strategy away from traditional on-site branch libraries.

- Desktop access to the full range of materials including OPAC, full text and abstract databases, some developed in-house and an integrator for AT&T-wide locator service (online phone directory).
- Creation of an off-site storage facility for lesser-used materials with 24-hour turnaround delivery.
- Contract negotiation each year with internal customers for funding of services. The Library Network did this along with all other administrative support services.
- Introduction of a new array of external vendors who had to compete for contracts, just as we had to compete for our own internal customers. Our competition was not another Library Network, but other ways to spend funds that were now under the control of technical managers. They no longer had to pay overhead charges over which they had no control; they could now choose which and at what level of support they might receive.
- The Library Network provided information support to AT&T employees worldwide via e-mail and online services and in the process had to deal with transborder intellectual property issues for both paper and electronic materials.

D. Autopsy

The transformation of the internal information services into a corporate-wide Library Network operation was a success and continued to operate as a unified entity for some time. In the end, however, "the patient" (i.e., AT&T) died from a related disease—inability of the parent organization to adapt to the changing and highly competitive environment. AT&T was bought by one of the "spin-off" regional Bell operating companies—SBC. SBC chose to rebrand itself as AT&T, but the former corporate giant exists now in name only. The crown jewel of the entity, AT&T Bell Laboratories, that functioned as a monopoly supported national research laboratory no longer exists in the form it once did, but components have migrated, merged, separated, and transformed. This has been true for the Library Network as well. Throughout all this change at the corporate level the information entity continues to exist, but with a new name "Integrated Information Solutions." The staff has shrunk and satellite physical libraries have disappeared, but the organization has continued to deliver high-quality information and information services throughout the company via the Web and other Internet technologies (J. J. Simon, personal communication, 2011).

III. UB School of Informatics, 2001–2006

Beginning September 2001, the author served as Dean of the School of Informatics at the University at Buffalo. *The challenge was to integrate two entirely separate academic departments with a total of 26 faculty members and to create a third program (informatics) using existing resources.* Enrollment was slightly under 1000 students with bachelors, masters, and PhD programs involving communication, and a master's program in library science. Funded research programs were minimal and for the most part came through library-related studies. At the outset, external grant funding did not exceed $30K per year.

A. Environment at Arrival

- The "School" was a loosely knit structure of two departments that had come together as a School of Communication and Information over a year previously.
- The then Provost had suggested this newly created school become the School of Informatics (or she would create such a school in any case perhaps using programs already in this school). Computer science and media studies had already rejected being part of this new school with computer science merging with a computer engineering program in the College of Engineering while media studies remained on its own in the College of Arts and Sciences.
- An ongoing search for a permanent dean of the newly formed school had not been successful previously and it had operated for over a year under an interim dean, a faculty member in communication).
- Each of the two departments operated as separate stand-alone entities without a program in informatics despite plans for such a program being on the books but not implemented.
- The existing two departments were physically separated by two floors and philosophically by much more than physical distance. The separation might as well have been two miles! The communication department prided itself on a theoretical, quantitative approach to the study of communication (but with little or no funded work in the area) while the library science program was focused on graduating practicing librarians with a focus on application—not research. The bachelors of communication and the masters of library science constituted the vast majority of enrollments in the merged entity.

B. Strategies for Change

- The departments needed to share resources to create a strong school—combining financial, development, and administrative staff at the School (not department) level. This required co-opting some space and administrative staff from departments for School-level functions—a move resisted and resented by the departments.
- New hires in either department had to agree to also teach in the informatics program (this was one way to circumvent resistance from legacy faculty).
- New hires were required to have clear research agendas and a willingness to seek grant support. In addition, they should reflect an interest in technology and its intersection with information and people.
- Legacy faculty were required to seek grant support for work if such were available in their area. They were also required to pursue an aggressive publication program.
- Efforts were made to resolve workload inequities with more teaching for faculty members not doing research and/or publishing. A consistent workload policy was attempted but it was resisted by both legacy faculty as well as their union, United University Professions (UUP).
- The School sought to attract students who had considered the computer science program but who wanted more applied or socially relevant challenges and related coursework.

C. Environment Prior to Dissolution of School

In June 2006, a new provost (who replaced the previous champion for the School of Informatics) operating with the support of a new president removed me from the leadership position of dean and within a matter of days announced the dissolution of the School of Informatics. The action was taken despite the following accomplishments within the School.

- Formal informatics degree programs (B.S., M.A.) with strong enrollment at the master's level and beginning to gear up for the undergraduate program that had received initial ABET accreditation.
- Administrative resources had been combined to support the three academic programs (communication, library science, and informatics).
- Newly hired faculty were prepared to teach in their home program (communication or LIS) and also participate in the informatics program.
- Research funding increased from $30K/year upon my arrival to over $2 million/year on my departure including research in health information systems, communication sciences, and library usage as well as digital libraries and data mining.
- Financial and other (e.g., internships) support from corporate and alumni sources was increasing.
- Strong and supportive dean's advisory board comprised of representatives from industry and other academic entities including AT&T, Welch-Allyn, Rich Products, and the UB Medical School.

D. Upon Dissolution

With the announced closure of the School, despite assurances from the Provost that "not only will these academic programs continue in their current manifestation, but they will progress and flourish" (Tripathi, 2006) several collateral results occurred:

- Faculty attracted by informatics program left the university.
- The two founding departments were separated and moved to different home colleges. Both rejected support of the informatics program under the new structure and focused their resources on their preinformatics degree programs.
- Alumni who supported the School (and not just one of the programs) withdrew funding as did corporate supporters.
- The Dean's Advisory Board was disbanded by the provost after members spoke out against dissolution of the School of Informatics.
- The library science program was given ALA conditional accreditation (the parent School was dissolved in the middle of the accrediting process) and has been on conditional status for two consecutive evaluations.
- Degree programs in informatics had enrollments frozen and then were eliminated.
- The Communication program emerged stronger than before creation of School due to the School's investment in new hires with strong research agendas (meant to serve as the core of health and other informatics activities).

E. Autopsy

A number of forces served to contribute to the demise of the School of Informatics despite its positive performance metrics. These are listed below with a candid appraisal of the strategic aspects of each

- New university administration was not supportive of the fledgling school (previous provost had been the champion of this program—and most of her initiatives were disbanded or reversed under new leadership)
- Competition with computer science was a strategic error on my part as the new provost was tenured in that program and not at all supportive of "informatics"—especially the social aspects of the emerging field.
- Enrollments in informatics were on the rise while computer science was declining. Informatics also was attracting more women and minorities—areas in which computer science was less successful. It was apparent that this emerging field was a threat to the more traditional computer science program.

Funding for academic programs under the previous administration was based on metrics such as enrollment and research income. This was changed to a subjective model channeling money and new faculty positions to programs deemed important by the new administration. This created a complete disconnect from the past reward system and in some cases pitted deans against each other for favored treatment.

- Failure on my part to see clearly the political agenda at play in which the more successful the School was in attracting students away from computer science, the more vulnerable it was as a threat. My belief that attracting students and strong new faculty along with a growing base of funded research would carry the argument was incorrect. This failure at the political level was a significant factor in the School's demise

While the School of Informatics no longer exists at the University at Buffalo, others have survived (Indiana) or emerged (Northern KY) and the concept is still extremely viable. What is required is a way to reconcile (or absorb) computer science into the mix such as Indiana where this may be under way with a dean with credibility in this domain.

IV. Nylink (A Study in "Retrenchment")

In September 2007, the author became Executive Director of Nylink (a statewide multi-type library consortium serving libraries in the State of New York). Nylink had an operating budget of $2.4 million and was entirely self-supporting even though the program existed within the Office of the Provost of the SUNY System Administration. Nylink contracted and delivered automation services to over 300 institutional members reaching over 2000 libraries throughout the State. It had a staff of 24 including professional librarians, information technology staff, and financial administrators. The program served libraries in higher education (public and private), public libraries, and K-12 libraries as well as special libraries and cultural heritage organizations. *The challenge was to transform the organization through a new business model involving internal product development, and new vendor relationships.*

A. Environment at Arrival

The author was hired to transform the organization from one primarily dedicated to serving marketing, implementation, and training needs of OCLC customers, into an organization focused on non-OCLC services and products. This represented a significant culture change for the employees. All but three of them were members of a union and, by contract, they were protected from dismissal except for reasons of financial exigency or retrenchment. The characteristics of Nylink were as follows:

- A 35-year-old-organization, previously called SUNY/OCLC, with heavy focus on a single vendor, representing over 40% of revenue with much of the additional revenue tightly coupled to the OCLC relationship.
- The organization was staffed for this focus and level of activity, with dedicated OCLC-centric professional staff, most of whom held "permanent" appointments.
- Nylink membership (300 institutions) perceived the organization as an arm of OCLC with some other "useful" services such as cooperative service agreements with various database vendors.
- Functioned as a fully self-supporting organization with no budgeted funds from SUNY and a healthy reserve resulting from operating "in the black" most years in the past decade.
- A very high level of uncertainty existed regarding the future relationship with OCLC. It was clear, however, that OCLC would not be a primary source of revenue. This was obvious after the first meeting with OCLC in October of 2007, but not obvious to many on staff. The same process of denial articulated by Kübler-Ross (1969) existed, as it had at AT&T Bell Laboratories after divestiture.

B. Strategies for Change

- Introduction of transparency in all matters to staff and to board (including financial realities and dealings with key vendors). Most staff and board had not been privy to the financial details including how much of the revenue came from each source and how it was spent, with over 80% on salary and benefits.
- Commitment to clear and frequent communication with the membership regarding the changing relationship with OCLC.
- Introduction of a clear *mission for the organization*: To support the information community through collaboration and innovation.
- and likewise a clear *vision*: To connect the resources, tools, and expertise of libraries and cultural heritage organizations throughout New York State for the economic and educational benefit of these institutions, the state, and its citizens.

- Articulation of a clear set of *operating principles*:
  Provide lowest cost services meeting member expectations
  (no favored vendor or product/service, provide choices where available)
  Operate on full cost recovery basis
  (understand all internal costs and price services accordingly—reduce cost where necessary)
  Maintain vendor relations that benefit our members
  (clear contracts, trusted partners)
  Treat all resources as assets for the benefit of members
  (continuous member input on what they need and want, responsible financial management)
- Creation of a structure that allowed for disruptive change while maintaining status quo for current services per Christensen (2003) and Martin (2007). This included the creation of a "skunk works" team operating outside the normal hierarchy that reported to the Director. This team was composed of individuals not so emotionally tied to OCLC and the history of serving its needs. It was charged with exploring new ventures and developing business plans for those offering the greatest promise.
- Introduction of business planning processes and development of a three-year transition plan to migrate the organization to full self-support once more without reliance on single vendor.
- Shift to strong member-focused services/products rather than vendor-focused support.
- Introduction of key performance indicators (financial, membership, professional solutions, training, etc.) that quantified the gap existing between old sources of revenue and existing expenditures. This clearly brought into focus the potential demise of the organization should new products and services not be developed in a timely manner.
- Draw on reserve for no more than two years while new products and services were introduced. This timeframe required extremely aggressive action, something the organization was unaccustomed to and resisted at most levels.

C. Environment Upon Announcement of Closure

In March 2010, the Provost's Office of SUNY System Administration determined that they would "retrench" Nylink rather than risk having to support it during a transition period that might extend beyond the limits of Nylink's cash reserve. In other words, SUNY was unwilling to invest its own resources in an organization that provided services beyond the SUNY institutions.

Retrenchment, in academic parlance, is usually applied to departments that a college wishes to close. The process allows the institution to dismiss employees even if tenured or otherwise protected (as in the case of Nylink) by unions. This was an unusual move for the SUNY System Administration, since it was breaking new ground by implementing retrenchment of an administrative unit supported by external funds. Nylink in essence was a guinea pig.

At the time of this decision (which was not made public or presented to the employees until May of 2010 for reasons involving sensitive union issues) the following situation existed:

- Nylink staff had been reduced by 25% using attrition—with a hiring freeze imposed by SUNY. The organization could not hire new blood for its transformation process and had to rely on temporary employees and consultants to fill gaps.

- Revenue dropped by 40% as anticipated. An aggressive business plan projected replacement at less than one-third of the shortfall with no clear sources of additional revenue within the time available based on spending down the cash reserves and no support from SUNY.
- There were new products/services in the pipeline or already in the marketplace (see, e.g., True Serials™, an electronic resource management service), but they needed at least two years to "stability."
- Introduction of a clear branding of Nylink services separate from vendor services. For example, Nylink Professional Solutions was introduced as the formal branding of the consulting services traditionally bundled in with vendor support and now offered as a stand-alone service for a fee.
- Member retention held at 95% during the first year of transition but was likely to decline further as OCLC pulled back its billing function, the last remaining significant revenue generator from that vendor.
- Staff were informed they would be terminated by May 2011 with the exception of a "skeleton crew" to handle final billing and collection of past due accounts. This crew had to leave by the end of Summer 2011.

D. Autopsy

Nylink ran out of time before the proposed new services could find foothold in the marketplace and ultimately would have also run out of reserve funds without support from SUNY. It could be argued that without offering "core services" such as cataloging and resource sharing, the replacement of OCLC revenue was impossible.

If that were the case, then the planned strategies for change were unrealistic and bound to be unsuccessful. There were, however, other factors beyond those of OCLC that were at play:

- A reengineering initiative driven by the SUNY board that indicated Nylink, if no longer self-supporting, should be eliminated.
  A new chancellor and new provost for the SUNY System faced with serious budgetary issues and an urgent need to cut SUNY costs.
- A contractual requirement to support "retrenched" staff belonging to the UUP union for one year after termination notice. This added a significant constraint on the lead time (and cost) needed to shut down the organization.
- A SUNY mission that did not include support of broader functions of a statewide Library Network reaching beyond its own institutions and requiring financial support during a transition period.

There was no clear home for the reinvented organization outside of SUNY. All assets (financial reserve, staff, equipment, and other items of value) were claimed by SUNY and could not have been transferred to an external entity despite the fact that these assets came from earnings via Nylink services to members within and outside of SUNY. This precluded Nylink from pursuing merger options external to SUNY. In the final analysis, Nylink was boxed in by its own structure and origin. It was born as a project within the Provost's Office of SUNY and remained such until its demise via retrenchment. A decade-old evaluation regarding moving Nylink out from under SUNY by becoming a separate 501c3 organization was not pursued at that time due to similar legal and organizational constraints. These constraints included Nylink's staff being SUNY employees with union protection and the difficulty of moving the cash reserve to a non-SUNY entity.

Despite the legitimate reasons for disbanding Nylink, there were some serious miscalculations concerning the collateral damage of doing so. As has recently become clear, without Nylink or a similarly positioned entity within the state government, purchase of services from organizations such as OCLC will be extremely difficult and will require the initiation of a lengthy and complex contracting process affecting SUNY, CUNY, the NY State Library, and other similar entities. Justifying a sole–source relationship with any vendor, including OCLC, will also require considerable effort and time and potential objections from other vendors in the same market space.

One could argue that effective decisions are made with the best available information and lead to the desired results. Because Nylink was not involved in the decision to disband its operations, the complexities of dissolving its services, replacing its contracts, and moving its statewide delivery system were not adequately considered. The decision led to a significant "scramble" to find other ways to replace services while the clock was running out. The decision to disband Nylink did not meet the criterion stated above for an "effective decision." In the long run, the cost of replacement may well exceed the cost of supporting Nylink during even a lengthy transformation process.

V. Conclusion

Looking at three examples of organizational change involving different environments (corporate, academic-single institution, and academic-system-wide) is instructive in understanding the forces at play for and against successful change. The failures far outnumber the successes both in the broader perspective of other studies and in the three examples discussed here.

To single out one or two reasons for failure oversimplifies the situations illustrated in this chapter and in other similar analyses (Kotter, 1995). The themes, however, are interesting to itemize. Here are the ones the author would emphasize:

- *If you cannot change the people* (in terms of their mindset and orientation to new realities), *then change the people* (to a new set of individuals ready and willing to embrace change).

- *Never ignore the ability of culture to trump strategy.* There is a reason why organizations spend much time and energy on creating and nurturing a culture (sometimes without even knowing they are doing so), but they should be careful what they create. Building a "stable" culture can lend a sense of security to an organization. What may be needed, however, for true security, is a resilient organization staffed with people demonstrating a willingness to embrace change on a continual basis. Reinforcing the wrong culture can be a fatal error.
- *Recognize that the stages of grief apply well beyond death and dying.* Denial, anger, bargaining, depression, and acceptance are also a normal for organizational change as well. While each stage must be acknowledged, staff should not be allowed to get stuck in one of the stages. Acceptance must be pursued by the leader to move an organization beyond continual resistance to change. For those unable to "move on," help them find new places to "move on to."
- *Leaders cannot bring about change by themselves.* Find the (few?) staff ready to embrace change and bring them onto the team. Get the right people "on the bus" and then get moving as articulated by Collins (2001).
- *Convey a sense of realism and urgency in every manner possible.* Be totally transparent about the seriousness of the situation confronting the organization. Do not deliver only bad news, but present a realistic assessment and then talk about strategies for change that can deal with the situation. Give everyone a chance to "get it."
- *When (and if) it becomes clear that the strategies are not working, engage everyone in creating new strategies.* Remember that change applies to you as well as your staff.
- *Learn from mistakes (and you will make some).* Related to the previous point, do not ignore mistakes. Use them as a lesson. There will likely be a "next time" *and you will be better prepared by taking a realistic look at your past efforts.*

The future will belong to those who can embrace change. I always think of my grandmother who rode to her new home in a horse and buggy as the bride of a country doctor at the end of the 19th century. Before she died in the mid-twentieth century she was a passenger on a commercial jet airliner flying to see relatives in California whom she had never met before. She understood change and embraced it. We should too.

References

Christensen, C. M. (2003). *The innovator's dilemma: The revolutionary book that will change the way you do business*. New York, NY: Harper Collins.

Collins, J. C. (2001). *Good to great: Why some companies make the leap—And others don't*. New York, NY: HarperBusiness.

Hersey, P. (1984). *Situational leadership: The other 59 minutes*. Escondido, CA: Center for Leadership Studies.

Kotter, J. P. (1995). Leading change: Why transformations fail. *Harvard Business Review, March–April*, 59–67.

Kübler-Ross, E. (1969). *On death and dying*. New York, NY: Macmillan.

Martin, R. L. (2007). *The opposable mind: How successful leaders win through integrative thinking*. Boston, MA: Harvard Business School Press.

Penniman, W. D. (1987). Tomorrow's library today. *Special Libraries*, 78(3), 195–205.

Schneider, W. (1999, May). Why good management ideas fail: Understanding your corporate culture. *Otherwise, Featured Guest.* Questa, NM: Paradigm Shift International. Retrieved from http://www.parshift.com/Speakers/Speak016.htm

Schein, E. H. (2004). *Organizational culture and leadership* (3rd ed.). San Francisco, CA: Jossey-Bass.

Smith, M. E. (2002). Success rates for different types of organizational change. *Performance Improvement, 41*(1), 26–33.

Tripathi, S. (2006, June 16). Provost announces reorganization of school of informatics. University at Buffalo news release. Retrieved from http://www.buffalo.edu/news/8012

True Serials™: See Trueserials.com for details on this product now offered by an independent software as a service provider.

Suggested Further Reading with Annotations

Chaleff, I. (1995). *The courageous follower: Standing up to and for our leaders.* San Francisco, CA: Berrett-Koehler.

How to pursue success when being led, leading from within the organization, and knowing when to stand up for your beliefs.

Christensen, C. M. (2003). *The innovator's dilemma: The revolutionary book that will change the way you do business.* New York, NY: Harper Collins.

Balancing the current practices of a successful organization with the need to introduce "disruptive" technologies and processes.

Frankl, V. E. (1997). *Man's search for meaning.* New York, NY: Pocket Books.

While we have little control over what happens to us, we are in complete control over how we choose to respond.

Greenleaf, R. K., Frick, D. M., & Spears, L. C. (1991). *The servant as leader.* Indianapolis, IN: Robert. K. Greenleaf Center.

An essay on leaders as servants of those being led as written by an ex-AT&T executive. Pamphlet useful for classroom instruction.

Greenleaf, R. K. (1996). *On becoming a servant leader.* San Francisco, CA: Jossey-Bass.

A vastly expanded version of the essay cited above.

Hersey, P. (1984). *Situational leadership: The other 59 minutes.* Escondido, CA: Center for Leadership Studies.

A useful model for understanding the need to change strategies depending on the readiness (capability) and willingness (mindset) of those being led.

Martin, R. L. (2007). *The opposable mind: How successful leaders win through integrative thinking.* Boston, MA: Harvard Business School Press.

Understanding how to carry two opposing concepts simultaneously within a set of strategies. The world is not always "either/or"!

Schein, E. H. (2004). *Organizational culture and leadership* (3rd ed.). San Francisco, CA: Jossey-Bass.

Source of excellent definition of culture, to wit:

> The culture of a group can now be defined as a pattern of shared basic assumptions that was learned by a group as it solved its problems of external adaptation and internal integration, that has worked well enough to be considered valid and, therefore, to be taught to new members as the correct way to perceive, think, and feel in relation to those problems. (p. 17)

Schneider, W. E. (1999, May). Why good management ideas fail: Understanding your corporate culture. *Otherwise, Featured Guest.* Questa, NM: Paradigm Shift International. Retrieved from http://www.parshift.com/Speakers/Speak016.htm

An argument for building around existing culture rather than trying to change it. An opposing view to many of my experiences.

Refocusing Distinctive Capabilities: Strategic Shifts in Harvard's Baker Library Services

Cynthia Churchwell, Mallory Stark and Debra Wallace
Knowledge and Library Services, Harvard Business School,
Boston, MA, USA

Abstract

This chapter presents a case study of how Baker Library Services, a department of Harvard Business School's Knowledge and Library Services, has refocused its distinctive capabilities in order to become better integrated with research and course development and increase the value of its human and material resources' contributions to research, teaching, and learning. As part of a multipronged strategy, this chapter has developed new individual and organizational capabilities, including Research Support Continuum, Research Services Delivery Model, the Project Management Office, and services to support collaborative research and course development environments. The chapter is presented as a journey with reference to an earlier report on the development of the Curriculum Services Group, an update on current initiatives, and an outline of future plans for continuing to review the priorities needed to achieve the group's strategic shifts.

Keywords: Strategic alignment; capability development; research support; academic information services; library and faculty collaboration

I. Introduction

The genesis of this chapter was a challenge presented by the 8th Annual Columbia University Libraries Reference Services Symposium (March 2010), and its theme was "Doing More with Less." The Reference Services Symposium became a catalyst for Baker Library Services (BLS) to reflect on its work moving forward in the rapidly changing internal and external environments. At the same symposium in 2007, we presented a first look at a new BLS service that proactively engaged with faculty to integrate resources into information-rich learning opportunities. This work entailed

LIBRARIANSHIP IN TIMES OF CRISIS
ADVANCES IN LIBRARIANSHIP, VOL. 34
© 2011 by Emerald Group Publishing Limited
ISSN: 0065-2830
DOI: 10.1108/S0065-2830(2011)0000034009

collaborating with faculty throughout the design, development, and implementation of Masters of Business Administration (MBA) and Executive education courses. The 2007 paper, *Shifting Gears* (Wallace, Cullen, & Esty, 2007), presented a case study of the development of a Curriculum Services Group—a group of business librarians who were moved out of the reference environment and tasked with integrating information and information research skill development into courses and curriculum-related learning activities. Four years later, the world was very different.

The 2008 economic crisis has had, as in many institutions, an impact on our approach to providing services. The 2010 symposium's theme, "Doing More with Less," is a sobering reminder that it is not "business as usual" in academic institutions. However, we argue that we are neither "doing more with less" nor even "less with less." Rather, we took, and are continuing to take, the opportunity to fine tune an original transition strategy and rethink how to position distinctive capabilities, leverage human and material resources, set priorities, and become even more closely aligned with the Harvard Business School's (HBS) mission by creating value for faculty, students, and the broader Harvard University and HBS communities.

BLS is one of six departments within Knowledge and Library Services (KLS). The other five are Baker Library Collections, Information Management Services, Information Products, Executive Office, and Business Operations with a total staff of 54. These functional departments provide an array of services such as research assistance, acquiring and licensing resources, and publishing a Web site and an online newsletter highlighting faculty research. To accomplish this work, KLS has a diverse staff, including librarians, educators, journalists, taxonomists, computer programmers, and statisticians.

Due to the complexities of its products and services, collaboration across KLS groups is a norm. With one of the world's most comprehensive collections of contemporary and historical business information, KLS provides services to the HBS community of approximately 250 faculty plus their staff who support teaching and research, 1800 MBA students, 9000 executive education participants, and 113 doctoral students. Over 70,000 alumni also have access to KLS as do 13 administrative units at HBS, the greater Harvard community, and scholars from around the world.

II. Charting a Course

Worth a paper on its own, KLS's vision is articulated in a comprehensive description of a *Future State*, which was first created in 2008 and updated in 2010 (see Appendix A). It was the result of a multiyear, collaborative strategic planning process in which the entire staff participated. *Future State* outlines KLS's direction based on changes expected within the information environment, stakeholder, partner groups, and HBS as a whole. It describes what KLS will look like in order to meet these changing needs. *Future State* became a "beacon"—or stretch point—that provided strategic focus for setting priorities, allocating resources, and developing staff.

Achieving this vision relied on six primary strategic shifts to

- Integrate KLS with research and course development;
- Organize the School's priority information;
- Develop an enterprise Web service;
- Move to electronic products and services;
- Support global research and education; and
- Increase the reach of faculty knowledge dissemination.

The transition from Baker Library to KLS was guided by strategic shifts that began in Fall 2004. Recognizing that change of this magnitude takes time, KLS's Senior Management Team (SMT) developed the chart in Table 1 as a means of explaining progress to the Dean's office, partners, and stakeholders.

In addition to *Future State*, KLS had three enduring goals that provided consistency throughout the transition. They helped set the context for prioritizing BLS's efforts and ensured a customer-centric focus. These goals were to

1. Deliver the greatest possible value to KLS customers by integrating our expertise and resources in support of their teaching, learning, and research;
2. Build and enrich a knowledge and information ecosystem that delivers what customers need when they need it, seamlessly; and
3. Be the "trusted advisor" for HBS in knowledge, information, and learning practices.

This chapter highlights one of the strategic-shift streams and outlines how distinctive capabilities in BLS were refocused in order to become more integrated with research and course development. This transition is part of a long-term process, a journey that started in 1927, with the birth of Baker Library and continues today with constant assessment of stakeholder objectives and priorities, realignment of capabilities, and discovery of new ways to leverage distinctive capabilities in order to meet users' needs.

III. Baker Library Services–Then and Now

Baker Library Services (BLS) was formed in 2005, a combination of the outward-facing service-delivery points related to the contemporary collections. BLS was responsible for oversight of physical and virtual spaces as well as three functional groups: research services, reference services, and access

Table 1
KLS Strategic Shifts

Strategic Shifts	FY07	FY08	FY09	FY10
Integrate with research and course development	Three pilot MBA projects	34 projects Model developed	Develop—9 Revise—9 Enhance—60	10% growth Focus MBA and Exec Ed
Organize the School's priority information	Catalog books	Catalog electronic information: Institutional Memory (IM)	IM and Centennial Assets	Scholarly assets
	Socialize information management	Information Lifecycle Management Program	Scholarly Asset Standards for SharePoint (Intranet)	Information management standards and governance Expert resource
Develop an enterprise Web service	Ad hoc—mainly work for KLS	iTRAC 89 projects	74+ projects Intranet Program Office	Transferred to ITG
Move to electronic products and services	Status quo 2.5X $ electronic vs. print	First Knowledge Center—BBOP HC Web properties 2.9X $ electronic vs. print	Institutional Memory Agribusiness KC OPM eBaker 2.9X $ electronic vs. print	Deliver our products in SharePoint 2.3X $ electronic vs. print

	No focus	European universities	Chinese Universities	GKEN +
Support global research and education		Research centers	Harvard collaborations; Launch GKEN—40; 269 global research requirements	China, Europe, India; China Knowledge Center; Strategy for knowledge dissemination
Increase reach of faculty knowledge dissemination	*Working Knowledge* (*WK*) Web site and newsletter	Global content (China, India); *WK* for Exec Ed, Publishing, news media; *WK* moved to daily content	*Economic Crisis* site; *WK* for School's Initiatives; Align with HBS Marketing; Scholarly Communications Task Force	*WK* stakeholder analysis; "Platform" management; Healthcare collaboration; Scholarly communications

services. The staff included approximately 15 professionals (e.g., librarians, statisticians, economists, and MBAs), 10 paraprofessionals, and a rotation of temporary staff to supplement library operations.

By early 2011, as part of the 2009 workforce reduction and refocusing, BLS has 20 full-time equivalent staff with 17 professional and 3 paraprofessional staff (see Table 2). Areas of responsibility are the same as they were in 2005 except that primary responsibility for BLS' Bloomberg Center Web site now resides with Information Products, a relatively new KLS department.

Within this reduced headcount, services were repositioned to achieve an overarching goal to

Leverage our distinctive capabilities through strategic shifts aligned with HBS priorities in order to institutionalize the integration of research and course development, creating greater value for our faculty, students, and community.

Achieving this goal is enabled by the development of four new individual and organizational capabilities:

1. Research Support Continuum—a shift in focus from reference to research enabled by the provision of self-service tools.
2. Service Delivery Model—staff and procedural shifts emphasizing research instead of reference.
3. Project Management Office—new individual and organizational capabilities to support proactive, project-driven work needed for curriculum services.
4. Collaborative Research and Course Development Environments—introduction of new technology to enable research and course development via a Microsoft SharePoint platform and services that emphasize a customer-centric approach to service delivery.

A. Research Support Continuum

Analysis of customer research behavior data from our reference question tracking system identified a significant shift in the types of questions being asked across our major communication channels (i.e., through web forms and e-mail, in person, and via phone). It also pointed to an increase in both the time to engage with users and the level of expertise required to satisfy queries. To help refine service offerings, inform our staffing approach, and identify our professional development needs, we developed the Research Support Continuum as in Fig. 1.

The continuum defines progressive levels of assistance performed by a range of service staff. It enables more effective targeting of products and services to meet customer needs and to provide greater understanding of customer behaviors. Five tiers of service were identified from self-service

Table 2
Baker Library Services Organizational Chart

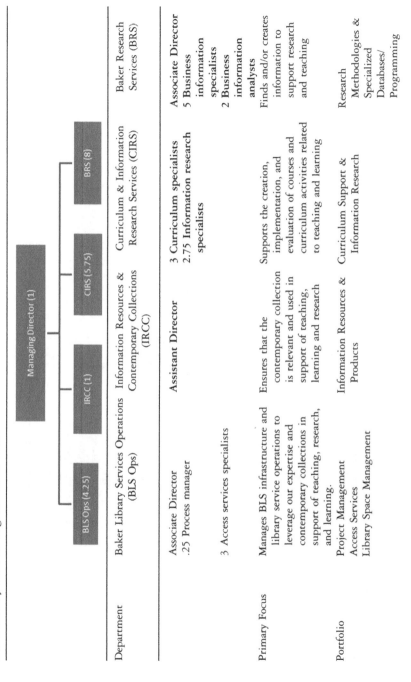

	BLS Ops (4.25)	IRCC (1)	CIRS (5.75)	BRS (8)
Department	Baker Library Services Operations (BLS Ops)	Information Resources & Contemporary Collections (IRCC)	Curriculum & Information Research Services (CIRS)	Baker Research Services (BRS)
	Associate Director .25 Process manager 3 Access services specialists	Assistant Director	3 Curriculum specialists 2.75 Information research specialists	Associate Director 5 Business information specialists 2 Business information analysts
Primary Focus	Manages BLS infrastructure and library service operations to leverage our expertise and contemporary collections in support of teaching, research, and learning.	Ensures that the contemporary collection is relevant and used in support of teaching, learning and research	Supports the creation, implementation, and evaluation of courses and curriculum activities related to teaching and learning	Finds and/or creates information to support research and teaching
Portfolio	Project Management Access Services Library Space Management	Information Resources & Products	Curriculum Support & Information Research	Research Methodologies & Specialized Databases/Programming

(Org chart top node: Managing Director (1))

Table 2. (*Continued*)

Department	Baker Library Services Operations (BLS Ops)	Information Resources & Contemporary Collections (IRCC)	Curriculum & Information Research Services (CIRS)	Baker Research Services (BRS)
Work	Develops and maintains project management processes, tools	Provides intellectual oversight for collections	Positions business information, creates information products, and enables information research capability development for lifelong learning	Provides information research support to faculty, doctoral students, HBS administrators
	Manages project pipeline	Educates KLS about the contemporary collection contents	Supports student and alumni information research needs	
	Manages & tracks resource allocation	Develops self-service tools and learning resources		
	Collects and analyzes BLS statistics	Responsible for BL|BC Web site Content		
	Facilitates user access to information resources			
	Maintains Stamps Reading Room, Stacks, Exchange			
	Manages library systems			
	Provides DocDel/Ill Services			
Research Continuum*	1	0 & 1–4 support	1–4	1–4

*See Fig. 1

BLS Research Support Continuum

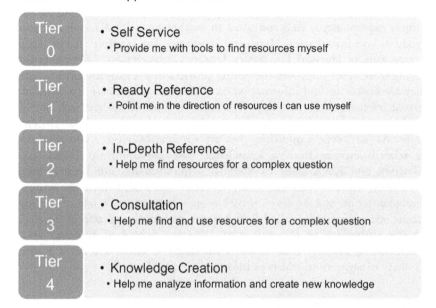

Fig. 1   Research support continuum.

(low touch) to knowledge creation (high touch). The tiers were based on the assumption that the largest number of customers served occurs at Tier 0—Self-Service, which is also the "lowest touch" tier characterized by the lowest level of personal contact and direct service effort. The higher tiers target fewer customers, but provide increasingly higher levels of service and usually require a larger investment of time interacting with customers from staff who provide the service as well as a higher degree of methodological and subject expertise.

1. Tier 0–Self-Service

Self-Service occurs when BLS provides assistance primarily via the Web site through self-service tools, with the transaction not mediated by staff members. The tools are targeted to assist users in identifying appropriate information resources such as research guides, frequently asked questions, and knowledge centers. While considered "low touch" because of the lack of staff mediation, the development of these tools is, in fact, quite labor intensive. The Information Resources and Contemporary Collections group (IRCC) is responsible for developing self-service tools with input from subject experts across BLS and often in partnership with KLS's Information Products and Information Management groups. For example, Baker Library is now part of Harvard University Library's subscription, *LibAnswers* from SpringShare. This improves the ability of users to get assistance from staff if they are unable to find information on their own. *LibAnswers* is a web-based virtual reference tool that supports questions received via the web or SMS/texting. It is an intuitive system featuring a single search box as the entry point. As users type a question, they are automatically presented with links to related answers from a knowledge base based on previously asked questions and FAQs built by staff. If a question has not been answered previously, users can submit a new question via a web form. In KLS, the implementation of *LibAnswers* serves as an enhancement to one of our most robust self-service tools called *Fast Answers*, previously a platform developed by the University of Pennsylvania's Wharton School of Business at the University of Pennsylvania. It was a collaborative effort that built a shared database of answers to business information questions.

2. Tier 1–Ready Reference

Ready Reference includes staff members providing assistance to straightforward directional and reference questions, such as citation verification, use of primary catalogs and databases, and location of specific materials or collections such as corporate reports. All BLS staff members (i.e., paraprofessional and professional) provide this service.

3. Tier 2–In-Depth Reference Service

In-Depth Reference consists of reference interactions requiring a higher volume of resources and/or higher degree of subject expertise. Staffing levels required to provide the service are differentiated in Tier 2. While all research support specialists function in this role, questions may be referred to specific subject matter experts, process owners, or product managers.

4. Tier 3–Consultation Service

Consultation represents the move from reference to research support. All consultations are provided by appointment and involve advance preparation on the part of the Information Research Support Specialist. A wide range of queries fall into this tier, spanning the reference—research divide depending on the client. In the case of MBA and doctoral students, research is not completed on their behalf. For faculty, faculty proxies, alumni, and HBS administrators, research results, including analysis and findings, are completed.

5. Tier 4–Knowledge Creation

This is the highest level of research support and includes a fee-based service used primarily by HBS faculty and their proxies. Doctoral students are also advised on research design and literature review approaches. Researchers provide contract deliverables, including consulting on research methodologies; database creation, clean-up, and merging; fact-checking; teaching preparation; creation of charts, graphs, or other exhibits for published work; and coauthoring of papers. Baker Research Services (BRS) takes the lead in providing this service tier.

6. Observations

Customer use of higher tiered services, across all communication channels and service-delivery points (e.g., e-mail, web forms, phone, and personal contact), has increased as more information is digitized and as web technology and our self-service tools have improved and increased in number. As well, staffing public service points with professionals versus paraprofessionals have decreased the number of "dead-ended" ready reference and directional questions and increased our ability to add value, moving a Tier 1 query to a Tier 2 and sometimes Tier 3 level. Therefore, investment in development of effective self-service tools results in a higher level of difficulty of questions being asked at higher level tiers. This trend is expected to continue. The phenomenon is significant because it suggests that staff working at the Information Services Desk require higher level skills and because it informs the Service Delivery Model, which is discussed in the next section.

The Research Support Continuum language provides a clear message to users that BLS adds value beyond its traditional reference role. As partners engaged in research processes, both the Continuum and the Research Services Delivery Model are key components of the information ecosystem designed to meet customers' needs seamlessly and enhance library staff roles as trusted advisors for knowledge, information, and learning practices (per the enduring goals).

B. Research Services Delivery Model

Multiple factors converged in BLS, causing new thinking about how service is provided and subsequent revision of the service model. In addition to the

Research Support Continuum discussed in the previous section, engagement in curriculum and course support (Wallace et al., 2007) increased from 3 pilot projects in 2007 to 78 projects at the end of the 2009 academic year, and 83 by the end of the 2010 academic year. This increased involvement generated more use of KLS's research services by students (e.g., MBA, Doctoral, and Executive Education) due to the integration of information resources and information research intensive assignments in course design. As well, there was a domino effect where students requested support for additional coursework based on exposure to BLS integration in other courses.

Student queries were at Tiers 2–3 on the Research Support Continuum and required deeper knowledge of resources and course content, especially the faculty's teaching points and student learning objectives related to assignments. Reference services statistics also showed an increase in higher tiered questions in general. This increase is believed to be related to the fact that lower tiered questions are often answered by self-service tools (Tier 0) as seen from our web analytics. Thus, customers who cannot find the answer to queries using Tier 0 move up the continuum and use higher tiered services. Finally, the economic downturn prompted a Harvard University-wide reduction in workforce. Directly affected by this mandate, BLS eliminated several positions. Driven by usage statistics and the enduring goals, a conscious decision was made to align staff capabilities with customer needs and to reduce the number of paraprofessional positions supporting customers at the lower end of the Research Support Continuum.

These factors led to the reconfiguration of a Service Delivery Model in 2009, shown in Fig. 2. Recent trends in statistics and prior analysis related to the Research Support Continuum indicated need for a service delivery model to leverage distinctive capabilities through individual knowledge and skills of staff members. Increased engagement in course development required a change in organizational infrastructure that supported the management of upward of 40 simultaneous projects. The reorganization included merging curriculum and research support services specialists into one group, Curriculum and Information Research Support (CIRS). To reflect and support changing transactional service levels, the focus of Access Services staff shifted to Baker Library Operations (BL Ops).

This realignment has led to improved communication of project status and service needs. Simultaneously, the new structure provided flexibility to allocate staff resources more efficiently and to leverage subject expertise across projects and services. Staffing at the services desk now includes two information research support specialists at the busiest times of the day with BL Ops staff "on call." In this way research librarians, who were formerly "on call," are proactively positioned directly at the point of service. Since the

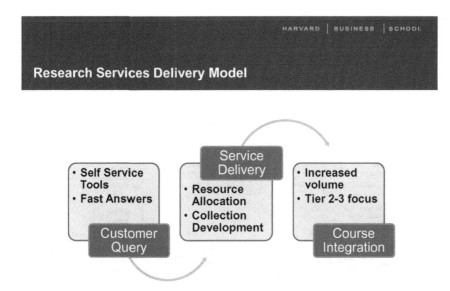

Fig. 2   BLS services delivery model.

realignment, statistics continue to show an increase in higher tiered questions being asked and an increase in the ability to move a Tier 1 question to a Tier 2 and often Tier 3 service. This once again indicates how KLS staff members add value to research, teaching, and learning activities at HBS.

C. Project Management

A third factor contributing to the strategic shift in BLS was creation of a Project Management Office (PMO). This office is responsible for managing a growing number of internal and customer-facing projects, developing tools and procedures to facilitate effective project management, collecting statistics on project work, and implementing a consistent approach to acquiring projects and efficiently shepherding them to successful completion.

Soon after establishing the PMO, training was provided for staff to learn basic project management skills, outline methodologies for clearly defining projects and assigning responsibilities, and develop consistent terminology, templates, and approaches department-wide.

Due to the growing numbers of projects and the need to allocate resources, a toolkit was developed to support project work, including a Work Process Design Flow shown in Fig. 3. This diagram maps how all projects are

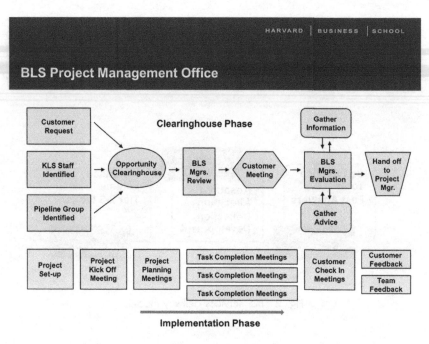

Fig. 3   BLS PMO: Work process design ow diagram.

funneled through an Opportunity Clearinghouse and considered for acceptance. Projects meeting KLS's strategic objectives and aligned with areas of responsibility are assigned a project manager who facilitates the process from launch to completion.

A Project Charter or Statement of Work (SOW) is a key component of the toolkit. The SOW ensures that project components are clearly articulated, including scope, deliverables, team member roles and responsibilities, and time frames for completion. Once possible projects are identified, they are logged into Project Pipeline, an Excel spreadsheet that tracks the project's life cycle from opportunity through launch to completion. Having all project information consolidated in one place facilitates successful completion of a project and identifies synergies across projects, statistics, and analyses, which in turn improves service quality levels.

With the creation of the PMO came a cross-department system for tracking time. Staff members keep track of the time spent by categories, which include customer service such as quick reference, in-depth research assistance, and consultations; administrative time (e.g., meetings, reading e-mail, and other types of communications); and professional development activities such as formal and informal learning and liaison with a specific customer group or faculty unit.

There is a separate category of time tracking for project work. Each project is tracked as a subcategory. Having staff keep track of time spent on various kinds of projects provides a more accurate picture of the work done in the organization and informs subsequent resource allocation. Tracking each project provides the ability to see not only how many people are working on the same project, but how much time each project requires. At project completion, it is possible to provide concrete data when considering acceptance of similar projects in the future and specifications of future projects can be adjusted accordingly. This system provides a consistent way of tracking and allocating human resources for subsequent projects and informs our Service Delivery Model.

Another aspect of the PMO is that everyone is informed of current projects. Initially weekly Stand-Up Project Meetings were held. The meetings were attended by all staff engaged in or supporting project work, including the department manager and director of the PMO. They were structured similar to an Agile software development approach to daily "quick check-in" where no one sat down, emphasizing the need for focused, concise information exchanges. Staff provided updates on projects, highlighting issues and opportunities related to their work. These meetings allowed the staff to be updated on each other's work and be alerted to any synergies that could be created from multiple staff working on the same project or leveraging work done for one project to another project. The meetings were also a knowledge-sharing opportunity to leverage team members and managers' experiences, providing tips on overcoming hurdles and recommending enhancements to projects and opportunities for new projects.

After having separate weekly Stand-Up Project Meetings for six months, it was found to be more effective to integrate these discussions into biweekly department meetings. The ultimate goal was to have individual staff update the Project Pipeline as they progress, recording a project's status from active to complete then archiving details to be used for new projects—a function now being managed in BLS's Microsoft *ShareSite* developed in 2010. This led to more effective in-person meetings and as project work increased, these meetings became weekly.

The implementation of a PMO resulted in several benefits. It provided a streamlined and consistent approach to considering the viability of projects when there are not enough resources to meet all project requests. Therefore, a process was needed to assess opportunities, prioritize them against the School's and KLS's objectives, and set up projects for success. Focus on resource allocation ensures that individual staff project workloads are easily identified and the ebb and flow of cyclical workflow is effectively managed, based on the academic year and faculty research behavior. This standardized process started in BLS and is now used across KLS. It ensures a consistent approach to methods across all projects and cross-functional departmental teams having uniform knowledge of the project management approach. As individuals lead projects, they develop capabilities transferable to future projects. Having a view of project life cycles allows staff to be proactive in generating new project work. Overall, the PMO keeps the work of individuals connected to the overall work of the organization and enables more efficient delivery of customer products and service.

The work of PMO is also critical to compiling statistics for KLS customer portfolio reports that are used throughout the year to review KLS engagement and plan customer priorities.

D. Collaborative Research and Course Development Environment

KLS is engaging in more and more collaborative activities with HBS faculty and units of the School. These activities strengthen KLS's position as a trusted advisor as we fulfill our mission to support the School by enabling the creation and exchange of ideas, expertise, and information.

1. Online Collaborative Research Spaces

HBS implemented Microsoft's *SharePoint* environment in early Fall 2009. In addition to setting HBS-wide information management standards for this new application, KLS took the lead in positioning this new technology with faculty as a collaborative research and course development environment. With a cross-functional team of KLS staff, our Information Resources and Contemporary Collections manager established 10 pilot projects with the goal of identifying models of cost-effective, easy-to-use collaborative research spaces. Given the unique characteristics of faculty research, it was anticipated that the faculty would need guidance in design, building, and ongoing support of these sites. As such, this opportunity was expected to enable KLS to

- Establish a boutique service that adds value to faculty research;
- Embed KLS products, services, and expertise into the research process;
- Integrate information management principles and practices into research environments in *ShareSite*;
- Identify research use models and create templates and guidelines for easy replication by other faculty;

- Identify opportunities to engage other KLS projects and services to meet faculty needs while strengthening faculty relationships; and
- Build *ShareSite* expertise in KLS staff for use in our own projects and information delivery sites.

The pilot project phase was completed in early 2010 with an evaluation of user satisfaction. After an analysis of the data, KLS developed:

- Standards for research collaboration sites, including life cycle management and analytics guidelines for site owners;
- A Case Research Template used for developing research collaboration spaces when writing HBS Cases. The template includes a KLS toolkit and selected resources to meet research needs;
- Training and guidance for IT help desk staff to support faculty requests for research ShareSites; and
- Gap analysis of ShareSite functionality and faculty research needs.

While each of the 10 pilot projects provided an opportunity to learn how to more effectively support faculty research collaborations, one project in particular yielded a proverbial "mother lode" in that it encompasses multiple research initiatives and audiences—all of which are spawned by one faculty research program.

A research collaboration between two HBS faculty members who were swamped with e-mail exchanges of documents and other information management challenges was identified. Upon discussion with the faculty, we found that creating a central site on the research program topic could then feed multiple subsites in support of related teaching, writing, and outreach activities. The collaboration included not only multiple HBS community members, but partners in other academic institutions and private/public sector firms. Fourteen related initiatives across seven audiences were identified. For the pilot project it was decided to focus on three components, by building interconnected spaces for the overarching research program (i.e., sustainable urbanization); a private space for creating a case about a sustainable city development firm; and a course support space for one of the faculty member's doctoral seminar as shown in Fig. 4.

This multifaceted research project provided an extremely rich test environment that is fairly typical of how faculty members are starting to engage in digital scholarship. They were enthusiastic about the opportunities that *ShareSite* offered to enable collaborative research. They readily acknowledged the need to leverage technology, especially with multiple partners and contributors collaborating on a research project. Specifically, they were looking for ways to manage their collection of resources, share materials, and facilitate multiple people working on the research output. The opportunity to integrate KLS products and services that utilize all of its distinctive capabilities and further all three of its enduring goals is extremely

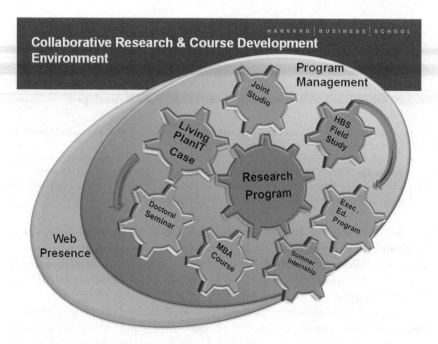

Fig. 4   Research and course development collaboration environment: Pilot project example.

energizing—but also both challenging and rewarding. With a steep learning curve on *ShareSite* functions, it was helpful to have Information Research Specialists knowledgeable about it. However, it was found that the selection of the *ShareSite* environment was best driven by faculty request rather than KLS suggestion. A new *ShareSite* pilot focusing on the information resource needs of one of HBS's Global Research Centers was in progress early in 2011.

E. Embedded Information and Tools

KLS is partnering with and leading projects to extend its support to HBS students and users of the HBS Web site by improving the ability to locate relevant information in a way that is convenient and timely. First, with the HBS's selection and implementation of a commercially available Learning Management System, *Desire2Learn*, KLS is partnering with the Information Technology Group to pilot innovations in course content and delivery. Also, KLS continues to create durable links to full-text content in subscription resources, which are referred to in course assignments or class preparation activities. This helps embed information in course platform environments, which is vital to student achievement. The complexity involved in creating links to the variety of resources available with differing authentication methods allows KLS to guide students to course content specified by professors. Second, KLS is expanding the reach of its capabilities in identifying relevant information for users by broadening and improving the search function at HBS. While the search function is limited to technical aspects of language and algorithms, "findability" is a broader process that includes indexing and metadata, the psychology and behavior of users, and the tools and processes of search creators. The Findability Services Project, led by the Information Management group, will improve our ability to find information across HBS's many information sources—its Web sites, Intranet, and applications. These are examples of how KLS is integrating expertise across the School.

1. Embedded Information Research Specialist

HBS includes as part of its MBA curriculum an optional Immersion Experience Program (IXP). IXP, based on experiential learning, provides an opportunity for MBA students to engage in off-campus, field-based activities that allow them to apply leading business ideas directly in the communities they visit. Begun in 2005, IXP destinations have included Brazil, China, Costa Rica, Europe, India, Israel, Mexico, New Orleans, Peru, Rwanda, Silicon Valley, United Arab Emirates, and Vietnam. In January 2011, 14 IXPs were offered.

There are three main types of IXPs:

1. Ideas in Management: management issue awareness building accomplished through applying and assessing leading frameworks in management theory in a global context;
2. Career: understanding the practice of a particular career or function in an organization; and
3. Project-Based: short-term project consulting.

KLS support of IXPs includes creating knowledge centers and working with student project teams before they leave. KLS foresees that it can leverage its expertise and collections significantly and become more integrated with the projects' information research needs—to enhance student productivity and performance in the relatively short time in which they have to "produce" a solution. To that end, a KLS Information Research Specialist accompanied the IXP to Vietnam in January 2011. It was an exciting opportunity to "embed" an information research specialist directly into learning activities. In Fall 2010, a *ShareSite* was developed in support of the activities of this IXP to help participants to learn about resources likely needed for their research. From this real-time, customer-centric pilot, it is expected that more can be learned about identifying and supporting the information needs of IXPs and developing new ways of leveraging our capabilities. For more information about the IXP experience, see the HBS IXP site at http://mba.hbs.edu/IXP/.

IV. Conclusion

As noted in the introduction to this chapter, strategic shifts are part of a journey. As next steps in this journey, BLS plans to

1. Continue to develop individual and organizational capabilities in research support, use of information in course development, project management, subject matter expertise, collaboration research environments, and digital scholarship;
2. Build out a research and course development toolkit: self-service tools, project templates, resource allocation methods, statistics gathering and reporting, assessment/evaluation feedback, and analysis loops;
3. Expand targeted marketing and outreach to faculty;
4. Develop a broader knowledge-sharing community on course development and digital scholarship;
5. Align KLS strategic initiatives to support the new centralized management structure of the Harvard University Library System.[1] There are several examples of KLS's alignment with this new structure. The subscription to *LibAnswers* illustrates how the Harvard Library is positioned to create a more consistent experience for all customers. Seven libraries were included in the Phase I pilot. In addition, KLS collaborated with colleagues throughout the University including the Harvard Art Museums' educational unit and the Harvard Center for Geographic Analysis (CGA). KLS was instrumental in incorporating collections of the Harvard Art Museums into the curriculum of "The Moral Leader," an MBA elective course. HBS researchers work cooperatively with staff at the CGA to share data and expertise on spatial datasets; and
6. Position KLS products and services in alignment with our new dean's priorities. Nitin Nohria became the school's 10th dean in July 2010. From conversations with HBS faculty staff, students, alumni, business leaders, and other educators, Dean Nohria recognizes that the School is at a crucial point in its history, and outlined five areas for change (Innovation Takes, 2010). These are:

   • Innovation in educational programs starting with the MBA program—developing new approaches to learning that are experiential, field-based, and immersive;
   • Intellectual Ambition—continuing mission of shaping the world of business scholarship;

[1]The centralized Harvard University Library receives direction from a University Library Board comprising faculty and deans and chaired by the Provost. The Library's Executive Director is appointed by and reports to the Board and is responsible for the University Library System (10 Named, 2010).

- Internationalization—expanding global focus;
- Inclusion—capitalizing on the diversity represented by students in the MBA program so that the culture is such that all can thrive; and
- Integration—enhancing our cross-disciplinary presence by developing closer ties with other schools in the University.

These priorities offer exciting opportunities for KLS. At the time of this writing, we are in the planning stage of defining how KLS will specifically align with these areas. We have little doubt that as the priorities identified by the dean become operational, KLS will continue to transform through strategic shifts starting with engagement in MBA curricular innovations.

As stewards of this particular part of the journey, BLS and other KLS colleagues are constantly challenged to rethink, refocus, and renew. Any notion of "business as usual" has been discarded and energies are being channeled into a cycle of continuous improvement through building new individual and organizational capabilities that enable all of us to add value, and in collaboration with our partners help our customers achieve their goals while advancing the role of knowledge and library services in higher education.

Appendix:. KLS Future State

KLS Future State 2011

External Information Environment

In 2011, the reach of the web and the effects of globalization, among other factors, have further transformed the way we live and work, learn, and educate. User-created and self-published content such as blogs and posts on the web have become far more accepted as a means of disseminating scholarly work, and the web itself is the starting point for most information research. The sheer volume of electronic information available overwhelms attempts at filtering, finding, and managing it. Moreover, less and less digital content has a paper equivalent. New avenues have opened with advances in search and metadata technologies, as well as in mobile devices, virtual worlds, and social software (collaboration tools). These advances allow greater personalization of services and products in all segments of the information industry. They also enable more innovative research and teaching environments, in which geographically dispersed communities of scholars and students can, in real-time, jointly create information and aggregate data.

Answering the question of who owns the information on the web has been trailing behind the technologies that have spurred new forms of content creation and use. The forms of copyright-based ownership model of the publishing industry continue to be debated within the scholarly community. New attempts to regulate and standardize "open-source publishing" have not yet taken firm hold, nor has academic recognition of new forms of publishing to include in metrics for scholarly authority and attribution. Peer-reviewed publications still drive the US scholarly infrastructure; however, a new, powerful wave of open-access peer review is gaining strength across the globe, pressing for new forms of financing scholarly work. Europe is embracing the open-access model by centralizing institutional publications in a single repository open freely to all European universities. Such universal access encourages global research and collaboration, and provides a forum for questions of intellectual property rights, collection policies, and archival preservation. Individual ownership of intellectual property continues to be complicated by the ease with which information is shared and "repurposed."

Harvard is active in opening access to scholarly research results. The Office of Scholarly Communications, established in 2008 as an open-access university-wide institutional repository, is capturing a significant percentage of scholarly output of several Harvard faculties. Discussions now focus on the inclusion of new forms, such as simulations, software, datasets, annotations, and aggregates thereof. In various pockets, the University already leverages text analysis and data mining techniques to uncover information patterns and research trends, particularly where interdisciplinary research and education occur. Datasets created in the research process are now available alongside the analysis and findings. Metadata registries make it easier to find the information, although a managed repository is seen to increase this capability. University librarians are examining the appropriate modes of research support, trying to balance their investments in commercial content against "in-progress" online-only resources created by scholars.

Greater cross-University collaboration and integration have resulted in new joint degree programs. The University is building rich networks of data and people, and firms hungry for innovation are joining through new forms of cross-sector partnerships.

Harvard Business School (HBS)

The Global Initiative has grown and thrives. It includes efforts such as the Global Database on International Business and Global Research and Education Centers. The growth in demand for management education in new and emerging as well as existing markets has prompted HBS to establish classroom facilities in China, India, and Europe, supporting a small portion of programs and other HBS activities. Research initiatives in healthcare management and the sciences, as well as in social enterprise, leadership, and entrepreneurship continue to grow and deliver significant new knowledge for those involved. January Immersion Experiences supplement on-campus education by providing practical "immersion" in academic, cultural, and corporate- or organization-based fieldwork around the world.

Blended learning and lifelong learning communities have created strong networks connecting faculty and practitioners. MBA programs are hands-on and especially in the EC year, experimental, with a growing number of students cross-registering into the MBA program to "build their own" joint degree programs, notably in engineering and life sciences; new dual degree programs have been created for business/real estate, business/urban planning, business/education, and business/public health. The doctoral programs have intensified efforts to increase the number of scholars who are prepared to join the faculty. Through all of these programs, the alumni remain active and even more involved in HBS teaching and learning.

At HBS, faculty remains focused on teaching and research. Case-based teaching remains the defining characteristic of HBS, enriched through the use of new information technology and social software. The impact of faculty's research is measured increasingly in ways that reflect the collaborative and dynamic digital nature of knowledge creation and dissemination evident in the sciences. eResearch, particularly in interdisciplinary and global work, is the preferred mode for many of the younger faculty members.

New types of students have entered our doors, in part due to the HBS 2+2 Program and a new fellowship program. The MBA class of 2011 includes more students who have work experience in world-class, knowledge-based science, and engineering organizations, and are accustomed to employing a full spectrum of cutting-edge IT technologies. They prefer to work collaboratively and expect information to be easily accessible. HBS has responded to student's changing expectations by offering web-based tools, video cases, simulations, and virtual communities in the classroom. This working environment seems to be preferred by young faculty and doctoral students as well. Executive Education participants have varying comfort levels with new learning technologies; new programs adopt similar technologies and approaches popular in the MBA.

Knowledge and Library Services (KLS)

KLS is a team of experts passionate about its mission, collaborative, innovative, service-oriented, and accountable to its customers, partners, and team members. It is committed to the School's values and to the importance of lifelong learning. Success requires spanning disciplines, risk taking, flexibility, innovation, and transparency. Success also requires reflection, evaluation, critical thinking, and knowledge sharing, as well as meeting expectations through planning, program and project management. KLS team members recognize the value of partnering with each other and with other organizations in the design, development, and delivery of products and services. Strategic partnerships with ITG and with Marketing and Communications have delivered significant value to HBS. KLS is a meritocracy where collaboration, knowledge sharing, team work, idea exploration, and delivering on commitments are recognized and rewarded. Within the realities of the economic environment and given the dynamic nature of the information industry, KLS tests what is core and noncore to its customers, and adjusts its products and services accordingly. Customers working around the globe benefit from services available virtually 24×7, and from staff, as appropriate. The powerful combination of process, technology, information, and expertise ensures that the integration of our work continues to deliver the support needed for world-class teaching and research.

Through its own work and the advisory role it provides to others, KLS supports the full cycle of knowledge creation, information management, presentation and information, and knowledge use. True to its mission, KLS' impact is best reflected in the ease with which multiple types and disparate sets of unique information, ideas, and expertise are used to support HBS' research and educational objectives. It is this uniqueness and multi-disciplinary expertise that puts HBS at an information advantage over others.

KLS leads its peer organizations in innovations in Scholarly Communications, knowledge asset management, web and Intranet design and development, and the application of deep subject and information expertise in support of global business research and education. KLS champions new collaborative approaches to research and knowledge sharing; it has created its first multidisciplinary Knowledge Commons and a prediction market that aggregates knowledge of information professionals about future trends in the information industry. Along with its strategic partners, KLS has completed the 2009 initiative to build a 2.0 version of the Intranet and the web for HBS. KLS continues to experiment with new methods of knowledge sharing, such as creating targeted, web-delivered, content "databases," expressly designed for user exploration and research, including end-user tools for linguistic analyses. Successful examples include the ongoing Institutional Memory program and next-generation Working Knowledge products.

KLS' customers (faculty, students, alums, staff, and business practitioners) recognize our high standards of quality and expertise in designing the user experience, supporting the development of courses and curricula, supporting the creation of new knowledge through research, and in developing, managing, and disseminating authoritative information and data products in a world marked by a deluge of digital content. KLS products and services span research and course support, knowledge and information access, information management, web development, and knowledge sharing.

Since 2008, KLS has developed advanced capabilities in data and digital content management, program management, web "interaction design," and information retrieval and visualization. Our capabilities in product management and information research are now mature. In terms of data management, KLS professionals include experts in knowledge asset management, data preservation and curation, text mining, and other forms of large dataset analyses. KLS has partnered with DRFD to create a global, collaborative network of information, archives, and datasets on international business. KLS chairs the governance of information and knowledge asset management at HBS.

Strong project and program management skills as well as deep subject expertise and knowledge of the audience requirements ensures the integration of our expertise into the primary processes of HBS, including course development, research, learning, and administration. KLS programmatically supports the enhancement, revision, and development of new courses and educational programs. Under the leadership program of KLS, and in partnership with ITG and M&C, the web and Intranet now deliver a world-class experience aligned with key HBS processes, giving staff, students, and faculty a competitive advantage. HBS recently won awards for the world-class user experience.

The KLS web development experts now have very strong interaction design and information retrieval/visualization expertise. Personalization prevails. Our customers have now full access to HBS web and Intranet resources on mobile devices; they can easily interact with and search across HBS applications and web properties, including locating and using knowledge assets available anywhere.

KLS is well-positioned to continue to lead in knowledge and information services for the next decade, having taken an approach to innovation based on rigor and discipline, strategic partnerships, focused on the customer and the HBS priorities.

References

10 Named to New Harvard Library Board. (2010). *Harvard gazette*, December 10. Retrieved from http://news.harvard.edu/gazette/story/2010/12/10-named-to-new-harvard-library-board/

Churchwell, C., Stark, M., & Wallace, D. (2010, March). Refocusing distinctive capabilities: Strategic shifts in Baker library services. Paper presented at the 8th Columbia University Libraries Reference Services Symposium, New York, NY. Retrieved from https://www1.columbia.edu/sec/cu/libraries/bts/symposia/reference/2010/index.html

Innovation takes center stage. (2010, December). *Harvard Business School Alumni Bulletin*. Retrieved from http://www.alumni.hbs.edu/bulletin/2010/december/deannohria.html

Wallace, D., Cullen, A., & Esty, B. (2007, March). Shifting gears—The role of reference and research services in curriculum design: A case study of faculty and library collaboration at the Harvard Business School. Paper presented at the 5th Columbia University Libraries Reference Services Symposium, New York, NY. Retrieved from https://www1.columbia.edu/sec/cu/libraries/bts/symposia/reference/2007/index.html

The Best Things in Life Are Free (Or Pretty Cheap): Three Mobile Initiatives That Can Be Done Now

Lilia Murray

Libraries, Murray State University, Murray, KY, USA

Abstract

The purpose of this chapter is to present a general review of free or inexpensive methods of implementing the following mobile services in libraries: Library Websites, Short Message Service (SMS) reference, and Mobile Online Public Access Catalogs (MOPACs). The findings were based on a literature review of materials that discussed mobile technologies in libraries. The findings conclude that libraries with tight budgets should approach their mobilization project in terms of stages, developing content and services sequentially from passive formats, which require little input, to more dynamic items, which entail greater interaction. Most free and inexpensive mobile services are geared toward passive formats, providing a starting point for libraries with limited budgets. Scope of the chapter is limited to public and university libraries and initiatives for smartphones. Prices listed are in USD as of January 2011 and may be subject to change. The costs of training, management, and development time by libraries were not factored into the costs. Mobile services have become one of the biggest new library trends. Simply keeping abreast of library service options made possible through advances in mobile technology can be a challenge. In addition, tough economic times have prevented many libraries from actually implementing mobile services. This chapter discusses a number of ways for libraries to create their own mobile initiative with little to no money at all—except of course for the hidden cost of staff effort.

Keywords: Mobile devices; Mobile phones; Smartphones; SMS; MOPACS; Libraries

I. Introduction

"May you live in interesting times" (Chinese proverb and curse).

When talking of tough economic times, people often refer to the Great Depression of the early 1900s. For libraries, it was both the best and worst of times. Even though there were severe budget cuts, patronage was never higher (Novotny, 2010). The same phenomenon is happening today.

LIBRARIANSHIP IN TIMES OF CRISIS
ADVANCES IN LIBRARIANSHIP, VOL. 34
© 2011 by Emerald Group Publishing Limited
ISSN: 0065-2830
DOI: 10.1108/S0065-2830(2011)0000034010

The American Library Association's (ALA) (2010) *State of America's Libraries Report 2010* indicates there has been a decade-long trend of increased library usage despite shrinking resources. Many libraries face financial hardships and are forced to make tough decisions about new services they can offer and maintain, particularly when it comes to technology.

According to a Pew Research Report *Mobile Access2010* (Smith, 2010), eight in ten American adults now have a cell phone and of them, 40% access the Internet on mobile devices. The report indicated that 65% of 18 to 29-year olds access the Internet on their mobile device. The 30 to 49-year old group had a 12% increase in use of mobile applications from 2009, the largest increase in any group, with 43% accessing the Internet in this manner. Worldwide, the mobile device market had increased 30% since 2009, and it was predicted that mobile data traffic would double annually through 2014 (Cisco, 2010; International Data Group, 2010). These statistics show that implementing mobile services should be of major interest to libraries. Yet, tight budgets have prevented many libraries from doing so. This chapter discusses a number of ways for libraries to create their own mobile initiatives for little to no money. The prices listed are in US dollars as of January 2011. The costs of training, management, development, and maintenance are not discussed since they will vary with technology skill levels and experience of the staff who work with these applications.

II. Literature Review

A. Initial Success Stories

A review of periodical articles, books, blogs, and Websites discussing mobile technologies in libraries revealed two major trends. The first focused on an array of success stories, showcasing a wide variety of mobile services. Kroski (2008) prepared a comprehensive report about incorporating mobile applications into library services, such as Websites, reference, and OPACS. Fox (2009), Lippincott (2008), Vila, Gálvez, and Campos (2010), Wilson and McCarthy (2010), and Zylstra and Thero (2010) detailed various mobile services at their libraries. Most of the literature contained recommendations for designing mobile projects and included reasons for their success. Oregon State University Libraries created a list of 10 design recommendations based on the Mobile Web Best Practices Report that includes hierarchy, links, navigation, page layout, and image tips (Griggs, Bridges, & Rempel, 2009).

B. Making the Case, Marketing and Assessment

The second trend focused on developing strategies and proposals aimed at obtaining support for mobile projects. These were described by Kroski (2008), Ragon (2009), Smith, Jacobs, Murphy, and Armstrong (2010), and Bridges, Remple, and Griggs (2010). They emphasized the importance of persuading administrators, managers, and coworkers of the importance and advantages of joining the mobile landscape. Proposals included literature reviews, problem statements and proposed solutions, possible resources, timelines, and examples of library mobile initiatives. These data help to build more convincing cases, and helped audiences gain an understanding of the value of mobile undertakings. Some projects included pilot periods ranging anywhere from three months (Bridges et al., 2010) to a year (Smith et al., 2010).

Part of the second trend focused on the importance of marketing and assessment of mobile initiatives to justify their existence. With many libraries experiencing constrained budgets, services that are not heavily used are likely to be eliminated. Therefore, it was recommended that proposals describe promotional efforts and assessment plans for verifying successes (Bridges et al., 2010). At the University of California Los Angeles Library, publicity included a short video, purchase of an ad in the student newspaper, as well as posting fliers in various offices, departments, and student gathering areas (Smith et al., 2010). Oregon State University Libraries promoted their mobile services on the library homepage, a Facebook fan page, and via a press release from the university's media relations office (Bridges et al., 2010). The latter resulted in the library being recognized in the local evening news and an article in the student newspaper. Assessment plans generally included focus groups, surveys, and usage statistics.

Both of these trends shared a common element: they attempted to prove the value of a mobile initiative, either through success stories or ways to convince reluctant colleagues. For those already convinced of the importance of a mobile project, the choices available can seem endless. Yet, inexpensive or free options can be very difficult to find. This chapter seeks to fill this gap by reviewing existing services and vendors particularly cheap or free ones.

III. Library Mobile Initiatives

Because of market growth, Bridges et al. (2010), Greenall (2010), and Wisniewski (2010) suggested focusing mobile efforts on smartphones, like the iPhone and Android instead of feature phones. The latter have smaller screens, less powerful processors, limited browser capabilities, and cannot download applications or software. In addition, they do not have a QWERTY keypad and lack touch-screen functions. Although libraries would reach the broadest user population by casting a wide net for mobile initiatives, this would be the more expensive and more time consuming choice (Murphy, 2010). Non-smartphone users will still be able to use many of these resources, despite a less than optimal experience (Wisniewski, 2010). The following three mobile initiatives are examined and listed in order of prevalence in the literature: Library Websites, Short Message Service (SMS) reference, and mobile OPACS (MOPACS).

A. Library Websites

Analysts claim that by 2015 Web use will be greater on mobile devices than that on desktops (O'Dell, 2010). In 2009, mobile data traffic surpassed mobile voice traffic, indicating that people are using their devices more for information access than for calls (Chetan Sharma Consulting, 2010). Thus, at the very minimum, most libraries are trying to create at least a mobile version of their Website (Baumann, 2010). The entire library Website should not be made mobile. Instead, it should be simple and straightforward to use and have content that makes sense to mobile users such as directions, hours, or contact information. "To put it another way, no mobile user wants to read your circulation policy on his or her handheld while standing in line at the dry cleaners, but he or she does want to know if you're open later than 5 p.m" (Wisniewski, 2010, p. 54).

Aldrich (2010) notes there have been few studies examining the creation and application of library mobile Websites. Among them are University of Cambridge in the United Kingdom and Kent State University. They asked users to identify the services they would find most useful for a mobile phone. At Cambridge most wanted access to flat information, with hours, a map of the library, and contact information at the top of their list. This passive information requires little input and can be done easily and quickly. Kent State's users also wanted a map of the building with call number locations and the ability to contact a librarian, but they ranked access to databases as the most desired. Aldrich suggested that these opposed rankings might be a normal evolution as technology improves. Cambridge's study was done a year earlier than Kent's, with respondents using primarily first-generation smartphones, whereas Kent users had access to third-generation smartphones. Therefore, it is important for each library to learn which mobile web resources library patrons consider most useful. An easy way of doing that is to evaluate usage statistics from the regular library website.

Aldrich (2010) surveyed 111 Association of Research Libraries (ARL) universities, and found 24 libraries with mobile sites. The five most accessed services, in order of prevalence, were the following:

- Library hours;
- Library directories (addresses of all campus libraries);

- Library catalog;
- Contact information; and
- The Main library's Website.

Out of these, library hours, library directories, and contact information require passive input, whereas the library catalog and the main library Website are more dynamic involving more work and time.

There are a number of ways to create a mobile Website, including free and inexpensive proprietary services from online vendors, open-source codes, and RSS feed conversion tools. In addition, collaboration with other libraries can help offset local technical expertise and work involved.

1. Vendors

Instant Mobilizer claims to be "the fastest, easiest, and most cost-effective way to create a mobile website" (dotMobi, 2011). Only registration of a .mobi domain name through one of their many partners is required. *Instant Mobilizer* can also be used for already registered .mobi domain names. As of January 2011, prices could be compared from 19 partners, with 11 more "coming soon." Annual prices for a .mobi domain name ranged from $7.99 to $24.99, with most offering discounts if registering for more than one year. After registering, users can access the library's .mobi site where *Instant Mobilizer* converts the desktop Website and maintains branding, colors, and logos of the library. Unless the regular Website already had a simple architecture, users would do a lot of scrolling. Thus, it is advisable to take advantage of the mobile site preview and plan for adjustments. On a positive note, it adds two convenient mobile functions: Google Maps are automatically added to addresses and "click to call" abilities are provided for phone numbers.

Another online tool is Zinadoo (2009a). This mobile website builder provides a free site creation tool, free Zinadoo.mobi domain, and free hosting. However, to help fund the free service, *Zinadoo* Websites display advertisements and to disable ads was approximately $66 per year in 2009. For libraries wishing to have a unique .mobi domain, the annual cost is $22.11 (Zinadoo, 2009b). This tool offers the most customization features, with choices of templates, colors, fonts, etc., and also allows the ability to add widgets and videos. In addition, it includes options to link to another URL, "click to call," and RSS feeds.

For customization and price, the best mobile Website builder is *mobiSiteGalore* (Akmin Technologies, 2011a). This service claims an average creation time of 54 minutes to create a mobile design (Akmin Technologies, 2011c). Like *Instant Mobilizer* and *Zinadoo*, no technical knowledge is required due to its WYSIWYG (what you see is what you get) mode. There are no software or plug-ins to be downloaded or installed. Although there are no extensive customization features, it does provide choices of readymade design templates, colors, fonts, and layouts. Pricing depends on the pack selected (Akmin Technologies, 2011b):

- 3 Page Basic Pack is limited to 3 pages; has limited features, designs, hosting, and support; but is 100% free.
- 10 Page Pack is limited to 10 pages; has all the features, 2 GB hosting space and regular online support; cost is $16.99 per month with a 25% discount for yearly subscriptions.
- Unlimited Pack offers unlimited pages; has all the features plus unlimited hosting and 24/7 priority online support; cost is $24.99 per month with a 25% discount for yearly subscriptions.

For libraries with little or no budget or technical expertise, *mobiSiteGalore* offers an easy means of creating a mobile Website with customization features, all without automatic ads.

Another approach to developing a mobile Website is to create an app. *AppBreeder* is an online iPhone app builder that requires no coding or programming knowledge. Their Website states, "if you can write a blog, you can build an app" (AppBreeder, 2010). It is free and will create a free iPhone Web app as long as it contains ads. However, there is a $99 one-time publishing fee per app once it is published to the App Store. *AppBreeder* can create a more customized app starting at $499.

2. RSS Feeds

An easy method for developing a mobile website is to create one via a library's existing RSS feeds. If the primary goal is to syndicate the library's stories, pictures, and/ or videos, this approach is suitable. *AppMakr* is a free browser based product that takes existing content feeds and creates an iPhone app in minutes (PointAbout, 2011). It can use any RSS or Media RSS feed to publish content to the app. Users can choose from various templates, upload logos and images, use custom banners, and choose interface colors. It provides an advanced algorithm that shows the likelihood of Apple's approval for iTunes AppStore publication with recommendations for improvements.

The only cost for this is publishing. There are two options—self-published apps and *AppMakr* published apps. In order to self-publish the app, users must create and load an Apple Developer account into *AppMakr*. An Apple Developer account costs $99 per year. For libraries in higher education, there is a free iPhone Developer University Program. Self-published apps are approved quickly, in days versus weeks, and show the home institution, rather than *AppMakr*, as the author (Suhy, 2009). There is an option to have *AppMakr* publish the app for $999. Since they handle the submission process, they deal with a large volume of apps that must be queued, resulting in a longer approval time. Therefore, choosing to self-publish is not only cheaper but faster as well.

ISites (Generation Wireless, 2011) also creates an app via RSS feeds and supports *Twitter*, *Blogger*, *YouTube*, and *Flickr*. It allows for banner, status bar, and text customization with colors and images. *iSites* has two pricing options: Smart and Pro. The Smart version costs $49 per month with a $100 discount for a yearly payment. The Pro option is $99 per month with a $180 discount for a yearly payment. Both choices come with the App Management System, a native iPhone App, an Android Market App, as well as the ability to update on-the-fly. What makes *iSites* unique is its ability for users to also create an Instant App for iPhones. This requires no App store submission and is free from the constraints dictating acceptance to native app stores. Instead, Instant Apps are issued through vanity URLs, requiring no approvals. The main difference lies with the full-service submission feature in the Pro version and the "Bump n Share" capability for app users to immediately share the app with others.

Table 1 shows the services described above, prices, and other costs from the least to most expensive options as of early 2011.

3. Open Source Codes

Creating code to develop a mobile Website in-house can be time consuming and expensive. Therefore, a potential strategy could be to use the numerous open source software that is available. Services such as *MyMobileWeb* (Morfeo Competence Center, 2011), *HAWHAW* (Huffschmid, 2010), *Wireless Abstraction Library* (WALL) (Passani, 2010), and the *MIT Mobile Web Open Source Project* (SourceForge, 2008) are all free and can be modified without restrictions. However, they can be quite complex and are best suited for libraries with code and programming expertise.

Simpler alternatives are *iWebkit* (2010) and *PhoneGap* (2011). *iWebkit* uses the same tools used to create a regular Website (HTML, CSS, and JavaScript) and needs a few more steps. *"iWebkit* is a package designed to help create an iPhone, iPodTouch and iPad compatible website" and it is limited to Apple mobile devices (iWebkit, 2010). Users simply download the latest version of it with a *User Guide* and then follow step-by-step directions. Their site claims that people without any HTML knowledge can create a full and professional Website in a couple of minutes. As an open source project under the Lesser General Public License (LGPL) it is not only free, but its code can be freely copied, distributed, and modified. Libraries looking to build their

Table 1
Mobile Web Services

Services	Free Option	Price Options	Other Costs
mobiSiteGalore	Yes (3 Pg. Basic Pack)	• 10 Pg. Pack: $152.91 per year • Unlimited Pack: $224.91 per year	
Zinadoo	Yes (but with ads)	• Without Ads: $66 per year • Unique .mobi domain: $22.11 per year	
Instant Mobilizer	Yes		Requires .mobi domain Name: $7.99 to $24.99 per year
AppBreeder	Yes (but with ads)		$99 one-time publishing fee
AppMakr (RSS)	Yes (App Developer Account is free to higher education libraries only)	• Self-published: free, but requires an Apple Developer Account at $99 per year • AppMakr Published: $999	
iSites (RSS)	No	• Smart: $488 per year • Pro: $1008 per year	

own Website app should look at *PhoneGap*. It provides free downloadable open source code, "with open standards like HTML, CSS and JavaScript so that you can focus on the app you're building, not on authoring complex platform compatibility layers" (PhoneGap, 2011).

4. Collaborative Approach

One means of sharing cost is to work with another institution. The Open University (OU) Library in the UK and Athabasca University (AU) Library in Canada shared development work and expertise about mobile resources and services (Sheik & Tin, 2010). The AU Library created an auto-detect and reformat software that allows developers to make Websites suitable for small-screen viewing. This software is used by the OU Library that can now use the same content for both normal and small screens.

Another approach is to collaborate with or within an organization. Canada's Ryerson University Library (Wilson & McCarthy, 2010) and Duke University Libraries decided against a freestanding mobile presence of their own and instead joined their institutions broader mobile initiatives. While not truly library-centric, these libraries received a link or spot on their campus' mobile site, potentially reaching a greater audience while minimizing mobile development costs. The University of Houston Libraries teamed with a computer science professor's class to develop mobile applications for real-world environments (Coombs, Arellano, Bennett, Dasler, & Vacek, 2010). There the librarians asked for hours, librarian contact information, and a mobile version of their catalog.

5. Do Nothing

Perhaps the least expensive and easiest method is to do nothing. Feature phones are going the way of dial-up, and smartphones will soon become ubiquitous. Each generation of smartphones has improved browser capabilities that will automatically adapt regular sites. Thus, "if you have a Web site, you are already a part of the mobile Web" (Kroski, 2008, p. 40).

In addition, many major search engines, including Google, have automatic transcoding so that a regular Website might not display so badly on a mobile device. Oftentimes, these pages resemble a "text-only" version of the desktop site and will omit items that may cause browser issues, such as big images, animations, or videos. To see what a site looks like when Google transcodes it, simply enter the URL into Google's tool: http://www.goo gle.com/gwt/n from either a desktop or mobile phone.

The main drawback to a "do nothing" approach might be the requirement of extra clicks and more scrolling due to small screens, making page navigation more difficult. Patrons accessing a library mobile Website generally want "specific facts and answers, with as little as typing as possible" (Fox, 2008, p. 2). In addition, since many who use mobile devices are actively moving or engaged in other activities, ease of use and accessibility of information are vital (Aldrich, 2010). Therefore, it is recommended to first create a solid body of content via normal desktop delivery with the possibility of redesigning the entire current Website for clearer mobile navigation (Chudnov, 2010).

IV. Short Message Service (SMS) Reference

SMS, or text messaging, has become one of the most popular forms of mobile communication. According to Pew's Internet Report, 72% of cell phone owners send or receive text messages. Ninety-five percent of 18 to 29-year olds, 82% of 30 to 49-year olds, 57% of 50 to 64-year olds, and 19% of those over 65 years old use their mobile phone's text messaging feature (Smith, 2010). "SMS is used for so much more than communication: it's now a major medium for seeking, applying and transferring content" (Smith et al., 2010, p. 245). Thus, SMS reference can complement other reference services, such as in-person, phone, e-mail, and chat, by providing users an accessible service via a familiar device.

Many libraries are using vendor services, such as AltaRama's (2009) *SMSreference*, Mosio's (2011a) *Text a Librarian*, and Springshare's (2011) *LibAnswers* with the SMS Module. Depending on a library's budget, a few of these services may be considered inexpensive. However, there are also some free alternatives, including *Broadtexter* (2011), SMS to instant message (IM) mashups, and *Google Voice*. These free options do not offer additional features included in most vendor products, but they do provide libraries with a means of establishing a cost-free text messaging service.

A. Vendor Services

AltaRama's *SMSreference* service provides a dedicated mobile phone number that libraries can distribute as their text number with texts sent to an email address specified by the library. Librarians' replies to the email are automatically sent to users mobile devices via text. Its start-up bundle, which includes implementation, training, one-year software subscription, phone number use, and 5000 use-or-lose messages, is the most expensive at $3,250. Mosio and Springshare offer cheaper alternatives with more options.

Mosio's *Text a Librarian* (2011a) is quite similar to Altarama's *SMSreference*, but is not limited to email. It offers a multimodal real-time notification service whereby librarians are alerted to texts by email, chat, text, and/ or a Web-based microboard. This microboard is not only searchable but archived indefinitely, providing a wonderful online knowledge database for training. Librarians can also create auto-responses for immediate greetings and reference service hours.

However, a unique number is not assigned to the library. All Mosio client patrons dial 66746 ("mosio") to text their libraries. Mosio sends the text to the appropriate library via a "keyword" chosen by each library. For example, Murray State University Libraries chose "msulib" as its keyword. Users have only to enter that "keyword" at the beginning of their first message with Mosio subsequently recognizing that mobile phone as connected to a particular library.

There are four pricing plans with *Text a Librarian*: Premium, Standard, Lite, and Cooperative (Mosio, 2011b). Libraries involved in a consortium have to contact Mosio for co-op pricing. The Premium, Standard, and Lite plans all come with one dedicated microboard, free inbound texts, free custom auto-responders, and patron marketing materials. The main differences lie in the amount of user logins and outbound texts per month. The Premium plan includes 20 user logins and 4000 outbound texts. It costs $199.92 per month with a $199 one-time setup fee, billed annually at $2,399. Their most popular plan, the Standard plan, allows 10 user logins with 1000 outbound texts per month. Its price is $99.92 per month with a $199 one-time setup fee, billed annually at $1,199. Lastly, their Lite plan is just $65 per month, billed annually at $780. It includes 3 user logins with 350 outbound texts per month.

LibAnswers is from Springshare, the makers of *LibGuides*. The price for *LibAnswers* is determined by the size of the institution (FTE for academic libraries or number of cardholders for public libraries), and ranges from $599 to $1099 per year (Springshare, 2010a). Besides a $149 one-time setup fee, the addition of the SMS Module is free for the first year. After that it is $30 monthly for the 600 messages per month plan or $50 monthly for the 1,200 messages per month plan (Springshare, 2010b). Like *SMSreference*, each library is given a unique phone number with no special keywords to remember. There are no limits to login accounts and an entire library staff can be logged in simultaneously.

B. Free Services

Each of the above vendor products requires a yearly subscription. However, a number of free text applications also exist. One such service is *Broadtexter* (2011). Although it does not offer the advanced reference capabilities of vendor services, it is a way to connect to users via mobile devices. Users must join the library's "mobile club" (also free) where they can post comments and reply to a library alert via text. Messages are shown on the library's *Broadtexter* page, which is viewable on both desktop and mobile phones. The biggest drawback is lack of user privacy because "mobile club" members can view *Broadtexter* pages, and read everyone's questions and answers. Those wanting anonymity would have to create an alias username. There are no limits to the amount of members a library can have, although the service does ask to be contacted if a "mobile club" is in the thousands, so it can support an institution's special needs.

The SMS to IM mashup is another free alternative. Perhaps one of the most popular types is the "AIM hack method." According to Farkas (2010), almost 50 libraries use this as their SMS reference tool. It is free to libraries that have an AOL Instant Messenger account and requires little to no training. Users send their text messages to the library's AOL Instant Messenger account, text in a short code with the library's AOL Instant Messenger name, enter a colon, and then text their question. Librarians see the text in their chat message box, integrated into an existing reference service. Libraries using this method report low usage, possibly due to the awkward combination of having to text a short code, the library's AOL screen name, and punctuation, before one can actually text a question (Weimer, 2010).

Table 2
SMS Services, from Least to Most Expensive Options

Services	Free Option	Price Options	Other Costs
Broadtexter	Yes		
(IM) mashups	Yes		
Google Voice	Yes		
Text a Librarian	No	• Lite: $780 per year • Standard: $1,199 per year • Premium: $2,399 per year • Cooperative: Contact vendor	Standard and Premium Plans: $199 one-time setup fee
LibAnswers	No	Based on FTE or # of cardholders; Ranges from $599 to $1099 per year	
with SMS Module	No	• 600 message plan: $360 per year • 1,200 message plan: $600 per year	SMS Module FREE for 1st year, but has $149 one-time setup fee
SMSreference	No	$3000	$250 one-time setup and 1 year training

Google Voice (Google, 2011) is one of a myriad communication and collaborative tools offered free by Google. It is a combination phone and Internet service where one number is used to manage all of one's phones, and voicemail can be recorded and saved as an email transcription. It also provides free unlimited text messages to and from domestic and international numbers. *Google Voice* texts work the same as regular texting, with all messages being received and sent using actual phone numbers. There are no clunky additional steps required. For librarians, it functions similarly to desktop IM, with texts appearing in the chat text box for replies. Libraries can choose a *Google Voice* number based on their area or zip code, or one that has specific word or phrase in it. "Although *Google Voice* is primarily intended for personal use, it has the potential to extend and enrich services by enabling libraries with limited means to establish sophisticated telecommunications operations without having to commit a lot of time, money, or resources" (Johnson, 2010). Table 2 lists SMS services from the least to the most expensive. The prices were current as of early 2011.

It is clear, upon review of both vendor-supported and free texting services, that the integration of texting into existing reference delivery methods is becoming increasingly seamless. It allows libraries to easily "stay relevant and maintain their role as information centers in the evolving mobile environment" (Smith et al., 2010, p. 245).

V. Mobile Online Public Access Catalogs (MOPACs)

"While providing access to the library's hours, staff contact information, and directions to the library is an important first step, what users typically want from a library is direct access to research materials" (Bridges et al., 2010, p. 315). Therefore, a mobile catalog should still be a priority when planning a mobile presence. Because of cost, however, mobile library catalogs are not as common as other mobile initiatives. Their use is on the rise due to more vendor-supplied versions of mobile catalogs becoming available, such as the *AirPAC* from Innovative Interfaces, *BookMyne* from SirsiDynix (2010), *Library Anywhere* from Library Thing, and *WorldCat Mobile* from OCLC.

A. AirPac

AirPac was designed to work on feature phones to appeal to a wider range of mobile devices. The search interface was a smaller version of a desktop interface with users clicking through three or four screens to get a call number. *AirPAC for Smartphones* is a free upgrade for customers who already have the classic *AirPAC* product. It has many of the search delimiters found in regular OPACS such as keyword and title. The results page lists author, title, resource type, publishing date, availability, and occasionally a book cover image. Users can also request items and see their personal accounts. However, they are unable to email or text results. As of November 2010, more than 70 libraries worldwide use *AirPAC for Smartphones*, allowing access to the Millennium catalog (News, 2010).

B. BookMyne

Although it is only available as an iPhone or iPod Touch app, *BookMyne* (*SirsiDynix,* 2010) is free from the iTunes store. It has some unique features such as the ability to scan a book's barcode and get availability information from the user's library of choice. In addition, users can place holds and view fines or fees on an Apple mobile device. In order to benefit from this service, libraries must have Symphony version 3.3 or higher. They can then install SirsiDynix's *Web Services* for free, which allows library to be accessed by the *BookMyne* app.

C. MobileBridge and Library Anywhere

Quipu Group's (2010) *MobileBridge* and *Library Anywhere* from Library Thing for Libraries (2011) can be choices for libraries with OPAC vendors who do not offer a mobile version of their catalogs. *MobileBridge* communicates with the catalog via a library's Z39.50 server, and can read and display RSS reading lists. For all normal catalog functions, such as searching and viewing item records, the base price is $2000 with a $400 annual maintenance fee. Functions such as placing holds and viewing account information can be added for $1000 with a $200 annual maintenance fee. *Library Anywhere* is less expensive and works with 90% of current OPACS, including those from ExLibris, Follett, Innovative Interfaces, and SirsiDynix (Spalding, 2010). No installation is needed and the mobile catalog can be "up and running in minutes" (2010). It is available for Android, Blackberry, and iPhone, but works on any phone with a Web-browsing feature. It is also compliant with Section 508 and other accessibility standards. Although it is proprietary, their prices are relatively inexpensive. As of January 3, 2011, annual subscription fees included the following (Blachly, 2011):

- Schools are $150, plus $50 for each additional location.
- Public libraries are $350 for main library, plus $50 per branch.
- Two- and four-year colleges are $750, plus $150 for each additional library building.
- Universities are $1000, plus $150 for each additional library building.

D. WorldCat Mobile

OCLC's (2011) *WorldCat Mobile* is a free Android and iPhone application that allows searches using keywords, author, or title. Since it only offers one search box, it is best for simple searches. By entering a location or postal code, it finds a WorldCat library nearby that owns the item. Additional features include click-to-call and map routing options. Most unique, however, is a "smart prefix" component that allows users to enter the first few letters of a search and get possible results while continuing to type. Lack of call numbers and the inability to limit a search by resource type are drawbacks of *WorldCat Mobile*.

Although vendor solutions may be the easiest option, there can be some limitations. Many of these services lack customization and mobile features, like exporting results from within the mobile program. Users want MOPACS that "fit into their established mobile lives by including core mobile concepts and will judge the mobile search platform by what it does not do well" (Murphy, 2010, p. 17). Therefore, some libraries may opt to create their own MOPAC if they have or can afford the needed technical expertise. Using open source codes, like those offered by The District of Columbia Public Library (DCPL), can be a great help. DCPL shares their code so that other libraries can build their own iPhone apps for MOPACs (2011). Their application is a free iTunes download and is called *DCPL*. The *DCPL* app allows for keyword searching, the ability to see availability, to place holds, and an option to view hours of operation.

VI. Conclusion

"In a generation, desktop content and catalog access moved from an impressive new technology to something that cannot sufficiently serve users effectively, a trend that should be on the minds of librarians across the country" (Baumann, 2010, p. 30).

In 2010, *Library Journal* conducted a mobile survey of academic and public libraries with results from 483 respondents. While 44% of academic and 34% of public libraries provided a mobile service to their patrons, 39% reported not having, and not planning for, any mobile initiatives (Thomas, 2010). Fifty-three percent of academic and 56% of public libraries stated "no budget" as a main factor in "not choosing to offer any services designed specifically for handheld devices" according to Thomas (p. 32). Yet, mobile devices are increasingly becoming the primary connection tool for most people. "Libraries cannot afford to ignore this medium if they are to keep in step with their patrons. There has never been a more relevant user-driven technology for libraries to adopt" (Greenall, 2010, p. 16). Fortunately, there are inexpensive and free options available to libraries.

Much of the literature (Bridges et al., 2010; How to create a mobile experience, 2008; Ragon, 2009; Smith et al., 2010) have divided various mobile applications into "passive or flat formats," which require little input, and "dynamic or active formats," which permit greater interaction. It is therefore recommended that libraries approach mobilization projects in stages developing content and services sequentially from passive to more complex items (Bridges et al., 2010).

According to Kroski (2008) "A smart strategy to adopt when developing for the mobile Web is starting small and allowing room to learn" (p. 39). For example, Oregon State University Libraries started out with location-based information, such as address, contact information, floor maps, and hours, and in phase two added more complex features such as a mobile catalog (MOPAC) where users can text or email for call numbers (Bridges et al., 2010). Most free and inexpensive mobile services are geared toward passive formats and provide a starting point for those with tight budgets. With more people turning to libraries for cost-effective ways to obtain information, library services that are accessible through mobile devices are becoming critical.

References

Akmin Technologies. (2011a). *A truly revolutionary service poised to change the way we all use the mobile internet.* Retrieved from http://www.mobisitegalore.com/index.html

Akmin Technologies. (2011b). *Packs and pricing.* Retrieved from http://www.mobisitegalore.com/pack_pricing.htm

Akmin Technologies. (2011c). *Why mobiSiteGalore.* Retrieved from http://www.mobisitegalore.com/why.htm

Aldrich, A. W. (2010). Universities and libraries move to the mobile web. *EDUCAUSE Quarterly, 33*(2). Retrieved from http://www.educause.edu/EDUCAUSE+QuarterlyMagazineVolum/UniversitiesandLibrariesMoveto/206531

Altarama Information Systems. (2009). *SMS reference.* Retrieved from http://www.altarama.com/page/SMSreference.aspx

American Library Association. (2010, April 11). *State of America's libraries report 2010.* Retrieved from http://www.ala.org/ala/newspresscenter/mediapresscenter/americaslibraries/index.cfm

AppBreeder. (2010). *Build-Your-Own iPhone App. Online!* Retrieved from http://appbreeder.com/default.aspx

Baumann, M. (2010). ALA report: Libraries gear up for mobile. *Information Today, 27*(8), 29–30.

Blachly, A. (2011, January 3). *Library anywhere prices.* Retrieved from http://www.librarything.com/blogs/thingology/category/library-anywhere/

Bridges, L., Remple, H. G., & Griggs, K. (2010). Making the case for a fully mobile library web site: From floor maps to the catalog. *Reference Services Review*, 38(2), 309–320.

Broadtexter. (2011). *Broadtexter*. Retrieved from http://www.broadtexter.com/

Chetan Sharma Consulting. (2010, March 31). *Global mobile data market update 2009*. Retrieved from http://www.chetansharma.com/blog/2010/03/31/global-mobile-data-market-update-2009/

Chudnov, D. (2010). Libraries in computers: A mobile strategy web developers will love. *Computers in Libraries*, 30(4), 24–26.

Cisco. (2010, February 9). *Cisco visual networking index: Global mobile data traffic forecast update, 2009–2014*. Retrieved from http://www.cisco.com/en/US/solutions/collateral/ns341/ns525/ns537/ns705/ns827/white_paper_c11-520862.html

Coombs, K. A., Arellano, V., Bennett, M., Dasler, R., & Vacek, R. (2010). Piloting mobile services at University of Houston Libraries. In A. Mohamed & G. Needham (Eds.), *M-libraries 2* (pp. 51–58). London, England: Facet.

District of Columbia Public Library. (2011). *iPhone application*. Retrieved from http://dclibrarylabs.org/projects/iphone

dotMobi. (2011). *Instant mobilizer*. Retrieved from http://instantmobilizer.com/

Farkas, M. (2010). *Libraries offering SMS reference services*. Retrieved from http://www.libsuccess.org/index.php?title=Libraries_Offering_SMS_Reference_Services

Fox, M. K. (2008, October 15). Mobile delivery: Information anywhere. *Netconnect*, pp. 2–5.

Fox, M. K. (2009). *Mobile technology in libraries: How the academic library is using PDA'S, handhelds, and other mobile technologies*. Retrieved from http://web.simmons.edu/~fox/pda/

Generation Wireless. (2011). *iSites: Create your app now*. Retrieved from http://isites.us/

Google. (2011). *Google voice*. Retrieved from www.google.com/voice

Greenall, R. (2010). Mobiles in libraries. *Online, Exploring Technology & Resources for Information Professionals*, 34(2), 16.

Griggs, K., Bridges, L. M., & Rempel, H. G. (2009). Library/mobile: Tips on designing and developing mobile web sites. *The Code4Lib Journal*, 8. Retrieved from: http://journal.code4lib.org/articles/2055

How to create a mobile experience. (2008). *Library Technology Reports*, 44(5), 39.

Huffschmid, N. (2010). *HAWHAW*. Retrieved from http://www.hawhaw.de/

International Data Group. (2010, January 28). *Mobile phone shipments rebound to double digit growth in fourth quarter, according to IDC*. Retrieved from http://www.idg.com/www/pr.nsf/0/220E6A3FF9F1E835852576BA0055D2E6

iWebkit. (2010). *iWebkit simple*. Retrieved from http://iwebkit.net/

Johnson, B. E. (2010). Google voice: Connecting your telephone to the 21st century. *Computers in Libraries*, 30(5), 21–25.

Kroski, E. (2008). On the move with the mobile web: Libraries and mobile technologies. *Library Technology Reports*, 44(5).

Library Thing for Libraries. (2011). *Library anywhere*. Retrieved from http://www.librarything.com/forlibraries

Lippincott, J. K. (2008). Mobile technologies, mobile users: Implications for academic libraries. *A Bimonthly Report on Research Library Issues & Actions from ARL, CNI, and SPARC*, (261), 1–4.

Morfeo Competence Center. (2011). *MyMobileWeb*. Retrieved from http://mymobi leweb.morfeo-project.org/mymobileweb

Mosio. (2011a). *Text a librarian*. Retrieved from http://www.textalibrarian.com/

Mosio. (2011b). *Text a librarian: Flexible plans for all libraries*. Retrieved from http://www.textalibrarian.com/pricing.php

Murphy, J. (2010). Using mobile devices for research: Smartphones, databases, and libraries. *Online: Exploring Technology & Resources for Information Professionals, 34*(3), 14–18.

News. (2010, November 17). Library news: AirPAC for smartphones now in 70 libraries. *Research Information*. Retrieved from http://www.researchinformatio n.info/news/news_story.php?news_id = 689

Novotny, E. (2010). Hard choices in hard times: Lessons from the great depression. *Reference & User Services Quarterly, 49*(3), 222–224.

OCLC. (2011). *WorldCat mobile*. Retrieved from www.worldcat.org/m

O'Dell, J. (2010, May). *New study shows the mobile web will rule by 2015*. Retrieved from http://mashable.com/2010/04/13/mobile-web-stats/

Passani, L. (2010). *Introducing WALL: A library to multiserve applications on the wireless web*. Retrieved from http://wurfl.sourceforge.net/java/tutorial.php

PointAbout. (2011). *AppMakr: Learn more*. Retrieved from http://www.appmakr. com/learn_more/

PhoneGap. (2011). *About PhoneGap*. Retrieved from http://www.phonegap.com/about

Quipu Group. (2010). *MobileBridge*. Retrieved from http://mobilebridge.quipu group.com/

Ragon, B. (2009). Designing for the mobile web. *Journal of Electronic Resources in Medical Libraries, 6*(4), 355–361.

Sheik, H., & Tin, T. (2010). A tale of two institutions: Collaborative approach to support and develop mobile library services and resources. In A. Mohamed & G. Needham (Eds.), *M-Libraries 2* (pp. 85–95). London, England: Facet.

SirsiDynix. (2010). *BookMyne*. Retrieved from http://www.sirsidynix.com/products/bookmyne

Smith, A. (2010). Mobile access 2010. *Pew Research Report*. Retrieved from http://www.pewinternet.org/ ~ /media//Files/Reports/2010/Mobile_Access_2010.aspx

Smith, B., Jacobs, M., Murphy, J., & Armstrong, A. (2010). UCLA and Yale Science Libraries data on cyber learning and reference services via mobile devices. In A. Mohamed & G. Needham (Eds.), *M-Libraries 2* (pp. 245–254). London, England: Facet.

SourceForge. (2008). *MIT Mobile Web Open Source Project*. Retrieved from http://mitmobileweb.sourceforge.net/

Spalding, T. (2010, January 16). *Library anywhere: A mobile catalog for everyone*. Retrieved from http://www.librarything.com/blogs/thingology/2010/01/library-anywhere-a-mobile-catalog-for-everyone/

Springshare. (2010a). *LibAnswers reference platform: Frequently asked questions*. Retrieved from http://www.springshare.com/libanswers/faq.html

Springshare. (2010b). *SMS/texting module—Free for 1st year!* Retrieved from http://www.springshare.com/libanswers/sms.html

Springshare. (2011). *LibAnswers—A self-service 24/7 reference tool*. Retrieved from http://www.springshare.com/libanswers/

Suhy, S. (2009, December 29). *Self-Published Apps vs. AppMakr Published Apps.* Retrieved from http://help.appmakr.com/entries/92975-what-are-the-differences-between-publishing-apps-with-appmakr-as-the-author-vs-self-publishing-apps-with-my-own-developer-account

Thomas, L. C. (2010, October 15). Gone mobile? (Mobile libraries survey 2010): Mobile catalogs, SMS reference, and QR codes are on the rise—How are libraries adapting to mobile culture? *Library Journal, 135*(17), 30–34.

Vila, M. C., Gálvez, A. P., & Campos, J. C. (2010). Mobile services in the Rector Gabriel Ferraté Library, Technical University of Catalonia. *Reference Services Review, 38*(2), 321–334.

Weimer, K. (2010). Text messaging the reference desk: Using upside wireless SMS-to-email to extend reference service. *The Reference Librarian, 51*(2), 108–123.

Wilson, S., & McCarthy, G. (2010). The mobile university: From the library to the campus. *Reference Service Review, 38*(2), 214–232.

Wisniewski, J. (2010). Mobile websites with minimum effort. *Online: ExploringTechnology & Resources for Information Professionals, 34*(1), 54–57. Retrieved from http://www.infotoday.com/online/jan10/index.shtml

Zinadoo. (2009a). *For all your mobile web needs.* Retrieved from http://www.zinadoo.com/

Zinadoo. (2009b). *Zinadoo pricing information.* Retrieved from http://www.zinadoo.com/Services/Prices.htm

Zylstra, R., & Thero, S. (2010). Libraries evolve to stay connected: Building the Your Library iPad app. *Feliciter, 56*(5), 204–206.

"Free Puppies": Integrating Web Resources into Online Catalogs

Robert L. Bothmann and Kellian Clink

Library Services, Minnesota State University, Mankato, Mankato, MN, USA

Abstract

This chapter describes means for selecting websites and the resources needed to add them to online catalogs. Reasons are given for including websites in online catalogs such as timeliness and geographic specificity. A historical overview of *Choice Reviews*, wikis, and web-based sources of websites is given along with an overview of Minnesota state resources from the point of view of using them as collection development tools for finding web resources. Social work librarians in the state were surveyed about their websites selection processes and the authors conducted time/cost studies of cataloging of online web resources. Findings were that librarians had little time to seek out websites and relied on *Choice* reviews to keep abreast of new and changing sites. Sources from the library literature and logs of staff time for cataloging of websites were used to approximate the costs of providing access. Although the cost/time study applied only to one library, the methodology and findings can be applied in almost any discipline and different types and sizes of libraries. While budgetary hardships will make librarians think hard about adding free resources to their catalogs, this chapter helps to quantify the necessary resources, implications, and reasons for inclusion of free web resources in online catalogs.

Keywords: Free web resources; web resources; collection development; cataloging costs; online catalogs

I. Introduction

We look differently at the cardboard box full of free puppies outside the super market once we become adults. As children what could be more fun than to get a puppy who is going to be your friend for life? Why not mom ... it's FREE!! But as adults we have learned the truth. We know that taking home that puppy is going to cost us in the end. The free price tag hides all the costs we are going to spend on food, training, shots, and a new couch once the puppy discovers you are not coming home at 5:00 every night to walk him. Open source WCM solutions are very similar. The free price tag is attractive at first, but for online strategies that have multiple initiatives (intranet, extranet, portal, landing pages, micro-sites, etc.), the hidden fees lie in the heavy customization, maintenance and engineering work. (Buytaert, n.d.)

LIBRARIANSHIP IN TIMES OF CRISIS
ADVANCES IN LIBRARIANSHIP, VOL. 34
© 2011 by Emerald Group Publishing Limited
ISSN: 0065-2830
DOI: 10.1108/S0065-2830(2011)0000034011

This is not a chapter about puppies nor is it about open source web content management (WCM) products. However, the concept of "free puppies" is one that can be applied to collection development and resource maintenance, particularly in terms of gift materials or freely available Internet and web resources. In fact, the last two sentences in the above quote could be rewritten as follows:

> Freely available Internet resources are very similar. The free price tag is attractive at first, but for collection developers and catalogers with limited budgets, time, and other resources, the hidden fees lie in the research, evaluation, description, access, and maintenance work.

Libraries of all kinds across the country are no stranger to budget cuts and limited funding since the 2008 economic downturn. Nicholas, Rowlands, Jubb, and Jamali (2010) spoke of alarm bells when they wrote "academia is the worst hit sector, with 43.8% libraries saying they are down from the previous year" (p. 377). The early twenty-first century context for libraries includes not only limited budgets but a strong, permanent upward trend toward using electronic information resources. Therefore one of the major challenges for librarians is how to acquire needed resources and to do so with limited budget support.

This chapter discusses, from the lens of one academic department (social work), collection development and technical services processes and the hidden costs of adding content from websites into online catalogs. The value of websites as sources of information is discussed along with a rationale for adding them to online catalogs. A short history of collection development tools for websites is also provided as well as a history of Minnesota's Legislative Reference Library (LRL) and its role in making relevant documents and websites from state, federal, and nongovernmental sources accessible. Findings from a brief survey of Minnesota social work librarians about their use of web resources are presented. Finally, the results of a study conducted in June 2010 Library Services at Minnesota State University, Mankato are reported to indicate how much staff time it takes to add and maintain a selection of "free puppies."

II. The Value of Websites as Resources

Websites fill a special role in the delivery of timely research reports and data that many other resources cannot. Books journey a long time from idea to bookshelf. Journal articles may also have a long lag time between idea and publication. Newspapers are written for general audiences and do not contain scholarly analyses or citations. In contrast, websites often provide data and reports quickly that may not be accessible through traditional library interfaces. Many nongovernmental organization (NGO) websites have statistics, research, and reports on current events which are not indexed in databases and are generally not accessible from the shallow web (Ratzan, 2006). While deep web content engines such as *Complete Planet* and *Turbo10* can help, can we expect our users to understand how to best use these? How many places should our users have to master to find valid and reliable information? How many will give up and just Google their queries? Federated searching is promising, as it may offer "a bridge between the reluctant searcher and the wealth of information in library databases, a best fit between the ideal and reality" (Curtis, 2005, p. 36). Even federated search engine databases however, do not include websites unless they have been added to online catalogs. For users to have the richest possible access to information, they need access through online catalogs so that all resources, including websites, can be found.

A study of 555 higher education faculty members in the United States and Canada by the Primary Research Group (2009) found that more than 53% of faculty members refer to websites in scholarly papers. Research university faculty members were the most likely among all kinds of institutions to refer to websites with 62% of them so doing. The study also found that about "46 percent of scholars are satisfied with college library efforts to preserve and catalog Websites" (p. 146).

Websites reviewed by *Choice* cards, referenced in *The Economist*, or on the "Links to the World" page at Minnesota's LRL contain information sources that are uploaded as soon as research has been completed. These are often authored by people whose full-time job is to perform research in a specific area and/or about a specific geographic area. For example, social workers using "Links to the World" will find many reports authored in 2010 about homelessness in Minnesota. For example, a search of Mankato's online catalog about homelessness and Minnesota yielded six websites from the Wilder Foundation, an organization that conducts research on homelessness in Minnesota. For social workers this is doubly valuable because the Foundation's work reflects Minnesota's laws, policies, social work processes, and populations.

III. The Value of Centralized Searching

Cataloging and providing access to Internet resources is not a new concept and has been a hot topic in library literature for many years, particularly during the late 1990s and early 2000s. The *Journal of Internet Cataloging* paid a lot of attention to cataloging and access issues related to Internet resources. It documented the history of OCLC's Cooperative Online Resource Catalog (CORC) initiative which went online in 1999 (Jordan, 2001). CORC evolved into a project to "encourage and enhance the description of Web resources to better serve library patrons" (Hickey, 2001, p. 6). At its fundamental level, CORC was meant to be a space where catalogers and reference librarians could collaborate and describe web resources in non-MARC metadata and thereby more efficiently catalog web resources which were perceived as valuable (Caldwell, Coulombe, Fark, & Jackson, 2001).

By 2002 the CORC initiative had more or less ceased (OCLC, 2002) and catalogers paid more attention to cataloging electronic journals and books than to web resources. More recently, a report by Calhoun (2006) predicted the slow demise of library catalogs and declining importance of cataloging given the growth of Internet search engines, particularly Google. Calhoun favored quick information-seeking behavior using a Google-like presentation based on key-word results. Mann (2006) refuted that assertion, noting that Google's relevance ranking cannot serve scholarly research needs. Scholars need an overview of all relevant sources, not simply the ones that have generated the most traffic and float to the top of a Google page. What Mann alluded to was that catalogs contain resources to which a library has access and that have been assessed, evaluated, and validated by experts such as collection development librarians with the knowledge to evaluate information.

The scope of library catalogs naturally varies from one institution to another. Some may question whether websites should be included in a catalog. As Wakimoto (2009) argued "what distinguishes the catalog from the Web is the *quality* of the resources, considered valuable to that library's users, carefully selected by subject specialists in the discipline to serve the curricular and research needs" of library users (p. 412). Since the inception of the web librarians have alerted users to valuable resources on the Internet through newsletters, pathfinders, and word of mouth. The trend toward using a central searchable database such as SerialsSolutions' *Summon* or EBSCO's *Complete Discovery Solution* containing books, articles, and everything else the library offers, means that it makes sense to include web resources as well.

Another reason to put websites in the catalog is that they can help to provide geographically specific subtopic resources for users. Too often students select a broad topic, such as homelessness, yet they only need to write a short paper. Searches could be narrowed by searching for state and/or NGO sites in a local catalog. For example, Mankato's online catalog yielded six reports on homelessness produced by the Wilder Foundation enabling searchers to find geographically relevant information.

IV. Collection Development Tools for "Free Puppies"

Librarians have access to many collection development tools for web resources. Among them are *Choice*, from the Association of College & Research Libraries (ACRL), and its "Internet Resources Wiki," and the "Internet Resources" column in *College & Research Libraries News*. "Reference and User Services" from the Reference and User Services Association (RUSA) website and *ipl2*'s website are also valuable sources of reviews.

A. ACRL and *Choice*

Choice is purchased by 3500 libraries according to *Ulrichsweb.com* and is described in *Magazines for Libraries* as "the selection tool of . . . thousands of academic libraries" (LaGuardia, 2009, p. 154). Fran Graf, managing editor of *Choice*, states that the push to review websites came from academic librarians who needed to keep track of the growing number of resources becoming available on the Internet (F. Graf, personal communication, October 23, 2010).

A special supplement of *Choice* was published in 1997 containing websites reviews. About this first foray into reviewing websites, Graf wrote in the introduction:

> Indeed, there is a wealth of excellent material on the WWW, but sites are appearing and mutating at such a spectacular rate that it is nearly impossible to keep up with them, let alone evaluate their quality. And there is probably no single group more intent on identifying, assessing, and organizing the best this revolutionary medium has to offer than librarians. (1997, p. 2)

Graf said there was great response to that first supplement with lots of interest and appreciation by users. By 1998, *Choice* had reviewed 420 websites (Graf, 1998; Rockwood, 1998). After the inaugural edition, every issue of *Choice* contained web reviews. The web edition evolved so that by 2005 it incorporated many ideas provided by users, including an indicator for fee-based websites, as well as indicators for previously visited sites (Graf, 2005). Now *Choice* cards come rolling in with a selection of websites in every batch. ACRL has also made websites available by topics since 1998 in the "Index to Internet Resources" in *College & Research Libraries News*.

B. *ipl2* as a Resource

ipl2 which was formed by merger in January 2010 of the *Internet Public Library* (IPL) and the *Librarians' Internet Index* (LII), can be a great way of finding valuable online resources. It makes available easily digestible information from governmental, mainstream news, and nongovernmental sources. *ipl2* is currently managed by 3 library schools (Drexel, Florida State, and University of Michigan) with 14 other library schools assisting with organizing and managing the site. The scope of *ipl2* is broad serving "people of all ages, nationalities, occupations, and levels of education" (The *ipl2* Consortium, n.d.). Entry is through five different portals: subjects, and magazines special collections created by *ipl2*, kids' stuff, and a teen corner. Libraries can either highlight this website on their home pages or use it as a collection development tool to add resources to their own online catalogs.

V. Minnesota State Resources

Although this section focuses on one state, many others and other states and government organizations have similar resources. The American Library Association's Government Documents Round Table keeps a wiki-searchable list of state documents, but each state's resources may vary in usefulness. Nevertheless, state and other government documents created for legislators can be valuable sources for users because web-based documents can narrow unwieldy topics to manageable, narrower, and geographically focused ones. While a number of states are experiencing recession-driven closings or scrutiny (Miller, 2010), Minnesota's LRL is going strong and its website makes a majority of Minnesota electronic state documents readily available.

A. The Minnesota Legislative Reference Library

In the spring of 2003 LRL began a pilot project to make digital copies of legislatively mandated reports and link them to its online catalog. Many mandated state agency publications and the Legislature's studies are acquired electronically, or if in print, scanned and added or linked to LRL's catalog. With the demise of the state depository microfiche distribution program, this project became even more important. In 2004 the program was expanded to all digital publications that met the definition of a state document. In addition to legislative reports, the LRL acquires other state agency publications and archives copies of those received in electronic format.

Online archiving soon posed several problems for LRL. Adding multiple links on the bibliographic records for online documents in several parts, or for successive issues of a serial, made the catalog records cluttered and confusing. Frequently there was not a one-to-one relationship between the paper document and the digital document which could be online in formats not amenable to archiving. The static link on the bibliographic record to the Library's archive file meant that the files could not be migrated to another server without breaking over 1000 links in the Library's catalog. Finally, no preservation metadata for the electronic files was being recorded.

In 2004 LRL received an LSTA (Library Services and Technology Act) grant to research and develop solutions to these problems. LRL investigated institutional repository software products and document management systems used by other states. It soon became obvious that most of the systems were too large, complicated, and—most importantly—far too expensive for LRL. The nature of many software products also conflicted with LRL's goal of using the catalog to provide access because they created separate collections with separate catalogs. In the end, LRL concluded that the system best suited to their needs would be the one they would build themselves.

LRL developed a simple, inexpensive yet robust electronic document management system. The database did not create a new catalog from scratch, but harnessed LRL's catalog of MARC 21 bibliographic metadata. Descriptive metadata remains in the catalog record. An Edocs database is used to record preservation and administrative metadata and to create links between separate URLs (as in the case of serial issues), solving the cataloging problems that the growing archive had presented. The array of topics, the speed with which documents are uploaded, and the quality of research make this a valuable site. LRL uploads digital versions of state documents quickly, along with legislative histories, historical data tables, and digitized state laws. Another valuable Minnesota resource is LRL's "Links to the World," a collection of topically arranged websites.

B. Links to the World

LRL's Links to the World presents sites under broad subjects listing first Minnesota documents, then federal documents, and after that NGO documents. It began around 1993 when Internet information was becoming readily available and organized on Gopher (Gopher (Protocol), 2011). The Gopher was hierarchical in nature and key-word searching was limited. Carol Blackburn (personal communication, November 19, 2010) at LRL indicated that the websites made available on Links to the World were the result of a combination of push–pull influences. It started when it was clear a question would be asked repeatedly or something happened that librarians knew would prompt reference questions at the desk. Initially the URL's were on Rolodex cards at the reference desk at LRL. Over time the entries were transcribed into a Word file and subsequently into an online version in 1995.

It morphed into a tool that provided legislators with immediate access to information directly from their computers. While LRL's primary audience was elected legislators, its resources are openly available on the web. They are particularly valuable for Minnesota social work students since most of them will practice in Minnesota. Links to the World is also an excellent place to obtain local vantage points on national or international topics.

Described simply as "A subject list of Internet resources selected for our legislative audience" (Minnesota Legislative Reference Library, 2008), it follows the same format for each topical cascade of websites. As seen in Fig. 1, it has 49 broad topics.

As shown in Fig. 2, Links to the World is heavily used. For example, from December 2, 2009 to December 2, 2010 the site was visited 18,181 times with the top three individual topics visited being K-12 education with 9629 visits, media 7679 times, and 6048 for special interest groups. Each LRL librarian maintains several topical pages and a link checker program is run once a month. Each librarian fixes the links/references on their pages. In the most recent report, a third of the 49 pages had broken links, with an average of two to three broken links per page. In terms of content updates on the topical pages, the librarians add/update pages as they become aware of new resources. One or two pages go through a formal content evaluation/update during weekly reference staff meetings. After reviewing all the Links to the World pages, evaluation of another related Minnesota Webography takes place. Between the review of these two resources, Blackburn estimated that the last total review took about a year and half to complete.

Agriculture and Rural Issues	Elderly and Retirement	Media
Alcohol, Drugs, and Tobacco	Energy	Minnesota Information
Arts and Culture	Environment	Minorities
Banking and Insurance	Federal Information	Politics and Elections
Business and Industry	Gambling	Public Utilities
Charities	Government Data Practices	Reference Sources
Children's Issues	Health	Special Interest Groups
Criminal Justice	Housing	Sports and Recreation
Demographics	International Information	State Information
Directories	Labor and Employment	Taxation
Disabilities	Land Use	Telecommunications
Economic Development	Law and Legislation	Transportation
Economics and Government Finance	Legislatures	Veterans and Military Affairs
Education (Early Childhood)	Libraries	Welfare and Low Income Issues
Education (Higher)	Local Government	Women's and Men's Issues
Education (K-12)		

Fig. 1 Topical areas in "Links to the World."

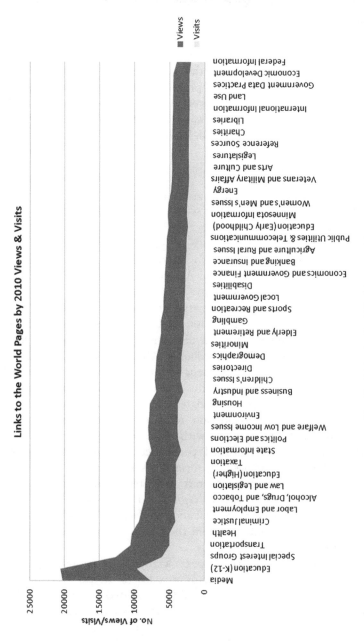

Fig. 2 Links to the World page visits.

VI. Survey of Social Work "Free Puppy" Collections in Minnesota

The authors surveyed social work librarians in Minnesota's academic libraries about websites and how they make them available to users. Fifteen colleges and universities with social work programs were identified through the National Association of Social Workers. If a social work librarian could be identified, an e-mail questionnaire was sent directly to that person. If not, the head of the library was contacted. They were asked about the following:

1. how they identify web sources;
2. how they promote websites;
3. how websites relate to social work curricula in their opinion;
4. what websites fill a particular need for social work students; and
5. how much time they expend identifying and maintaining websites.

Of the 15 contacted, 5 (33.3%) responded and indicated that *Choice* cards, *ACRL News*, and the National Association of Social Worker's website were searched for recommendations. *Choice* was used by everyone. One respondent relied on articles in newspapers such as the *New York Times*. A group of librarians at one institution responded collectively and listed the Federal Depository Library Program discussion list as a resource. Only one librarian responded that LRL was a source. All said that they relied heavily on faculty suggestions. One respondent commented that the web provides a variety of resources to research the development, implementation, and implication of issues and policies related to social work practice including government, media, and foundation websites. Three librarians reported promoting the use of websites with *LibGuide*, three through library instruction, and one with printed pathfinders. No one indicated which websites filled a particular need for social work students.

Because of the low response rate websites of the 15 schools were reviewed. Of the 15, eight used *LibGuides* and five used *LibData*. Table 1 shows the websites with a numerical indicator of the times that they were found. These, of course, only represent their presence on these pages and not in their online catalogs.

Most librarians stated they spent a couple of hours per semester identifying, promoting, and maintaining websites. It had been anticipated that the Links to the World site would be utilized by every social work librarian. This was not the case and, as one respondent indicated, its nonuse might simply be due to lack of time. Unlike most of the surveyed institutions, Minnesota State University (MSU), Mankato has a graduate

Table 1
Websites listed on Social Work library pages

National Association of Social Workers 4	Columbia University Social Work Library
Washington University (St. Louis) Websites 4	Disability and Independent Living Movement Collection
American Public Human Services Association 3	FedStats
Social Work Access Network 3	
American Public Human Services Association 3	Green Book (House Ways and Means)
Annie E. Casey Foundation 2	HUD User
Children's Defense Fund 2	International Federation of Social Workers
Compare Minnesota 2	MinCAVA
Family Violence Prevention Fund 2	Minnesota Board of Social Work
Information for Practice 2	Minnesota Community Foundation
Minnesota Department of Human Services 2	National Public Radio
U.S. Department of Health and Human Services 2	New Social Worker Online
Urban Institute 2	Rural Assistance Center
Blandin Foundation	Pat McClendon's Clinical Social Work Page
	SAMHSA's National Clearinghouse for Alcohol and Drug Information
Center for Economic and Policy Research	Society for Disabilities Studies
Child Welfare Information Gateway	U.S. Department of State
Childinfo (from UNICEF)	Wilder Foundation

social work program with strong focus on rural social work. For that reason, the library has sought out geographically relevant resources for students who will practice in Minnesota. There is regular review of links in LRL with a view to creating records in the library's catalog. In addition, the *Christian Science Monitor* (*CSM*) and *The Economist* are reviewed every week for web-based information sources.

VII. The Cost of Puppy Care and Feeding (Cataloging and Catalog Maintenance)

Adding freely available websites may seem like a great idea in times of budgetary difficulties and certainly it can be. However, if Ranganathan's fifth law of library science—that the library is a growing organism—is extended, the cost of adding free puppies to a growing catalog means staff time and money. The quantification of cataloging time, however, has not been well documented in recent years.

Reichmann (1953) noted that libraries had discussed the costs of cataloging at a "rate of one article every second year for almost a century" (p. 290). Some of his data show that the cost of cataloging one resource ranged from 72¢ to $1.37 between 1885 and 1934 (Table 2). Reichmann also included a table showing unit output for 1951–1952. Unit output was calculated as the number of titles processed, divided by the total number of production units, which in turn were counted as one (1) for professional staff and 0.6 for clerical staff. However, no monetary value was provided by Reichmann.

Nonetheless, as shown in Table 3, unit cost can be deduced by averaging the unit output for 1951–1952 (Reichmann, 1953) and comparing that to the 1952 annual salary of a librarian at a medium-sized academic library, as calculated by Terrell and Gregory (2003). A recent presentation by Skeen, Grover, and Woolcott (2010) shows that the average cost of unit output varies widely between a medium academic and small public library (Table 4). Harris (1989) found that self-reported cataloging costs in 1981 ranged between $53.00 and $14.67 (or $129.04 and $35.72 in 2011 values) for libraries that did not distinguish between monographs and serials. His research placed the median cataloging cost from 34 libraries at $15.00 (or $36.52 in 2011 USD). Similarly, Leung (1987) found that in 1983 the University of California at Riverside costs for cataloging averaged $14.65 per unit ($32.55 in 2011), ranging from $44.53 ($98.94 in 2011) for original cataloging down to $8.22–$10.40 ($18.26–$23.11 in 2011) for offline and online OCLC copy-cataloging respectively.

Table 2
Costs of cataloging prior to 1935

Year	Cost	2011 value
1885	$1.00	Not available
1913	$0.78	$17.44
1930	$0.726	$9.62
1934	$1.37	$22.63

2011 value based on CPI Inflation Calculator, United States Bureau of Labor Statistics.

Cataloging cost studies appear more sparsely in the literature after Leung although Morris, Hobert, Osmus, and Wool (2000) conducted a cost study with similar findings. Charbonneau's (2005) study of production benchmarks does not provide any unit costs of cataloging, but it provides examples of expected catalog record production that varies from one per hour to six per day to 100 per month. In its report for the Library of Congress R2 Consulting (2009) opted not to attempt to create a base cost of cataloging and chose to assume that an original catalog record costs USD $100.00.

In essence the literature simply proves that cataloging is expensive, ranging between $20.00 and $100.00 per resource cataloged, and that it is slow, ranging from 1 to 3 resources per hour, assuming 1950 hours per year for 1 FTE (see Tables 3 and 4). The sum findings of the literature as a whole compare to the cost of cataloging web resources at MSU, Mankato. This is for original and complex copy-cataloging performed by a professional cataloger and for basic copy-cataloging performed by a professional cataloger and for basic copy-cataloging performed by an experienced paraprofessional.

Table 3
Costs of cataloging in 1952

1951–1952 Average unit output	Average per hour	1952 Annual salary	1952 Average dollar per unit cost	2011 Inflation value
639	3	$3,300.00	$5.16	$43.09

Table 4
2010 Costs of cataloging at Utah State University and North Logan Public Library

	Total salary (2010)	Titles added (2010)	Average per hour	Average dollar per unit cost
USU academic	$464,240 (9.5 FTE)	~20,000	1	$23.21
NLC public	$35,000 (0.75 FTE)	~4,000	2.5	$8.75

A. Cataloging State Documents: Print and Electronic

Library Services at MSU, Mankato has been a long-time selective federal depository library and has a tradition of cataloging depository materials either using copy-cataloging or doing original cataloging. It also has a strong tradition of collecting and cataloging Minnesota state documents. During the days of print and microform, Library Services would derive the microform MARC 21 records from original print records. As more state documents were issued digitally, the number of microforms dwindled until they were discontinued in 2004. Thereafter most state documents were made available in digital form by producing agencies or were digitized and archived by LRL. With the move to electronic formats, review and selection of state documents became a larger part of the workflow, particularly for librarians responsible for social work collection development.

New arrivals were posted in e-mail announcements by LRL. The social work collection developer selected web resources from the list and forwarded the selections to a cataloger for addition to the online catalog. The list was usually a mixture of Minnesota state documents and other Minnesota-related websites or reports. However, the creation of MARC 21 records for the electronic state documents was much different from that of deriving print for microform records. Many of the resources selected had no print record for use as a derivation base, and thus required full original cataloging. Other selected resources were in fact component items of continuing resources, such as reports to the legislature, but the originating sites did not always provide title-level access. This meant that rather than cataloging a report as a serial once, catalogers had to search new issues and verify access, or add an issue-specific URL to the cataloged serial MARC 21 record.

Catalogers have to verify URL access for all resources, which is no easy feat considering that new state administrations or changes in nonprofit leadership often re-create the web presence of the state department or agency, agencies decide on a whim to re-design the website without providing re-directs from changed URL paths. Additionally the Minnesota legislature in recent years has mandated many mergers and closures and changes in oversight for many state bureaucracies. The cumulative effect is a host of descriptive surrogate records in the catalog with links to nowhere.

The maintenance for a collection of online resources is therefore far from free. Hours of staff time are required to run URLs through automated validity processes, to investigate the reports, to search for updated URLs, to write to agencies and wait for replies about updated links when necessary, and then to update the catalog records. Reviewing and resolving a monthly report of suspect URLs, can take from 1 to 8 hours. This process is by no means confined to state documents and applies to other websites, particularly for smaller NGOs and municipal or nonprofit websites. LRL's archival process with their stable URLs has alleviated much of this problem for Minnesota state documents, but not for other web resources.

At Mankato, a graduate assistant with an MLS degree and beginning experience in cataloging worked for 14 months between January 2007 and May 2008 to create about 500 catalog records for Minnesota state documents. Some were simple derivations from a print record to an electronic description record. Others were true original records and still others entailed complex copy-cataloging. This involved minimally verifying that the URL matched the resource described in the record, or in the extreme, finding a new URL or creating a continuing record for a set of serial reports. The graduate assistant worked 56 weeks, generally spending 5–10 hours per week on average at this specific cataloging task. This amounted to an average unit output of 9 records per week or 1–2 records per hour. At a 2009 professional librarian mid-level salary of $52,358 (Hadro, 2009) this equates to an hourly salary of $26.76, and the unit cost of a cataloged web resource.

B. Cataloging Web Sites from *Choice* Reviews

In a different snapshot, 86 *Choice* cards for electronic resources labeled "recommended" or better by reviewers were selected from science and technology disciplines. They had been culled from batches received between 2005 and 2011, with the bulk of them dated 2009–2010. *Choice* was used because of its prevalent use by social work collection developers. Over the course of 5 days in February 2010, an experienced paraprofessional copy-cataloger spent an average of 3 hours per day searching OCLC WorldCat for acceptable copy. The copy-cataloger found 35 (41%) that were acceptable and immediately exported those MARC 21 records into the catalog. Forty-seven of the remainder had less-than-acceptable copy and were placed in a local "save" file to wait for review and cataloging by a professional. Four were not found in WorldCat.

MSU, Mankato has defined acceptable copy in the following manner. The website must be cataloged according to current cataloging rules, meaning as set forth in *Anglo-American Cataloguing Rules*, 2nd edition, 2002 revision with 2005 updates. As shown in Fig. 3, acceptable copy should be cataloged as an integrating resource (Record type (Type) a, Bibliographic Level (BLvl) i, and Entry convention (S/L) 2), with the general material designation $h [electronic resource] in field 245. The record must contain the tags 006m and 007c for electronic resource nature and carrier descriptions respectively to facilitate limiting and facets in the online

```
(Bolded text shows elements for copy-cataloging review.)

Continuing Resources Workform

Type a   ELvl #   Srce #  GPub f    Ctrl #    Lang eng
BLvl i   Form o   Conf 0  Freq w    MRec #    Ctry dcu
S/L  2   Orig #   EntW #  Regl r    Alph #
Desc a   SrTp w   Cont ### DtSt c   Dates 1996 ,  9999

006          m       d
007          c  $b  r  $d c  $e  n
050  00  QE522
082  04  551.21    $2 21
245  00  Global Volcanism Program $h [electronic resource].
246  1#   $i Title on HTML header: $a Smithsonian Institution
Global Volcanism Program
260  ##  Washington, D.C. : $b Global Volcanism Program, Dept.
of Mineral Sciences, National Museum of NaturalHistory, $c
1996-
538  ## Mode of access: World Wide Web.
500  ##  The Smithsonian's Global Volcanism Program GVP) seeks
better understanding of all volcanoes through documenting
their eruptions during the past 10,000 years.
588  ##  Title from home page (viewed on July 12, 2004).
520  ##  This site is the homepage for the vulcanology program
at the Smithsonian Institution. It provides links to various
Smithsonian developed sites on the study and history of
volcanoes as well as to other sites dedicated to volcanoes.
Provides information of the volcanoes of the world, the
volcanic activity reports. Includes a volcano database
searchable by regions and names.
505  0# New features -- Preliminary notices of volcanic
activity -- Volcanic activity reports -- Volcanoes of the
world -- Products -- Site & program information -- Volcano
NetLinks.
650  #0  Volcanoes.
650  #0  Volcanological research.
650  #0  Paleogeography $y Holocene.
610  20  Smithsonian Institution.  $b Global Volcanism Program.
610  20  Smithsonian Institution. National Museum of Natural
History. Dept. of Mineral Sciences. Global Volcanism Program.
653  ##  Volcano $a volcanoes $a volcanology $a volcanism
$a eruption $a eruptive $a erupting $anewsletter $a Holocene.
710  2#  Smithsonian Institution. $b Global Volcanism Program.
856  40  $u http://www.volcano.si.edu/
```

Fig. 3   OCLC MARC record acceptable copy example.

catalog, with a Library of Congress Classification number to facilitate collection analysis, Library of Congress Subject Headings, and a valid URL in field 856. Having found 35 of 86 potential catalog records, the copy-cataloger was able to process 41% of the selected websites. The remaining websites were cataloged following OCLC's interim integrating resources practices on book work forms.

C. Cataloging Websites from News Publications

In a similar experiment to estimate time needed to assess and catalog websites, the authors reviewed the June 2010 issues of *CSM* and *The Economist* and identified 100 websites in each publication. Using standard collection development principles the list was winnowed down to 20 web resources with 10 from each publication.

Table 5
Cataloging availability of reviewed Websites

Web site	Review source	OCLC record exists	Current AACR2 rules	No. of OCLC holdings
Brookings Institution (www.brookings.edu)	*CSM*	Yes	No	24
Cato Institute (www.cato.org)	*CSM*	Yes	No	22
Legal Community Against Violence (www.lcav.org)	*CSM*	Yes	No	Yes
Tax Policy Center (www.taxpolicycenter.org)	*CSM*	Yes	No	Yes
Asian Carp Control (www.asiancarp.org)	*CSM*	No	N/A	No
GLBT Historical Society (www.glbthistory.org)	*CSM*	No	N/A	No
Gulf of Mexico Hypoxia Task Force (www.epa.gov/ owow_keep/msbasin/)	*CSM*	No	N/A	No
National Alliance for Public Charter Schools (www.publiccharters.org)	*CSM*	No	N/A	No
Pew Research Center's Internet & American Life Project (pewinternet.org)	*CSM*	No	N/A	No
University of Notre Dame's Institute for Latino Studies (latinostudies.nd.edu)	*CSM*	No	N/A	No

Table 5. (*Continued*)

Web site	Review source	OCLC record exists	Current AACR2 rules	No. of OCLC holdings
Harvard University's Joint Center for Housing Studies (www.jchs.harvard.edu)	*The Economist*	Yes	Yes	5
National Governors Association (www.nga.org)	*The Economist*	Yes	Yes	Yes 1
Pew Center on the States (www.pewcenteronthestates.org)	*The Economist*	Yes	Yes	9
Pew Research Center (pewresearch.org)	*The Economist*	Yes	Yes	9
American Academy of Pediatrics (www.aap.org)	*The Economist*	Yes	No	20
National Institutes of Health (www.nih.gov)	*The Economist*	Yes	No	49
Food and Agriculture Organization (www.fao.org)	*The Economist*	Yes	No	27
Institute for Public Policy Research www.ippr.org.uk)	*The Economist*	Yes	No	2
Interagency Council on Homelessness (www.ich.gov)	*The Economist*	Yes	No	Yes 1
National Center on Education and the Economy (www.ncee.org)	*The Economist*	Yes	No	Yes
Total		14	4	192
Average		70%	29%	

As the data in Table 5 show, 70% of these websites had MARC 21 descriptions in WorldCat, yet only 29% of those had been cataloged following current rules. While the data in Table 5 are not statistically significant, they do complement results seen from the *Choice* experiment, and general anecdotal evidence from catalogers—that more than half of the websites in WorldCat require more than basic copy-cataloging.

VIII. Discussion and Conclusion

Libraries have benefited over the past four decades from the Library of Congress' Cataloging in Publication (CIP) program (Library of Congress, 2010). It allows libraries to rely on preliminary cataloging of books. For nonprint media, such as video and sound recordings, catalogers rely on best practices and guidance from Online Audiovisual Catalogers, Inc. (OLAC) (Online Audiovisual Catalogers, 2011) to create MARC 21 records. Web site cataloging, as we have shown, has been spotty at best. Many libraries have created pathfinders or subject web guides, but have chosen not to catalog web resources. As the list of OCLC holdings in Table 5 demonstrated, very few libraries choose to catalog websites or even place their OCLC holding symbol on those records.

Just like real puppies bring an ineffable benefit to our human lives, free websites can add immeasurable value to users' research needs. websites can provide current, authoritative, and in-depth information. Our research showed there are hidden costs associated with collection development and cataloging of these websites. Once cataloged, URLs can break or change, additional hidden maintenance costs such as tracking broken links, and bringing catalog records up-to-date. The studies and experiments reported here did not attempt to quantify these added maintenance costs. Whether copy or original cataloging is involved, the average cost is in the range of $26.00–$100.00 per website. A nonquantified hidden cost associated with cataloged websites relates to collection development. If the site changes its content, it may need to be rereviewed in its entirety.

While the studies reported in this chapter focused primarily on resources for social work, the findings are extensible beyond social science. Use of mediated websites such as those in LRL's Links to the World, can help to ease local hidden costs.

Calhoun's prediction about declining use of catalogs and relying on Google-like search engines may or may not be in our future. Vaidhyanathan (2010) indicates that there are reasons to worry about Google search results. Information that populates the top of a Google search is not the most relevant, but rather the most popular. Yet end users have little understanding for how certain sites rise to the top. Another reason to worry about the "Googlization of everything" becomes evident in the context of information literacy. While the web provides a wealth of information, it cannot impart critical information literacy skills to users if they need to interpret various viewpoints and identify potential biases. In a recent conference keynote address Vaidhyanathan (2011) challenged librarians to create a framework to enable responsible cultural democracy on the web, similar to the way in which we have selectively cataloged web resources and in part through library/literacy instruction. *ipl2* could be a model for this since it assembles web resources which have been assessed by professional librarians.

Vaidhyanathan's challenge led to venues for further research not only exploring how librarians should think about the provision of access to the web information but also in constructing search environments that go beyond providing access to information that has been vetted only by commercial publishing establishments. The profession needs to think about provision of access to web resources, how to construct search environments that go beyond giving access to information vetted only by commercial publishers. As libraries look at their collection development policies, shrinking staff, and reduced materials budgets, they may need to consider internal paradigm changes, in which web resources are part of the richer universe of recorded knowledge, and are not treated as something odd, distasteful, or substandard.

One of the challenges for librarianship is making those paradigm changes happen. They can start by collection developers submitting websites for cataloging. Since cataloging processes and policies are typically reactive to collection development policies, the latter need to explicitly include/exclude websites. Institutional cultures in libraries may also need to change if web resources are included in altered collection development paradigms.

The research in this chapter indicates that few libraries are adding websites to their catalogs, and the reasons for this need to be teased out and evaluated. Is it the perceived paucity of reviewing sources? Is it habit to only add print resources and dismiss web resources? What do technical services policies, processes, and staff members do to encourage or discourage the addition of web resources in the catalog? How about users? Faculty use web resources in their own research (Dewald, 2005; Shpilko, 2011), but do they assign students to find credible and valid research results on the web? In short the entire institution in which academic libraries exist needs shifts in policies and practices.

These questions all beg for further research to be done. While this study found that only *Choice* is used consistently by social work librarians in Minnesota, other means of identifying and evaluating websites need to be explored. MSU, Mankato has 16 librarians and 14,500 full-time equivalent students. It would be helpful if institutions of other sizes and types were to explore the issues addressed in this chapter. Similarly, comparative data across institutions of the hidden costs of collection development and cataloging of web resources would better enable the field to make hard decisions.

Librarians are faced with two competing pressures. Budgets are decreasing, which would argue for increased inclusion of "free" resources. Yet they are faced with doing "more with less," which argues against having the time to find, evaluate, and process "free" resources. The inclusion of web resources in online catalogs also means that librarians need to be even more vigilant in their information literacy classes about developing skills for evaluation and validity of web resources. Per the ACRL standards for information literacy (2011) the profession must address both "resource literacy" (the ability to understand the form, format, location, and methods for accessing information resources) and "social-structural literacy" (knowledge of how information is socially situated and produced including understanding scholarly publishing processes).

Returning to Buytaert's free-puppy analogy at the beginning of this chapter, the library profession might rewrite the first two sentences to read:

> We need to look differently at the free Websites on the Internet once we outgrow our disdain for the work of tending these free resources. As professional librarians we have learned the truth. We know that taking home that puppy (adding that free Web site) is going to cost us in the end (but bring value to our users).

Acknowledgments

The authors would like to thank those who helped us by giving us their time, including Francine Graf of *Choice*, Carol Blackburn and Julie Dinger from the Minnesota Legislative Reference Library, and the social work librarians who informed us about their use of Websites.

References

Association of College and Research Libraries. (2011). *Information literacy for faculty and administrators*. Retrieved from http://www.ala.org/ala/mgrps/divs/acrl/issues/infolit/overview/faculty/faculty.cfm

Buytaert, D. (n.d.). *Open source and free puppies*. Retrieved from http://www.buytaertnet/open source and free puppies

Caldwell, A., Coulombe, D., Fark, R., & Jackson, M. (2001). Never the twain shall meet? Collaboration between catalogers and reference librarians in the OCLC CORC project at Brown university. *Journal of Internet Cataloging, 4*(1/2), 123–130.

Calhoun, K. (2006, March 17). *The changing nature of the catalog and its integration with other discovery tools*. Washington, DC: Library of Congress. Retrieved from http://www.loc.gov/catdir/calhoun-report-final.pdfwww.loc.gov/catdir/calhoun-report-final.pdf

Charbonneau, M. D. (2005). Production benchmarks for catalogers in academic libraries: Are we there yet? *Library Resources & Technical Services, 49*(1), 40–48.

Curtis, A. (2005). Why federated search. *Knowledge Quest, 33*(3), 35–47.

Dewald, N. H. (2005). What do they tell their students? Business faculty acceptance of the web and library databases for student research. *Journal of Academic Librarianship, 31*(3), 209–215.

Gopher (Protocol). (2011). *Wikipedia*. Retrieved from http://en.wikipedia.org/wiki/Gopher(protocol)

Graf, F. (1997). The web: Beyond "wow" [Supplement]. *Choice, 34*, 2.

Graf, F. (1998). Web II: A choice Internet reference tool [Supplement]. *Choice 35*, 3

Graf, F. (2005). About web IX [Special Issue]. *Choice, 42*, 5.

Hadro, J. (2009). *Academic librarian salary survey released: Mid-level salary survey*. Retrieved from http://www.libraryjournal.com/article/CA6656813.html

Harris, G. (1989). Historic cataloging costs, issues, and trends. *The Library Quarterly*, *59*(1), 1–21.

Hickey, T. B. (2001). Collaboration in CORC. *Journal of Internet Cataloging*, *4*(1/2), 5–16.

The ipl2 Consortium. (n.d.) *ipl2: Information You Can Trust*. Retrieved from http://ipl.org/

Jordan, J. (2001). Preface. *Journal of Internet Cataloging*, *4*(1/2), xix–xx.

LaGuardia, C. (Ed.) (2009). *Magazines for libraries* (18th ed.). New Providence, NJ: ProQuest.

Leung, S. W. (1987). Study of cataloging costs at the University of California, Riverside. *Technical Services Quarterly*, *5*(1), 57–66.

Library of Congress. (2010). *Cataloging in publication: Scope*. Retrieved from http://cip.loc.gov/scope.html

Mann, T. (2006, April 3). *The changing nature of the catalog and its integration with other discovery tools, final report, March 17, 2006: A critical review*. Washington, DC: Library of Congress Professional Guild. Retrieved October 1, 2007, from http://guild2910.org/AFSCMECalhounReviewREV.pdf

Miller, B. (2010). State and local documents spotlight: Whither goest thou, state and local notable documents. *DttP: Documents to the People*, *38*(2), 10–12.

Minnesota Legislative Reference Library. (2008). *Links to the world*. Retrieved from http://www.leg.state.mn.us/lrl/links/links.aspx

Morris, D. E., Hobert, C. B., Osmus, L., & Wool, G. (2000). Cataloging staff costs revisited. *Library Resources & Technical Services*, *44*(2), 70–83.

Nicholas, D., Rowlands, I., Jubb, M., & Jamali, H. (2010). The impact of the economic downturn on libraries: With special reference to university libraries. *The Journal of Academic Librarianship*, *36*(5), 376–382.

OCLC. (2002). Collections and technical services. *Bits & Pieces*, June, p. 264. Retrieved from http://www.oclcpica.org/?id=1162&In=uk

Online Audiovisual Catalogers. (2011). Publications and training materials. Retrieved from http://www.olacinc.org/drupal/?q=node/11

Primary Research Group. (2009). *The survey of higher education faculty: Evaluation of library efforts to index, preserve and catalog blogs, websites, email archives, and other cyber resources*. Retrieved from http://www.primaryresearch.com/uploaded/admin_reports/sample_reports/20100723_081306Excerpt_SHEF_Cyber_Resources.pdf. New York, NY: Author

R2 Consulting. (2009). *Study of the North American MARC records marketplace* (Retrieved from http://www.loc.gov/bibliographic-future/news/MARC_Record_Marketplace_2009-10.pdf). Washington, DC: Library of Congress

Ratzan, L. (2006). Mining the deep web: Search strategies that work. *Computerworld*. Retrieved from http://www.computerworld.com/s/article/print/9005757/

Reichmann, F. (1953). Costs of cataloging. *Library Trends*, *2*(2), 290–317Retrieved from http://www.ideals.illinois.edu/bitstream/handle/2142/5514/librarytrendsv2i2k_opt.pdf?sequence=1

Rockwood, I. E. (1998). Web redux [Supplement]. *Choice*, *35*, 2.

Shpilko, I. (2011). Assessing information-seeking patterns and needs of nutrition, food science, and dietetics faculty. *Library & Information Science Research*, *33*(2), 151–157.

Skeen, B., Grover, J., & Woolcott, L. (2010). *Making cents of cataloging: Are we getting what we are paying for?* Retrieved from http://works.bepress.com/julie_grover/2

Terrell, T., & Gregory, V. L. (2003, April). A look at now and then: Salaries of academic and research librarians. Paper presented at the ACRL 11th National Conference, Charlotte, NC. Retrieved from http://www.ala.org/ala/mgrps/divs/acrl/events/pdf/terrell.PDF

Ulrichsweb.com (2011). Retrieved from http://www.ulrichsweb.com

United States Bureau of Labor Statistics. *CPI inflation calculator*. Retrieved from http://www.bls.gov/data/inflation_calculator.htm

Vaidhyanathan, S. (2010). *The Googlization of everything (and why we should worry)*. Berkeley, CA: University of California Press.

Vaidhyanathan, S. (2011, March). Keynote speech presented at the Library Technology Conference, Macalester College, St. Paul, MN.

Wakimoto, J. C. (2009). Scope of the library catalog in times of transition. *Cataloging & Classification Quarterly*, 47(5), 409–426.

Bringing Order Out of Chaos: Benchmarking Tools Used in Merging University Libraries in Finland

Ari Muhonen[a], Ulla Nygrén[b] and Jarmo Saarti[c]
[a]Library, Aalto University, Espoo, Finland
[b]Library, University of Turku, Turku, Finland
[c]Library, University of Eastern Finland, Kuopio, Finland

Abstract

At the beginning of 2010, new higher education legislation was enacted in Finland. As a result, 17 state universities were consolidated into three newly formed and autonomous universities. This chapter describes the merger process of the libraries in these new universities, namely Aalto University, University of Eastern Finland, and the University of Turku. Using a case study approach, the chapter describes different aspects of the merger process, particularly how to manage cultural change in formerly independent libraries into a single new organization, as well as how to define the new structures and alter directives for management, leaving the past behind. Although this is based on Finnish experiences, it is helpful for other libraries considering or engaged in similar mergers by giving examples and tools for the actions needed for new structures to succeed. Also described are the challenges that the three libraries met in introducing innovations, the necessity for broad communication, and marketing of the new structures within their respective universities. Also included is a brief background description of the overall impact of the new legislation on universities as a whole. Higher education in Finland encompasses polytechnic institutes and universities. This chapter addresses library mergers only in universities.

Keywords: University libraries; Mergers; Restructuring; Management; Organizational culture; Finland

I. Introduction

From 1999 through 2003, the European Union provided impetus for its member states to refocus their policies and structures for higher education.

LIBRARIANSHIP IN TIMES OF CRISIS
ADVANCES IN LIBRARIANSHIP, VOL. 34
© 2011 by Emerald Group Publishing Limited
ISSN: 0065-2830
DOI: 10.1108/S0065-2830(2011)0000034012

In Finland, this resulted in a new University Act being passed in the summer of 2009 (Ministry of Education, 2009). The new act meant that formerly state-owned universities were to become more autonomous, especially in financial terms. In addition, the number of separate universities in Finland was reduced from 20 to 17 that were shaped into three new and larger entities at the beginning of 2010. The three new universities were Aalto University, the University of Eastern Finland (UEF), and the University of Turku. One of the main aims of the reform was to strengthen Finnish academic research and improve services (Fig. 1).

A merger necessarily brings about corporate change and leads to a rebuilding of an organization. According to Kotter (2007), a typical change process goes through a series of phases. One phase of crucial importance is

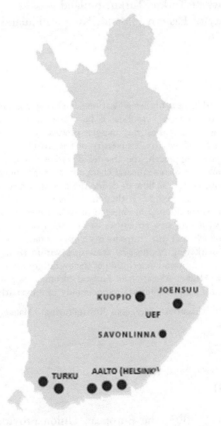

Fig. 1 Location of the three new universities.

the creation of new organizational cultures. It has been argued that the successful creation of a new organizational culture is the cornerstone of building a successful new organization. A merger of two universities—or three as in the case of Aalto—thus represents a huge task in restructuring preexisting cultures. This entails reorganizing staff positions, combining and creating new services, as well as restructuring management. This, combined with the fact that the legal status and working environments of the universities in Finland were changed at the same time, posed enormous challenges for management of the universities as well as their libraries.

The concept of *chaordic enterprise* has been introduced to describe the attempt to utilize chaos theory when analyzing complex organizational cultures and environments (Putnik & Van Eijnatten, 2004). A merging process can be seen as a chaotic phenomenon where the main mission of management is to create order so that the daily service production is enabled. A merger can also be seen as a crisis in the life cycle of an organization. There is evidence that successful recovery from a crisis is best advanced by being well prepared, which in turn requires planning and strategic leadership, mastery of organizational development, and clear decision-making processes (Hargis & Watt, 2010).

In Finland, the universities actually faced at least four new paradigms that changed their environments drastically. First, the University Act separated universities from the state. They became economically independent and their employees became employees of the universities instead of being civil servants. Simultaneously, the concept of leadership in universities underwent a thorough change. University boards no longer were made up only of members of the academic community but were mandated to include eminent individuals from business, arts, and society. As a whole, universities were to be more professionally managed. The same applied in university libraries which meant that library directors were no longer considered to be the top professionals, dealing only with library issues, or "chief librarians." Instead emphasis on leadership skills made library directors more like the CEO of a company.

Third, the economic downturn beginning in 2008 meant that many institutions and their libraries had to learn to cope on shoestring budgets. The fourth and the most important aspect of change was introduction of digital document dissemination and information and communication technologies (ICT) that changed the ways in which libraries functioned (Thompson, 2005). This paradigm shift for libraries moved libraries from a collection-based identity to one with service and access-based emphasis (Saarti, 2005). This meant that employees in universities and their libraries faced an identity crisis that needed to be managed in order to avoid operational paralysis.

The following sections describe the merger processes used in the three libraries along with the tools and methods they applied and benchmarks of the best practices used in this process.

II. Universities, Libraries, and Changes Leading up to 2010

A. Aalto University

The idea of merging design, technology, and economics into one university was introduced in September 2006 by Yrjö Sotamaa, then President of the University of Art and Design. Soon after this the Ministry of Education nominated a working group led by Raimo Sailas, the Permanent State Secretary of the Ministry of Finance, to develop the idea further. The working group gave its report in February 2007, suggesting that the University of Art and Design, Helsinki School of Economics and Helsinki University of Technology be merged. Presidents of the three universities met the Minister of Education in May 2007 and agreed to start planning work immediately.

Actual planning started in the three universities in September 2007, by forming 13 different task forces, namely:

- Teaching;
- Research;
- Societal impact;
- HR services;
- International affairs;
- Library and information services;
- Student services;
- Financial services;
- IT Services;
- Property and infrastructure services;
- Lifelong learning services;
- Marketing and communications; and
- Entrepreneurship and innovation services.

Their aim was to find new ways of performing research, teaching, and various services provided by the university. The three library directors had begun their planning in January 2007 when mergers were first in sight.

The university task forces reported in May 2008, and other groups were appointed in September 2008 to plan details. This time administration and services (including library matters) were the responsibility of a group called "Avoid bureaucracy." Altogether more than 500 people from the universities and their stakeholders were involved in planning for over a year and a half. The President of the University was appointed in January 1, 2009, and Aalto University was officially established in January 1, 2010 by merging the three institutions (Aalto, 2011). As of January 1, 2011, the university had 19,516 students, 338 professors and 4,113 other staff members, and consisted of 6 schools: Art and Design, Chemical Technology, Economics, Electrical Engineering, Engineering, and Science (Aalto, 2011).

B. University of Turku

The University of Turku was created when the University of Turku and the Turku School of Economics libraries (TSEL) merged on January 1, 2010. The process leading to the merger began in 2006 when a working group of university representatives, headed by Markku Linna from the Ministry of Education proposed that the two institutions form a consortium in order to better advance the competitiveness of high-quality research in the Turku region.

The concept of a consortium soon matured into preparation for a merger starting in 2008. The merger united two very different universities in terms of both size and disciplines. The University of Turku was founded in 1920 and is the third oldest university in Finland. For a long time, it had been one of the largest multidisciplinary universities in Finland. TSEL on the other hand, was founded in 1950 specializing in business administration. After merger the new university had 21,000 students, a staff of 3000, and ranked among the largest, and most broadly based in the country. It has the following Faculties: Education, Humanities, Law, Mathematics and Natural Sciences, Medicine, Social Sciences, and the TSEL.

The two libraries were the last to become involved during the merger process. In the summer of 2009, only about half a year before the merger was due to come into force, the rector of the university appointed a steering committee to clarify the libraries' situation. The committee consisted of experts in management, university administration, and representatives of the most important interest groups, such as the university board and the scientific community. The library director joined this committee after being appointed in December 2009. With respect to the approaching merger, the steering committee's task was to

- rebuild the management system of the library;
- construct a reform of the organizational structure of the library; and
- create a balanced policy for allocation of resources.

The timetable for merging the libraries in Turku was quite opposite of the situation in UEF, where building a new library organization started as soon as the merger was decided upon. At Turku, conducting affairs in a shorter time frame did have positive aspects. The processes of reforming the organization and evaluating services benefited from the fact that the structure of the parent organization had already taken shape.

C. University of Eastern Finland

Creation of the UEF began in 2007 when a working group, led by Reijo Vihko, submitted a report on how to intensify cooperation between two Universities: Joensuu and Kuopio. It was significant that the library was incorporated into

Table 1
Comparative Data for Three Universities in 2010

	Aalto	Turku	UEF
Total univ. student enrollment (FTE)	19,516	21,142	13,776
Total univ. staff (incl. professors)	4,300	3 296	2730
Libraries:			
Monograph print volumes	360,000	1,630,500	1,000,000
Serial titles—e-journals	26,000	33,000	19,000
Serial titles—print	1,800	33,790	2,500
Annual budget	million euro 10; USD $ 1,423 million	million euro 10; USD $ 1,423 million	million euro 7.1; USD $ 10.1 million
Physical space—sq. meters	11,300	18,000	14,000
Physical space—sq. feet	121,600	193,800	150,700
Previous number of library units	3	19	14
Current number of library units	3	15	14 (the year 2011 will mean a radical cut in the number of departmental libraries)

this process from the very outset. The library made a proposal on how it could contribute to the merger and what projects it would need to initiate. The universities started to discuss a total merger in the fall of 2007.

The year 2008 was a busy planning year. The organizational structure and strategy of the university were completed including the restructuring of the library's organization and its strategy. The library obtained funding from the university's management for two projects. The first one was to create a single merged database, a task that was completed in the summer of 2009. The second project was to develop a joint policy for information literacy and tutoring. Here, emphasis was put on building distance learning courses.

With approximately 14,000 students and 3000 employees, the UEF became one of the largest in Finland. It has three different campuses, situated about 130 km apart in Joensuu, Kuopio, and Savonlinna. There are four faculties: Science and Forestry, Health Sciences, Social Sciences and Business Studies, and the Philosophical Faculty that offer courses in more than 100 major subjects, with multidisciplinary emphasis.

1. Summary and Comparative Data as of 2010

Table 1 compares the three libraries in terms of the populations they serve and provides basic information about holdings, budgets, and physical units and space as of 2010.

III. Challenges in the Merger Process

A merger is an opportunity for chaos in any organization. Too often it is assumed that transitions will be straightforward and that only benefits and good practices will transfer from older organizations to merged units. Since this is not the case, it has been stated that most mergers are likely to fail. One of the most important reasons for failure is the lack of sound planning. The success or failure of mergers will be determined during the integration processes when new organizational cultures and structures are being created. Since every institution has its own history and culture, it seems that failure happens when one cannot make a sound transition from the old cultures to completely new ones (Nguyen & Kleiner, 2003, pp. 447–448).

What are the factors that contribute to the success of organizational change? Kotter (2007) listed the things that leaders do right in successfully transforming organizations. Even though the Kotter's studies were based on commercial enterprises, many of his steps for success are applicable to nonprofit organizations like libraries. For example, he pointed out that transformation programs do not start without motivation, and this requires good leaders with powerful guiding visions. Strengthening professional leadership in Finnish universities—and their libraries—is well in line with this concept.

Kotter also emphasized, that without a vision, all transformation efforts can seem just a list of separate and incompatible projects without anything to link them together. It is essential to communicate the vision by all possible means, both in word and deed, that is to say "walk the talk." New organization cultures then build on a shared understanding of the vision. The structure of the organization must also support the vision, meaning that changed structures should be put in place where needed and obstacles must be removed.

Libraries that are service-based have to build their visions so that they support the goals of the parent organization. It is essential for success in all steps that there be motivation and involvement of top management as well as staff. In order to implement cultural change, there needs to be an open culture of trust in which each person in the library is willing and able to share information and to learn from others (Mohr & Sengupta, 2002). In addition, time has to be allowed for bereavement, because staff is actually experiencing the death of their former organizations. Staff might fear that part of their identity will disappear in a merger unless their work in the old organization is part of the foundation for the new unit.

In the following section, the most important subprojects faced in the merging process are addressed:

- merging of the organization: building new organizational culture and leaving the old one behind;
- challenges of personnel management: changes from being a civil servant to an employee, changes in the chain of the command, building community and nurturing know-how, and managing job-related stress;
- service development and resource allocation: integrating and innovating services, reallocating resources and services, managing the economic downturn; and
- communication, marketing and lobbying internally and externally and lobbying for the library inside the university.

A. Merging Organizations and Creating New Structures

Organizational mergers happened in Finland at several levels. At the state level, all university legislation was reorganized. This meant that the funding of higher education institutions changed as did the status of employees. For universities, this meant restructuring their entire management systems. This was particularly challenging because at the same time that talks about the optimal number of universities in Finland started the economical downturn also began. The talks focused on reducing the number of higher education institutions in order to increase quality and efficiency, and to adapt to student populations that were declining due to decreasing birthrates.

1. At Aalto University

As already mentioned, the three library directors began planning for the merger at the end of 2006, well before the official announcement of a planning process by the university. They spent the spring of 2007 gathering background information and visioning a common future. Two brainstorming sessions with staff from all three libraries were held in the fall of 2007. These led to nomination of six working groups that were comprised of staff members. Four of the groups concentrated on users (students, teachers, researchers, and enterprises), one on library systems, and one on university publishing. During this phase, two concepts called "The customer life cycle" and "The book life cycle" were created that were used to produce a service portfolio for the new library.

The main part of planning was completed by the end of 2008 with the library being the first unit within the university to develop the "big picture" for the future. Being first was not a benefit, because it took about one year for other units to prepare their plans. This meant that the library had to wait and lost a lot of momentum. Nevertheless, it was still possible to do more detailed planning with 10 teams nominated by the library directors. Brainstorming sessions also continued. The main emphases were to discuss teamwork results and to acquaint people with each other.

Even though the library itself was able to prepare for the future, its work was not really acknowledged by the university management team. While library representatives took part in several of the eight university-level working groups, library matters were handled only as part of the "Avoid bureaucracy" group. The library was not able to influence the university's strategy or its bylaws. This led to a situation where several matters affecting the future of the library remain undecided as of the writing of this chapter. These included the learning center structure and the number of branch libraries. It also delayed creation of the new organization structure of the library that was finally decided in November 2010. The new organization is shown in Fig. 2.

All of this preliminary planning was under the leadership of three library directors, although the director of the Aalto University Library was not appointed until December 2009.

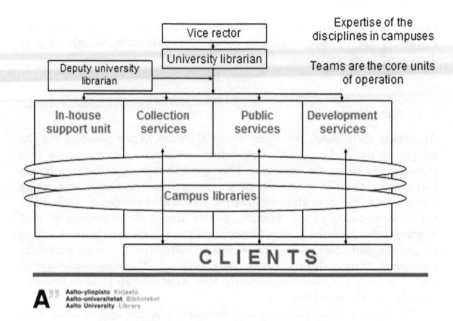

Fig. 2   Organization of Aalto University Library.

2. At University of Turku

During the first decade of 2000, the university had tried to work out the best ways to solve problems caused by an operational model with 19 separate library units, many of which had different procedures, and had a critical lack of space, especially in the main library that housed a statutory free copy collection of all material published in Finland from 1919 onwards. To supplement local planning efforts, the Finnish Ministry of Education appointed an expert reviewer in 2007, Dr. Jussi Nuorteva, to scrutinize the possibilities of intensified cooperation between higher education libraries in the Turku region with a special emphasis on the situation at Turku University Library.

The reviewer's final report stressed the importance of developing information management holistically, especially as it related to research. He pointed out that a consortium agreement between the University of Turku and TSEL should facilitate the creation of uniform procedures. The report included proposals for concentrating university library operations into four library and information service centers. This report was used as a base from which to start planning the organizational structure for two merged libraries (Nuoteva, 2008).

From the start, key interest groups, including the scientific community and students and the entire library staff, participated in reorganizing the library and creating a new organizational structure. In spring 2010, the library conducted a customer satisfaction study, LibQUAL™, and another enquiry specially tailored to the various disciplines, to obtain information on ways they use the library and their expectations about library services.

The results from these were taken into account during the planning process. During 2010, four whole-day sessions were held where library personnel analyzed customer feedback. Staff discussed alternative models of organizational structures, identified the key processes of the library, and debated detailed work processes, such as handling interlibrary loans or teaching information literacy to students.

In this way, personnel took responsibility into their own hands. Working together on these issues also helped staff members from two separate libraries get to know and understand each other better and to learn about different work processes. The new organization structure (Fig. 3) with three discipline-specified libraries has been functioning since the beginning of 2011. There still are things to do before the reorganization is complete. During 2011, decisions have to be made about now separate functions like acquisitions, cataloging, and whether to have them done by library-wide teams or be centralized.

3. At University of Eastern Finland

In the merger of the Joensuu and Kuopio Universities into the UEF, early decisions made by the university and library leaders helped considerably. For example, the management system of the university and its library were both finalized during 2009. A library director was appointed during the planning phase in December 2009. The library appointed heads of various services soon thereafter. As a result, the library's management team was functioning in 2009 before the official merger took place in 2010. The library's organization as it was redesigned is shown in Fig. 4.

Thus, when the new library started to function, it had a strategy for the library and its services, new Web pages, new Intranet, new work processes, and job descriptions for teams and personnel. In other words, the year 2009 was really the first year of joint operations and thus the library was able to be fully functional from the beginning of 2010.

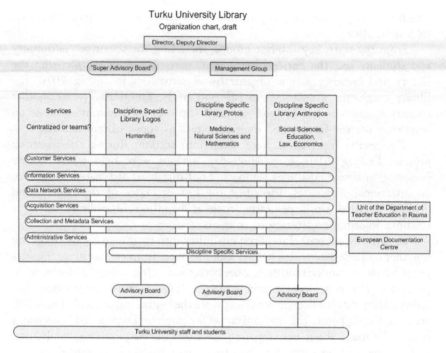

Fig. 3   Draft organization chart of Turku University Library.

B. Human Resource Management

1. Aalto University

The three libraries formed the University's Library were all leading ones in
their fields in Finland. All had high profiles and traditions spanning at least
100 years. Therefore, cultural change was one of the most difficult tasks in
merging. This was tackled mainly through broad cooperation with staff and
maintaining equality among the libraries.

Planning was undertaken in several working groups and in brainstorming
sessions where all staff members participated. Working groups had
representatives from all library units. In brainstorming sessions, staff members
were mixed together to enable mingling and getting acquainted. Planning
work was done efficiently and at this stage, cultural clashes did not affect
results in any negative way.

Most difficulties were encountered when deciding the names of the three
campus (former university) libraries and organizational structure, both being

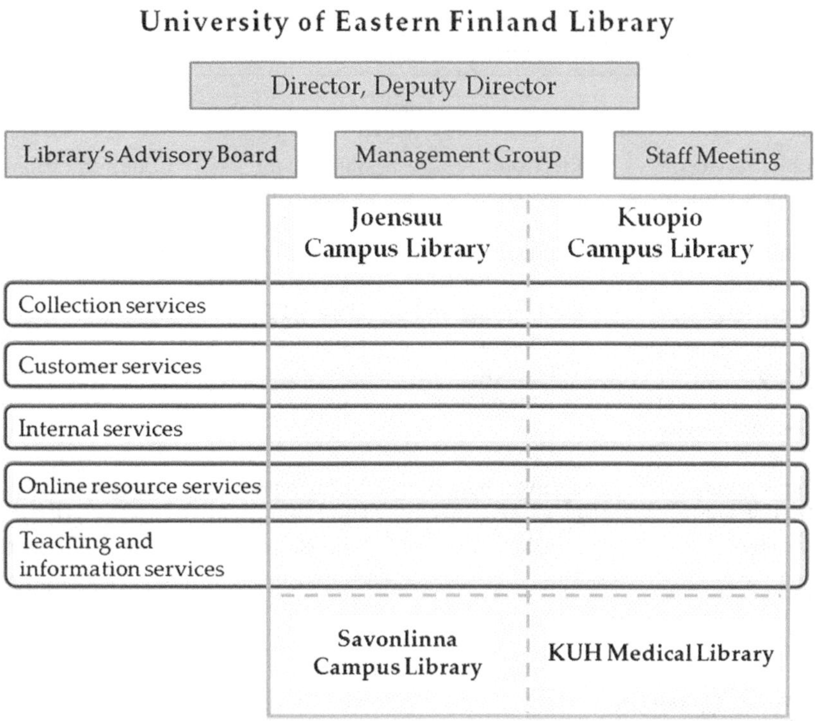

University of Eastern Finland Library

Fig. 4 Organization structure of University of Eastern Finland's Library.

strongly affected by past cultures and identities. Long, intense, and in some cases, even heated discussions took place to solve these problems. This was necessary, however, to develop a new organizational culture. Nonetheless, there were some dissatisfied individuals who thought their opinions were not heard.

Formation of a new culture did not really gather momentum until the fall of 2010, when the new organizational structure came into force. Sixteen teams operate across all three campuses with each team reporting to one of the heads of the library as depicted in Table 2. Staff members have become acquainted with fellow workers and they have been able to start planning new daily routines. The teams are self-organizing and have been given considerable responsibility for their own work. Work on structure is ongoing, but the teams have already demonstrated the ability to create new procedures and connections among the campuses.

Table 2
Team Structure of Aalto University Library

Teams			
Public services, Arabia campus	Electronic materials	Support for research and publishing	Communications
Public services, Töölö campus	Acquisition	Information literacy	Internal support
Public services, Otaniemi campus	Cataloguing and indexing	Library IT systems	
Faculty libraries, Otaniemi campus	Collection management	New digital services	
Reference service			
Resource sharing			
Teams report to:	Teams report to:	Teams report to:	Teams report to:
Head of public services	Head of collections	Head of development	Head of HR
			Head of finance

2. Turku University

In Turku, the library merger triggered overall reform of management and organization structure. Initially, this was felt more in the TSEL, the smaller unit, which lost its status as an independent university library. In the case of Turku University Library, no such identity change occurred. The challenge was, and remains—adopting a new identity as part of a bigger and essentially a multidisciplinary library. For TSEL, the change was rapid and fundamental. For example, within half a year its database and information retrieval portal were incorporated into those at Turku University Library. With this loss, it became important for TSEL staff to feel that they had contributed several good practices to the new library. Assimilation was helped by the fact that some TSEL staff moved to work in the "university side" of the library and the director of the new library was chosen from the TSEL.

For library personnel, the most significant impact of the merger occurred in the library's management. The task given to the steering committee, to reform the whole library organization, initially seemed somewhat theoretical and remote. Although plans to undertake such changes had been in the air for decades, they had not resulted in true change. It was therefore vital for management to share with staff information about work that had been done so far and to bring them up-to-date about the ideas, plans, and discussions that were underway. Staff also had to be made aware of approaching reforms, which involved creation of larger library units and centralization of work once done separately. They were informed how changes would affect them, how work-processes would be modified and inevitably alter the content of everyday work, as well as working environments.

All this was done to prepare personnel for the most important aspect of all, namely to make the change their own by participating in planning and ultimately motivating them to take change into their own hands. The engagement of staff grew gradually during common "development days," where all staff participated in planning the future organization. During those days, it became quite clear that even though changes could not be initiated without vision and encouragement from leaders, it is certain that they never could be accomplished without motivated staff. Working side by side in identifying, describing, and comparing work processes also stimulated the emergence of a common culture. Planning, and taking part in social events like the library's 90th anniversary, also had a unifying impact.

One of the obstacles to developing library services was a disproportionate personnel structure. During recent years, the number of staff in the Turku Library had been significantly reduced. This was out of step with requirements that the library focus more on supporting research and finding new and innovative means to achieve this goal. It was crucially important that the university's leadership realized this dissonance and gave the library full support in creating a more balanced personnel structure through which expert service can be offered. In budget negotiations for 2011, the library received permission to fill nine open vacancies for library professionals.

3. University of Eastern Finland

The shift of employees from civil servants to university employees resulted in redundancies during 2010 when the university started to balance its finances to new realities. The first decision made was that the level of funding was to be the same level as the years before. For the library, this meant reductions in the collection budget (about 15%) and about a 10 man-year reduction in staff. This created enormous challenges for personnel management.

Job descriptions had to be readjusted. For many employees, the merger meant that work they had done previously no longer existed. Therefore, managers had to help in the bereavement caused by the death of old jobs. The most important task for managers, however, was to rearrange job descriptions and define new roles for library staff. Some services, like interlibrary loans, were to be centralized as much as possible to one campus library. At the same time, information subject fields were rearranged based on the skills and knowledge of staff. Here the combined staff actually enabled better realignment of staff and their responsibilities. The fact that a lot of specialist work could be done via Internet helped a lot in this change.

Great effort was put into socializing and familiarizing staff members with each other because the campuses are quite distant from each other and staff members do not meet face to face very often. New technologies helped considerably. For example, most of the first year's 200 plus meetings were held via videoconferencing and Web technologies were widely used in dissemination of documentation and of ideas.

C. Developing Services

The most important characteristic of services is their process nature. Services can be defined as processes composed of a series of activities that involve the use of different types of resources, and often in direct interaction with customers (Grönroos, 2007). Libraries are, by nature, service-providing institutions. Almost all of the work done in them is connected with service delivery. A library therefore should assess its services constantly as part of its strategic planning and development. In a merger, evaluating services and generating new content is crucially important in order for library services university's mission and goals.

1. At Aalto University

Planning of a new service portfolio was done thoroughly at Aalto University Library. It was done in the first two phases of planning resulting in excellent internal reports. However, the loss of momentum during 2009 and 2010 meant that the work has not yet been fully implemented as of the writing of this chapter. The long pause meant that staff tended to forget the reasoning behind the planning and partly its results. Fortunately, these reports can be utilized to form the basis for the future work.

Another problem in developing new services was differences in working procedures and policies of three campus libraries. It was decided at the beginning of planning that best practices would be examined and the very best practices would be used by all. However, there was some reluctance to give up established practices and adopt unfamiliar routines. Fortunately, in many cases, teams have been able to create totally new working procedures that were accepted by all members.

2. At Turku University

Delivering quality service is fundamental for the survival and success of any organization. In order to improve services, many nonprofit organizations have introduced quality measures such as customer surveys. Applying a customer survey enables building upon the customers views and it means moving from a library-based view of services toward one that is customer-based (Hakala & Nygren, 2010).

One of the first tasks after the merger of the two universities was to find out what the customers, mainly university staff and students, thought about the library and its services, their expectations, and how well they were being met. Thus, a customer survey, LibQUAL, was undertaken in the spring of 2010. The results showed that customers were quite dissatisfied, particularly with the library's supply of information resources, namely the availability of print and electronic materials via the library's information search portal. One disturbing finding was that dissatisfaction was greatest in groups that were highest in the academic hierarchy, namely postgraduate and postdoctoral researchers, and professors. This result was unexpected because so many electronic resources were available to these groups.

Results indisputably revealed that something had gone wrong with development and marketing of library services. They strengthened the view expressed in the report from the Ministry of Education (2009) that there seemed to be a lack of understanding between the scientific community and the library. In an analysis of results by faculty, the TSEL scored highest, having the most satisfied users with regard to information resources and performance of library staff. It should be noted that when this survey was done, TSEL still had its own library database and portal for information retrieval. It will be interesting to learn how incorporation of these into Turku University Library will affect results in a follow-up assessment in 2012.

Survey results indicated that service development will be first and foremost in finding ways to win the trust and confidence of the academic community. Since this can be best achieved through cooperation, an active interaction through meetings is being established between disciplines/faculties and the library. This is a kind of informal "advisory board," composed of researchers, students, and library staff. Its aim is to offer a channel for academics to take a more active role in library's processes, such as evaluating and choosing electronic resources. Thus, the scientific community can influence acquisitions through their expertise, benefiting both users and the library. Faculties nominate representatives to these advisory boards in spring 2011 and, according to plan, they will start to meet autumn 2011.

It is recognized that the organization and contents of service delivery need to be developed holistically with special teams concentrating on different forms of service. In conjunction with organizational reform, internal services like administration, data network services, cataloguing, and metadata services also have to be altered to better serve a new structure.

3. At University of Eastern Finland

The best way of managing people in a changing situation is to engage them in service developments. The UEF library used a quality management system based on the ISO 9001 that was adopted by the university (Balagué & Saarti, 2009). Here the views and ideas of the staff were incorporated in forming strategy as well as in devising the main goals of the library. It was based on this strategy that the team structure of the library was established (see Fig. 2). Also a lot of teams were used for project work during the transitional period, with most being subsequently terminated.

Teams were responsible for harmonizing service production of the old universities and different campuses at the UEF library. Here the aim was to highlight best practices for the new university instead of wasting time arguing about the past. This meant forgetting the past and learning new ways.

Perhaps the most significant single project in developing services was unification of databases of the old universities into a joint one for the UEF library.

This sent a signal to both the staff and users that a new library had been born. At the same time, it also meant that the library staff had to create a joint culture, procedures, and regulations covering all three campuses. The time for excuses had passed.

D. Communication and Marketing

Earlier in this chapter, we referred to a merger as a crisis in the life of an organization. In a crisis situation, the importance of communication is heightened. One reason is that merger automatically affects and changes the image of the old organizations. The study of organizational perception management deals with image and reputation of organizations. Research has shown that there are reasons to believe that the reputation of an organization should be considered as a strategic resource and that there is a strong link between reputation and competitive edge (Hargis & Watt, 2010).

Perhaps the most challenging task for management in a merger is communication and marketing. The first task is to create a common language and communication culture. Although the libraries have specialized terms for their services during a merger, these terms can be used and interpreted in a many different ways.

1. Aalto University

Marketing of the library to management at Aalto University proved to be challenging. Individuals seemed to have their own ideas about library functions. Some originated in the distant past when books and printed journals were the primary tools of information dissemination. Others thought that everything was freely available on the Internet. Here again a common language became important in transmitting an understanding of the library's core functions.

One thing that changed considerably in the recent past was the way that the library demonstrates the value it adds to the university. Reports need to have more details, and more data are needed to clarify what the library has achieved and what it contributes to institutional outcomes. Gone is the traditional trust that a library is a "universal good." This is at least partly due to a new university management philosophy modeled after those in commercial enterprises.

2. Turku University

As pointed out earlier, the most important communication challenge is having a dialogue with customers. The library has to learn the right ways to convince the researchers and students about all the many ways they can benefit from library services. This will involve building a communication strategy and making it a part of everyday functions of the library. It also means closer integration of the library into research and study processes. The creation of a positive image must be done realistically and honestly and it usually takes a long time, although damage to a reputation can happen very quickly. A good image in the minds of powerful stakeholders is an asset for a library as much as it is for an enterprise competing in the marketplace.

3. University of Eastern Finland

In the library, lack of a common language was noted quite often during 2009 and 2010. This occurred at almost at all venues and levels—management, meetings, and e-mails. Thus, it became important that library management and teams spend a lot of time discussing the definition of terms. Management solely via an email culture can be especially vulnerable with quite a lot of battles of will traced to semantic misunderstandings, such as what a "loan" means in different libraries.

As mentioned before, Internet technologies were used widely in communication and marketing. The library began building a new corporate culture by publishing articles regularly in the university's online bulletin and started to utilize online social media such as blogs and wikis.

The independent financial status of universities meant that the struggle for resources within the institution became harder and, in turn, the library had to learn to lobby. This was especially important for two reasons. First, interpersonal networks changed radically with the hire of new top managers for the university. Second, organizations usually look for economic savings, from a merger. Thus, the library needed to provide facts to university managers. This was especially crucial during budget negotiations when the library provided information about other similar sized university libraries in Finland. The library actually managed to reassure the university managers about its efficiency.

At UEF, 2010 meant rather big cutbacks to financial resources. In the library, this resulted in a reduction in electronic library resources. Here the library received backing from the academic community to good effect in its efforts to avoid this reduction. Because of community support, the library received a 15% increase in its acquisition budget to add basic print and e-resources.

IV. Conclusion

Based on the experiences of three Finnish university library mergers, some best practices or benchmarks were identified as in Table 3.

The most important task faced by the three libraries was building new organizational cultures. Since this meant leaving old structures behind, library managers had to support staff through a kind of bereavement process due to loss old organizations. Having strategies for changes in work and building new organizations for merged libraries, along with prompt start-up to prepare services, were also important. If staff were shown that best practices from the older organizations were building blocks for a new library, it was easier to get commitment to the new organization.

The right timing of mergers cannot be understated, especially when libraries have to function as normally as possible during organizational changes. It was also found to be important that the parent organization make difficult decisions as quickly as possible. The delay at Aalto University of appointing a university library director, and making other critical decisions, led to an unacceptable hiatus in developing a merged library structure and operations. The university must identify the

Table 3
Best Practices in Library Merger Processes

Tasks	Best Practices

Merging the organization
- Rapid decisions about naming the director of the library
- Rapid decisions about teams and their leaders
- Defining the strategy and organization of the library
- Involve staff, stakeholders, and experts in the process
- Identify the need for professional management
- Manage termination of previous organizations and processes

Challenges in personnel management
- Defining tasks and roles of staff (revise job descriptions)
- Build a new organizational culture and new library identity
- Manage job-related stress
- Reallocate resources and redesign services
- Hold face-to-face meetings to socialize staff from different libraries
- Recognize the need for staff education

Develop services and reallocate resources
- Assess customer views on present and future services
- Integrate and innovate services
- Reallocate resources and redesign services
- Create efficiencies and eliminate overlaps
- Identify best practices
- End unproductive practices in previous organizations

Marketing, communication, and lobbying
- Build networking opportunities for academics
- Engage in cooperative ventures with students
- Build relationships with university administrators (esp. new ones)
- Set up efficient and effective communication structures
- Use new technologies such as blogs, apps, wikis, and video conferencing to enhance communication

individuals responsible for the library in its organizational structure and the university's strategy, change strategies, and work routines. The library can only function properly after these decisions have been made, because the library cannot prejudge them.

Understanding and support of senior university management is essential in restructuring libraries. At the same time, libraries have to maintain the best possible relations with university management to successfully convey the benefits and value that the library contributes to the institution. Similarly there must be genuine dialogue with academic communities. Customers must know the value that the library brings to their work in order to give their support.

Mergers that result in change in a university's leadership mean that the library will quickly lobby and inform management about library issues. Such a change also means that the interpersonal networks that used to be in the older organizations have to be at least renewed if not built anew. The most effective way to build connections is for libraries to ensure their involvement at the earliest possible stage of merger discussions.

In restructuring, libraries should build and develop services based on customers' needs. In other words past rules, regulations and practices that evolved without regard to customer needs lead to a library's isolation from clients. In new or restructured legal and operational environments, library directors need new skills such as human resources management, lobbying, marketing and communication, as well as leadership ability. They must recognize the need for further education of library staff members as emphasis is placed on teams and changes in jobs.

During the mergers, the three new libraries found that communication was key, not only inside the library but also externally. For example, when UEF communicated with their customers about a budget reduction in electronics resources, strong support groups emerged and successfully pressurized to reverse the reduction. Creating a common language became an important requirement for communication to work. Time for the staff and users to adapt to the changes also had to be provided. Library managers themselves found they had little or no time to adapt. They had to be willing and ready to use rhetoric of the new organization from the outset, such as using the new library name instead of older ones.

It is certain that future decades will see rapid changes due to unforeseeable factors and events. Not only are academic libraries going through a paradigm shift to accommodate fleeting technologies, so are students, faculty, and researchers in teaching, learning and communication processes. A digitally native and globalized generation has entered universities all over the world. Libraries that will not adapt their ways accordingly will soon be outdated. The mega challenge for libraries will be to be proactive change agents, ingratiating themselves into evolving teaching and learning processes, and doing so in colleges and universities that are experiencing reduced enrolments and income streams.

References

Aalto University. (2011). Retrieved from http://www.aalto.fi/en/about/statistics/

Balagué, N., & Saarti, J. (2009). Benchmarking quality systems in two European academic libraries. *Library Management*, *30*(4–5), 227–239.

Grönroos, C. (2007). *Service management and marketing: Customer management in service competition* (3rd ed.). Chichester, UK: Wiley.

Hakala, U., & Nygren, U. (2010). Customer satisfaction and the strategic role of university libraries. *International Journal of Consumer Studies*, *34*(2), 204–211.

Hargis, M., & Watt, J. D. (2010). Organizational perception management: A framework to overcome crisis events. *Organization Development Journal*, *28*(1), 73–87.

Kotter, J. P. (2007). Leading change: Why transformation efforts fail. *Harvard Business Review*, *85*(1), 96–103.

Ministry of Education. (2009). Proposal for the new Universities Act in brief. Helsinki, Finland: Ministry of Education. Retrieved from http://www.minedu.fi/export/sites/default/OPM/Koulutus/koulutuspolitiikka/Hankkeet/Yliopistolaitoksen_uudistaminen/liitteet/HE_yolaki_eng_20.2.2009.pdf

Mohr, J. J., & Sengupta, S. (2002). Managing the paradox of inter-firm learning: The role of governance mechanisms. *Journal of Business & Industrial Marketing*, *17*(4), 282–301.

Nguyen, H., & Kleiner, B. H. (2003). The effective management of mergers. *Leadership & Organization Development Journal*, *24*(8), 447–454.

Nuoteva, J. (2008). *Turun korkeakoulujen kirjasto- ja tietopalveluiden kehittäminen* [Development of the library and information services of higher education institutes in Turku] [Abstract]. Helsinki, Finland: Ministry of Education and Culture. Retrieved from http://www.minedu.fi/OPM/Julkaisut/2008/Turun_kkjen_kirjasto-_ja_tietopalveluiden_kehittaminen_.html?lang = en

Putnik, G. D., & Van Eijnatten, F. M. (2004). Chaos, complexity, learning, and the learning organization: Towards a chaordic enterprise. *The Learning Organization*, *11*(6), 418–429.

Saarti, J. (2005). From printed world to a digital environment: The role of the repository libraries in a changing environment [Special issue]. *Library Management*, *26*(1–2), 26–31.

Thompson, J. N. (2005). *Books in the digital age: The transformation of academic and higher education publishing in Britain and the United States*. Cambridge, UK: Polity Press.

Innovation for Survival: From Cooperation to Collaboration

Jennifer Rowley

Department of Information and Communications, Manchester Metropolitan University, Manchester, UK

Abstract

This chapter provides an overview of the value and management of collaborative innovation in the development of library services. Open or collaborative innovation is innovation that bridges organizational boundaries. It discusses key aspects of interorganizational innovation and its application in libraries, namely the essence of innovation, the imperative for collaborative innovation, choosing partners and innovation networks, successful management of collaborative innovation, and the barriers to collaborative innovation and their management. It is argued that innovation is pivotal to survival and success in dynamic and complex organizational environments. Increasingly organizations are seeking to pool resources and enter into collaborative alliances in order to achieve large-scale, radical, paradigm innovations. However, the success of such alliances is not guaranteed, and is dependent not only on choosing the right partners but also on the leadership and management of innovation teams, having an understanding of the challenges of collaborative knowledge creation, and negotiating organizational and interorganizational barriers to innovation. While library and information literature has seen much discussion of innovations in terms of the outputs of innovation processes, there has been little discussion of the innovation processes needed to achieve new service developments, and other innovations. This chapter encourages information professionals to think strategically about innovation activities, specifically the management of the performance of collaborative or open innovation.

Keywords: Open innovation; Creativity; Collaboration; innovation alliances; Libraries; Information services

I. Introduction

Innovation is pivotal to survival and success in dynamic and complex organizational environments. The library and information management literature has recognized the challenging and changing environment faced by libraries as a consequence of the impact of information technology on

LIBRARIANSHIP IN TIMES OF CRISIS
ADVANCES IN LIBRARIANSHIP, VOL. 34
© 2011 by Emerald Group Publishing Limited
ISSN: 0065-2830
DOI: 10.1108/S0065-2830(2011)0000034013

the information marketplace and, more recently, the public sector funding crises. This literature, however, has used the rhetoric of change management, rather than that of innovation in articulating its response.

This chapter promotes the value of enhancing focus on innovation and creativity in the development of library services and does so through a discussion of open or collaborative innovation, that is to say, innovation that bridges organizational boundaries. Such innovation is referred to as open innovation (Chesbrough & Schwartz, 2007) or collaborative innovation, and the groups of people, or innovation teams, who come together to progress such interorganizational innovations are referred to as innovation networks by Powell, Koput, and Smith-Doerr (1996), as learning alliances by Khanna, Gulati, and Nohria (1998), or collective knowledge development strategic alliances by Larsson, Bengtsson, Henriksson, and Sparks (1998).

Information organizations in the public sector (including public, academic, health, and other special libraries) have a long tradition of cooperation in areas associated with creation of metadata, development of standards, consortia licensing agreements for e-journals and other digital resources, performance enhancement and benchmarking, and in service delivery. In addition, national and public libraries often work in partnership with other public sector departments, agencies, and services on projects associated with promoting reading and learning, developing digital literacy, and variously contributing to cultural engagement in their communities. It is important, however, to understand that collaboration is philosophically and in practice different from cooperation. In cooperation, desired outcomes are relatively clear, the distribution of future returns and mutual benefits can be identified and negotiated in advance, and the cooperating parties act essentially in their own interest. Collaboration in innovation for new services and user experiences, on the other hand, often involves unpredictable outcomes, and as such, trust, honesty, and equity are pivotal, with collaborating parties committing to understand and taking into account each other's interests as well as their own.

The following key aspects of interorganizational innovation are discussed along with the exploration of its application in libraries:

1. *The essence of innovation*—This section explores the essence of innovation, by discussing the different types and scales of innovation, with particular emphasis on service innovation. It also argues for the strategic role of innovation and the need to manage innovation processes.
2. *The imperative for collaborative innovation*—The philosophy underlying collaborative innovation is that by opening up their innovation processes, searching beyond their boundaries, and developing and managing a rich set of network relationships, organizations enhance their capacity to innovate. This section discusses the mutual exchange of benefits in open innovation.

3. *Choosing partners and innovation networks*—Choosing the right partners for innovation is critical, with selection depending on the types of innovation related to type of innovation networks. Different types of innovation networks are discussed.

4. *Successful management of collaborative innovation*—Innovation teams, the group of people charged with taking an innovation forward, are pivotal to the success of an innovation. The factors that affect the level of group innovation, and the key issues that need to be addressed in managing an innovation network, are covered.

5. *Barriers to collaborative innovation and their management*—Open innovation teams, comprised of people from different organizations, have organizational diversity that can positively influence collaborative knowledge creation and idea generation. However, such diversity can also obstruct the process. This section reflects on barriers to successful collaboration, approaches to their negotiation, and some of the hindrances to successful innovation and entrepreneurship that are widespread in the public sector.

II. The Essence of Innovation

All organizations innovate to survive and succeed, but the types of innovation that they undertake, and the nature of their innovation processes, vary. In libraries most innovations are service innovations, which are designed to enhance the benefits delivered to library and information service users. Sometimes such innovations are triggered by evidence (often from staff or users) that there is scope for quality enhancement. On other occasions, innovation is provoked by changes in the broader consumer, economic, technological, or policy environment.

The essential diversity of innovation has led to considerable discussion about the precise nature of innovation. For example, innovations can be small scale and local, or they may involve whole organizations with complete shifts in their strategic direction. The notion of "newness" is often at the core of definitions of innovation, as is the idea that innovation will in some way make things better or improve them. Deiss (2004), for example, describes an innovation as something that changes the way we can do what we want to do, and that adds value to our lives. On the other hand, Damanpour (1996)'s much quoted definition of innovation focuses on innovation as a means of changing an organization, either as a response to changes in the external environment or as a preemptive action to influence the environment. Other commentators such as Barringer and Ireland (2008) associate innovation with creativity and entrepreneurial behavior, designed to contribute economic, social, or cultural value.

Most libraries are involved in a range of different innovation processes simultaneously. Indeed, organizations often have no option but to innovate in a number of directions at the same time. For example, to improve their service to users a library might develop a service to provide e-books to readers. This development might not only involve the design of the service (service innovation) but also innovation in approaches to budgets, metadata, and collection management. Innovations may vary considerably in scale with associated resource implications and strategic impact. They can range from modest service improvements such as changing the route of a mobile library service, redesigning an academic library student induction process, to the outsourcing of a library service, or the establishment of a consumers' association for libraries. Innovations also vary in the time period over which they are implemented, and the type and extent of resources required for development and implementation. Indeed, to survive and prosper, libraries must engage with and invest in a range of different types and scales of innovation. In short, they need to innovate at "every point of the compass."

In managing a portfolio of innovations, it is useful to be able to classify innovations. Two commonly used classifications are based on levels of newness or novelty, and on the outcome of the innovation process, respectively.

A. Newness

In terms of newness, innovations can be described as either incremental or radical. A *radical innovation* is a fundamental change that often is implemented through a specific project associated with the development of a new product or service. Depending on the significance of the new product or service, a radical innovation may impact on organizational culture, structure, resource allocation, and job roles. An *incremental innovation*, on the other hand, is an add-on to a previous innovation without changing its essential concept. In the service context, such innovation is often a response to information gathered through the regular cycles of feedback embedded in quality auditing and monitoring mechanisms such as surveys. It may also be triggered by a range of external factors such as the release of a new version of software that is key to the organization's processes and service delivery. An example might be development of Web 2.0 services as a result of the release of a new version of a library management system.

B. Outcome and Other Classification Types

In addition to classification on the basis of their newness, innovations can be categorized on the basis of the outcome of the innovation process. Two broad groups are external/tangible and internal/intangible innovations. *External innovations* are those in which the customer directly uses or benefits from the innovation. Product and service innovations are types of external innovation.

Internal innovations focus on enhancements in internal processes such as production systems, ordering and acquisition systems, and team working logistics. Customers benefit from such internal innovations indirectly either because they support enhanced service delivery or reduce the cost of a product or service. Francis and Bessant (2005) proposed two additional and more far-reaching types of innovation, position, and paradigm innovation. *Position innovation* is concerned with the role of innovation in exploiting new customer bases and markets and new ways of offering or introducing the innovation to the potential customer. For example, the rebranding of London Borough of Tower Hamlets' public libraries as Idea Stores was a position innovation, which involved not only rebranding at the level of the name but also a considerable shift in the services offered, and the targeted customer groups. *Paradigm innovation*, on the other hand, occurs when the way of looking at things is reframed or when the organization changes its business model (revenue generation model). Paradigm innovation requires that whole strategies and principles of the organization, or even a sector, have to change. Many would argue that newspaper and scholarly journal industries are in the middle of a paradigm change as they seek viable and sustainable business models in a digital world. Paradigm and position innovation often bring a series of internal and external innovations in their wake.

III. The Imperative for Collaborative Innovation

As discussed in the introduction, libraries have long traditions of cooperation and collaboration both in order to support new developments and to deliver greater effectiveness and efficiency. For example, libraries collaborate through consortia concerning licenses for e-journals, to establish and develop metadata standards for new media, and to form special interest groups to share experiences, monitor developments, and organize training and development activities. Public libraries collaborate with government bodies and community groups in regeneration projects, cultural initiatives, and other community activities. Academic libraries work with teaching and research staff in a diverse range of subject areas on innovations and projects that enhance teaching and learning, and capitalize on opportunities offered by digital resources of all kinds.

Nevertheless, there is an imperative to do more collaborative innovation, and to do it better. There is widespread recognition that the increasing complexity of change in organizational environments means that many innovations require resources from more than one organization. In the case of libraries, major service innovations that might be viewed as radical, and in terms of their impact and outcome that might lead to repositioning or paradigm change, will often be collaborative ventures. The following quote from Ketchen, Ireland, and Snow (2007) seems particularly apposite for information organizations:

> Accelerating trends in globalization and information technology have helped create competitive arenas whose demands are growing quickly and unpredictably, and competition in such settings exceeds the ability to keep pace of even the most agile individuals, small businesses, and corporate research and development units. (p. 375)

The philosophy underlying open innovation is that organizations enhance their capacity to innovate by opening up their innovation processes, searching beyond their boundaries, and developing and managing a rich set of network relationships. It is widely recognized that talking to and working with people in different organizations can widen horizons, challenge assumptions, and, in general, can facilitate innovation and creativity. Typically, in open innovation, there is a mutual exchange of benefits arising from a variety of factors:

- Bringing together different and complementary knowledge and skills sets;
- Enhancing capacity for creativity, and problem solving by enlisting more minds;
- Sharing of and reduction in the risks associated with exploring and exploiting new ideas, through sharing knowledge, skills, and costs;
- Access to new markets and technologies; and
- Shared learning and understanding, which may form a platform for future innovation.

It would be naïve, however, to assume that such benefits can be delivered without appropriate leadership and management. It is, after all, often difficult to get people to work together and welcome change when they are all employed by one organization. The challenges in delivering successful collaborative innovation are far from trivial. Some of the challenges associated with managing collaborative innovation, or innovation networks, are discussed further below.

IV. Choosing Partners and Innovation Networks

Like innovation, collaborative innovation comes in a wide range of different guises. Given that a library may be involved in a number of collaborative innovations of different scales and types at any one point in time, there is a real challenge in managing resources to support them, since they are probably running in tandem with in-house innovations. In addition, the exact benefits achieved through open and collaborative innovation depend on the nature of the innovation network, the knowledge and skills of the member organizations, and the anticipated innovation. Accordingly, prior to discussing the approaches to managing collaborative innovation and its inherent challenges, it is useful to reflect on some of the types of innovation networks with which information organizations may be involved. These include the following:

- *Spatial clusters*—networks that form because the members are geographically close to one another, and have a mutual interest in promoting the economic, social, and cultural development of their city or region. Typically, such networks involve partners from both the public and private sectors.
- *Sectoral networks*—networks that form because members perceive themselves to be in the same industry sector, and see collaboration and benchmarking as important for innovation, performance, and reputation building in political arenas for the sector.
- *Sectoral consortia*—networks that form to progress a specific innovation project, possibly provoked by a government policy initiative or funding opportunity.
- *Standards forums*—networks that form around the establishment and maintenance of standards, such as those associated with new technologies, metadata, and licensing.
- *New technology development network*—networks that form because the members (either individuals or organizations) are keen to share and learn about new emerging technologies and their applications.
- *Communities of practice*—networks of individuals that are informal, often across departments and organizations, which form because those individuals have shared interests and find it mutually beneficial to share knowledge and learn from each other. Members build relationships and trust through regular interaction and may develop shared resources, tools, and knowledge repositories.

These different types of networks differ in their objectives and outcomes that will, in turn, influence their optimum membership and processes.

A. Similarities

Another factor that impacts the levels of innovation and creativity that a network achieves is the relative similarity of the organizations involved. For example, networks composed of tightly coupled organizations possessing similar experiences and cultures are likely to have relatively low levels of innovation (Ketchen et al., 2007). Bessant and Tidd (2007) suggest that innovation networks can be categorized on the basis of the type of innovation (incremental or radical), and on the similarity of participating organizations, as shown in Table 1, and that this has consequences for managing the innovation network.

In Zone 1 innovation networks, organizations have a broadly similar background and context and are concerned with improving existing practices. As such it is important that they share experiences, disclose information, develop trust and transparency, and build a shared-sense of commitment to innovation. While superficially straightforward because the focus is on incremental innovation, Chapman and Corso (2005) suggest that

Table 1
Types of Innovation Networks

	Similar organizations	Heterogeneous organizations
Radical innovation	Zone 2 (e.g., sectoral consortia)	Zone 3 (e.g., new technology development network)
Incremental innovation	Zone 1 (e.g., sectoral networks)	Zone 4 (e.g., spatial clusters)
	Similar organizations	Heterogeneous organizations

Source: Adapted from Bessant and Tidd (2007).

to sustain such collaboration is challenging because it involves an alignment of organizational processes, and extends beyond selected innovation teams to other members of the organization. An example of a Zone 1 network might be a group of academic libraries working toward improvements in digital service delivery.

Zone 2 networks, on the other hand, are working toward a radical innovation associated with new products, services or processes, and possibly capitalizing on the opportunities offered by new technologies. An example might be public libraries working together with publishers and others to establish the principles and associated business models for digital rights management for e-books.

In Zone 4, participating organizations are very different from one another, and may need to spend some time understanding each other's agendas, surfacing potential conflicts and developing trust. An example might be a regional cluster working together to gradually build the infrastructure associated with a knowledge city, a city in which key stakeholders in private and public sectors acknowledge the centrality of knowledge to the economic, social, and cultural development of their city. They need to make careful judgments about what to reveal and share.

Finally, Zone 3 networks are likely to involve members from different sectors such as those in a supply chain, and are likely to bring different perspectives about priorities in the innovation process. An example of such a network might be a strategic alliance formed by a book publisher, a search engine organization, and a national library to provide access to e-books.

While the purpose of the innovation may to a large extent determine the membership of an innovation network, there is no doubt that participating organizations' experiences and competencies in innovation will also be a significant contributing factor in its success. Organizations that are good at innovation are described as "innovation orientated" or innovative. Lumpkin and Dess (2001) suggest that innovativeness is associated with willingness to move away from existing practices and to support new ideas, novelty, experimentation, and creative processes that may result in new products, services, and processes. Extending the findings from Light's (1998) study of nonprofit and governmental organizations, it is reasonable to suggest that innovative organizations are characterized by

1. a commitment to controlling their environment rather than reacting to environmental changes after they have occurred;
2. an organizational structure that creates the freedom to imagine, and think about how things might be different;
3. leadership that encourages and values innovation, and promotes an organizational culture in which questioning the status quo and engaging creativity is valued; and
4. management systems, procedures, and controls that serve the mission of the organization, rather than the other way round.

There are many other studies that investigate the characteristics of innovative, creative and entrepreneurial organizations. For example, Coveney (2008) suggests that library managers need to take responsibility for establishing the right work environment alongside adopting an innovation strategy in order to cultivate innovation and creativity. However, in terms of providing a practical list of the characteristics of an innovative organization, the list used in a recent survey about the role of innovation in economic recovery (Patterson & Kerrin, 2009) is useful (see Table 2).

Table 2
Factors that Drive Innovation in Organizations

Managers provide practical support for new ideas and their application
There is a "we are in it together" attitude
We strive for a reputation for being innovative
The general management style is participative and collaborative
The organizational goals are directly aligned with innovation
Management practices actively enhance innovation
There is a "no blame" culture—mistakes are talked about freely so that other people can learn from them
Resources and facilities are readily available for use in testing out new ideas
Personal development objectives explicitly related to innovation are set
Job assignments ensure that there is enough time and scope for trying out new ideas
The appraisal system is directly linked to rewarding creativity and innovation

---

Source: Extracted from Patterson and Kerrin (2009).

V. Successful Management of Collaborative Innovation

Some networks may be long-standing, and have other purposes in addition to innovation. In other instances, organizations or individuals will come together in response to a specific problem or opportunity. Nevertheless, in order to be successful, all innovation networks need commitment and management.

First and foremost it is important to acknowledge that innovation networks, certainly at the level of the individuals involved, are innovation teams. They are often "project teams" brought together for a specific innovation project over a given period. They are temporary, and individuals in the network have a keen sense of their responsibility and allegiance to their employing organizations, as well as personal and career consequences for them as individuals as a result of being a member of the team. West (2002) suggests that the following factors determine the level of group innovation:

1. *Task characteristics*—the nature of the task that the group is formed to achieve; innovation teams work well with whole tasks, with a start and an end point.
2. *Group knowledge diversity and skills*—skills and knowledge need to match the task. While innovation teams thrive on a certain level of diversity, an appropriate balance needs to be struck between the level of knowledge and skill diversity, to fuel creativity, and common ground to make it possible to operate as a team.
3. *Integrating group processes*—innovation teams need to go through the stages of group formation process as follows: forming, storming, norming, performing, and adjourning, during which they learn how to work with each other.
4. *External context and its demands*—including organizational climate, support systems, and the market environment.

Shaping and influencing these factors in order to optimize team performance is difficult at the best of times, but in innovation networks, where the members' allegiances and agendas might be diverse, there is opportunity for political maneuverings, disinterest, low levels of commitment, and poor delivery on objectives. It takes inspired and imaginative leadership to ensure that group processes and activities lead to the most successful outcome for all participating organizations.

Table 3 offers a checklist of the key issues that typically need to be addressed in managing an innovation network. It points to the importance of clarity of purpose and network boundaries, leadership, coordination and organization, and the management of group processes associated with participation, decision making, communication, knowledge management, risk, and conflict.

Knowledge creation and sharing is central to innovation processes. Du Chatenier, Verstegen, Biemans, Mulder, and Omta (2009) focus specifically on the issues of knowledge creation in open innovation teams. They

Table 3
Key Issues in Managing an Innovation Network

Key issue	Comment
The purpose of the network	The innovation network may have an ongoing purpose toward innovation in a sector, for example, or may be formed to execute a specific project. Without a clear purpose to which members can commit, the network will fall apart.
Network membership and boundaries	Network membership needs to be clearly defined and maintained. Agreed conventions are needed for changes and substitutions, and all organizations involved need to be and remain fully committed.
Leadership	Networks, like all innovative organizations, need leadership. An individual or a group needs to be granted the authority to resolve issues and conflicts that may endanger the achievement of the network's strategic objectives
Member participation	Networks will not work without participation and members need to be motivated to participate. Often members have different levels of participation, from full membership, through peripheral, to passive membership. Different levels of contribution may be required from different members at different times, but they must be willing to make the contribution required of them.
Coordination and organization	Networks need organization and coordination. Members need to understand how the network objectives are to be achieved (plans, budgets, time scales) and everyone's roles in achieving those objectives.
Communication	Communication processes and channels, their various purposes, and the level of openness, and confidentiality are an important aspect of building of relationships and trust.
Knowledge management	Attention needs to be directed toward how knowledge is created, captured, and shared across the network,
Risk/benefit sharing	Managing perceptions of the distribution of risks and benefits across the network is crucial to motivation, participation, and success.
Conflict resolution	Different network members will have different interests and seek different benefits from participation in the network. Success is critically dependent on negotiating toward a win-win situation for all concerned.

developed a model of collaborative knowledge creation, with the following four stages: sharing, interpretation, negotiation, and combination. Using this they explored the impact of various characteristics of open innovation teams in collaborative knowledge creation. On this basis, they identified the challenges listed below:

1. Being a good partner, but preventing free riding
2. Balancing openness and closure and building trust in a nontrusting environment
3. Balancing individual and alliance interests, creating common meanings, goals, and work plans
4. Balancing influencing and being out of influence
5. Fostering optimal team dynamics
6. Balancing being in control and being out of control
7. Deciding when to work together and when apart
8. Coping with role overload
9. Efficiently and effectively organizing teamwork
10. Rapidly building good relationships
11. Mobilizing commitment inside and outside mother organizations
12. Sharing complex information, knowing when to share and when to withhold
13. Balancing short- and long-term goals, stability, and risk
14. Sustaining good relationships (Du Chatenier et al., 2009, p. 358).

A. Leadership

So far this section has focussed on innovative teams and their management. Here, we take the opportunity to comment further on one of the key issues mentioned in Table 3, leadership. All innovation is a complex process that can consume considerable resources, involve many people, and have potentially significant consequences for organizations. In collaborative innovation, these resources, people, and consequences may be shared between two or more organizations. Leadership is viewed as pivotal by many in library and information fields (Akeroyd, 2000; Walton, 2008). Paul (2000) suggests that library managers need to be both creative and innovative themselves and be able to motivate and facilitate motivation in others. While there is little discussion of leadership specific to collaborative innovation, many general principles of leadership apply. First and foremost leadership is about influencing people, and is usually implicit that leaders influence people to do things differently. In other words, all leaders must be some extent innovators. According to Roberts and Rowley (2008), effective leaders are involved in the following:

- Creating, sharing, and communicating vision
- Shaping cultures
- Developing the potential of others
- Connecting with people and building successful relationships
- Taking a holistic and wide perspective.

In other words, in addition to managing a team, the innovative team leaders have a pivotal role in understanding and interpreting the context for innovation, and in building networks and alliances. The leader also needs to shape the culture of the innovation team, including its values and working practices. In addition, they need to challenge, stretch, and develop team members, and sometimes people outside of the team, to learn, achieve, and see things differently in ways that they had not dreamt possible.

VI. Barriers to Collaborative Innovation and Its Management

In addition to the challenges associated with managing innovation teams, there are a number of other challenges that arise from the fact that collaborative innovation is not simply about putting a new team together and leading it so that it works successfully. Open innovation requires management of the interfaces between the collaborating organizations. There is considerable potential that collaboration can make development more complicated and costly. It is therefore important to assess the likelihood that an innovation alliance will succeed, and to manage any potential barriers. According to Swink (2006), there are four categories of barriers to successful open innovation discussed below along with suggested as options for navigating them.

A. Physical and Temporal Barriers

Physical and temporal barriers can impede communication between team members. While information technology solutions can facilitate communication, according to Chapman and Corso (2005) they cannot resolve issues such as lack of trust or ineffective goal setting. There is need to encourage timely unstructured and informal interactions between team members to complement more formal communication. This is often most effectively achieved through physical colocation of a team. Arranging a dedicated location for a team and ensuring that everyone can make time to attend regular meetings in the same location can provoke a whole host of logistical challenges for each of the organizations involved.

B. Organizational and Hierarchical Barriers

Teams can easily be hampered by standard operating procedures, organizational structures, and budgetary controls. Different collaborating organizations, may, for example, have different budgetary cycles, and commit different levels of human resources to the innovation project. Different team members may have different levels of authority in their own organizations, and different decision-making processes (often linked to organizational structures and cultures) that might hinder and delay progress of the innovation. A separate organization for the project, with its own people and other resources, is one way to give the team the necessary autonomy. In addition, it may be necessary to realign reporting relationships within team members own organizations, and to support team members in negotiating conflicts between their allegiance to a functional or previous team and their allegiance to the project.

C. Relational and Cultural Barriers

Individual team members bring baggage to their role in a team. They may be unwilling to collaborate or participate as team members due to a perceived loss of power or status, or lack of interest or motivation. They may view being moved to a project team as being sidelined, especially if this reduces their opportunities for working with established and trusted colleagues within their own organization. They may perceive involvement in an innovation project that may or may not work as personally risky. Further, although they may have the requisite technical skills to contribute to a project, they may feel uncomfortable with the rather different experience and culture of an innovation team.

All of these potential barriers need to be managed. Leaders need to use a range of tactics to optimize motivation and engagement of team members. Selection of team members should be not only on the basis of their skills but also, whenever possible, on the basis of personality, enthusiasm for the project, personal development, and a desire for new experiences. Then attention needs to be paid to team development through the management of various aspects of integrating group processes, including coordination, participation, communication, and conflict resolution, as discussed in the previous section.

D. Knowledge, Information, and Data Management Systems-Related Barriers

Effectiveness of collaborative teams can be considerably hindered by the lack of technologies to support communication and access to data and information. Approval for and implementation of such technologies may be very challenging to achieve. This is needed to allow all organizations to participate equally and ensure there is no delay in starting projects.

In addition, it is necessary to make ongoing judgements about what data and information can be shared with people outside the organization, without compromising confidentiality or competitiveness.

Not all team members may have authority to make independent judgements and will have to refer decisions to a more senior manager at their home organization, thus hindering both group processes and progress on the task. Finally, many processes, values, and approaches within organizations, which may be the foundation for the innovation, are often found to be not recorded, and exist within organizations only as tacit knowledge. Even when they are willing to do so, organizations may find it difficult to make their knowledge available in a form that is accessible to innovation team members who do not share the organization's history and culture. Frequently organizations need to spend time and resources developing the knowledge of the how and why of their processes, before it can be shared with others.

E. Barriers Specific to the Public Sector

In addition to the barriers that can arise at the interface between organizations in open innovation, each organization in a partnership may have different predilections toward, or readiness for, innovation. In other words, their level of innovativeness or innovation may vary. Of particular relevance to libraries is the long-standing recognition that public sector organizations can be resistant to innovation and entrepreneurship. Many public sector organizations are large, and highly bureaucratized. According to Wilson (1989), they are structured to perform their core tasks with stability and consistency, and to resist change or disruption to these tasks. Many public sector organizations have neither the culture nor the structure to effectively support change, creativity, innovation, and entrepreneurship. They are risk-averse, quote public accountability as a defense, and often find it difficult to release resources to support imaginative and substantial innovation.

Some argue that the culture of control that is ingrained in such organizations is at odds with innovation. Organizational structures and processes designed to support efficiency in everyday operations are often inconsistent with innovation. Nevertheless, according to Taylor and Pask (2008), there is there is some evidence that public service organizations are changing rapidly due to increasing focus on citizens and community. Zampetakis and Moustakis (2007) state that a supportive context, with encouragement of initiatives and access to managerial information, an energetic working environment, change orientation, and strategic vision, can promote innovation and entrepreneurship.

Table 4
Barriers to Public Sector Innovation

Bureaucracy/Organization	Political environment	External environment
Hostile attitudes	Inadequate funding or resources	Public doubts about the effectiveness of the program
Turf fights	Legislative or regulatory constraints	Difficulty in reaching the program's target group
Difficulty in coordinating organizations	Political opposition	Opposition by those affected in the private sector
Logistical problems		General public opposition or skepticism
Difficulty in maintaining enthusiasm		
Difficulty in introducing new technology		
Union opposition		
Middle management resistance		
Opposition to entrepreneurial action		

Source: Based on Borins (2001).

Table 4 lists some of the barriers to public sector innovation, under three categories: bureaucracy/organization, political environment, and external environment. Public sector organizations will exhibit such barriers to varying extents, but innovators working in or with public sector organizations need to understand the organizational, political, and wider environmental contexts that may impact on the capacity of both their own organization and those with which they are collaborating to complete a successful and efficient innovation project.

VII. Conclusion

Innovation is pivotal to survival and success in dynamic and complex organizational environments. Increasingly organizations seek to pool resources and enter into collaborative alliances in order to achieve large-scale, radical, paradigm innovations. However, the success of such alliances is not guaranteed. Library and information service organizations need to think carefully and strategically about their innovation portfolio, and make well-considered decisions regarding the innovations in which they invest and engage. This involves consideration of a range of different types of innovations, including those that are the sole responsibility of the library service, and others in which they are working with other departments, information services, and other organizations. In this process, they are likely to be members of a number of different types of innovation networks, to which they will need to commit resources, and to continually monitor the benefits that participation delivers from the innovation.

The success of any collaborative innovation is dependent not only on the membership of the innovation network and the resources that members can bring to that network but also on the leadership and management of innovation teams, an appreciation of the challenges of collaborative knowledge creation, and the successful negotiation of organizational barriers to innovation.

References

Akeroyd, J. (2000, August). *The management of change in electronic libraries*. Paper presented at the 66th IFLA Council and General Conference, Jerusalem, Israel. Retrieved from http://archive.ifla.org/IV/ifla66/papers/037-110e.htm

Barringer, B. R., & Ireland, R. D. (2008). *Entrepreneurship: Successfully launching new ventures* (2nd ed.). Upper Saddle River, NJ: Pearson Education International.

Bessant, J., & Tidd, J. (2007). *Innovation and entrepreneurship*. Chichester, UK: Wiley.

Borins, S. (2001). *The challenge of innovating in government*. Arlington, VA: PricewaterhouseCoopers Endowment for the Business of Government.

Chapman, R. L., & Corso, M. (2005). From continuous improvement to collaborative innovation: The next challenge in supply chain management. *Production Planning & Control: The Management of Operations*, 16(4), 339–344.

Chesbrough, H. W., & Schwartz, K. (2007). Innovating business models with co-development partnerships. *Research Technology Management*, 50(1), 55–59.

Coveney, B. (2008). Assessing the organizational climate for creativity in public libraries: A case study. *Library and Information Research*, 32(1–2), 38–56.

Damanpour, F. (1996). Organizational complexity and innovation: Developing and testing multiple contingency models. *Management Science*, 42(5), 693–716.

Deiss, K. J. (2004). Innovation and strategy: Risk and choice in user-centered libraries. *Library Trends*, 53(1), 17–32.

Du Chatenier, E., Verstegen, J. A. A. M., Biemans, H. J. A., Mulder, M., & Omta, O. (2009). The challenge of collaborative knowledge creation in open innovation teams. *Human Resource Development Review*, 8(3), 350–381.

Francis, D., & Bessant, J. (2005). Targeting innovation and implications for capability development. *Technovation*, 25(3), 171–183.

Ketchen, D. I., Ireland, D. R., & Snow, C. C. (2007). Strategic entrepreneurship, collaborative innovation, and wealth creation. *Strategic Entrepreneurship Journal*, 1(3-4), 317–385.

Khanna, T., Gulati, R., & Nohria, N. (1998). The dynamics of learning alliances: Competitions, cooperation, and relative scope. *Strategic Management Journal*, 53(3), 193–210.

Larsson, R., Bengtsson, L., Henriksson, K., & Sparks, J. (1998). The inter-organizational learning dilemmas: Collective knowledge development in strategic alliances. *Organization Science*, 19(3), 285–305.

Light, P. C. (1998). *Sustaining innovation: Creating nonprofit and governmental organizations that innovate naturally*. San Francisco, CA: Jossey-Bass.

Lumpkin, G. T., & Dess, G. G. (2001). Linking two dimensions of entrepreneurial orientation to firm performance: The moderating role of environment and industry life cycle. *Journal of Business Venturing*, 16(5), 429–451.

Patterson, F., & Kerrin, M. (2009). *Innovation for the recovery: Enhancing innovative working practices*. London, UK: Chartered Management Institute.

Paul, G. (2000). Mobilising the potential for initiative and innovation by means of socially competent management: Results from research libraries in Berlin. *Library Management*, 21(2), 81–85.

Powell, W. W., Koput, K. W., & Smith-Doerr, L. (1996). Inter-organizational collaboration and the locus of innovation: Networks of learning in biotechnology. *Administrative Science Quarterly*, 41(1), 116–145.

Roberts, S., & Rowley, J. (2008). *Leadership: The challenge for the information profession*. London, UK: Facet Publishing.

Swink, M. (2006). Building collaborative innovation capability. *Research Technology Management*, 49(2), 37–47.

Taylor, B., & Pask, R. (2008). *Community libraries programme evaluation*. London, UK: Museum, Libraries and Archives Council.

Walton, G. (2008). Theory, research and practice in library management 4: Creativity. *Library Management*, 29(1/2), 125–131.

West, M. A. (2002). Sparkling fountains or stagnant ponds: An integrative model of creativity and innovation implementation in work groups. *Applied Psychology: An International Review*, 51(3), 355–424.

Wilson, J. (1989). *Bureaucracy: What government agencies do and why they do it*. New York, NY: Basic Books.

Zampetakis, L. A., & Moustakis, V. (2007). Entrepreneurial behaviour in the Greek public sector. *International Journal of Entrepreneurial Behaviour and Research*, 13(1), 19–38.

Author Index

Subject Index